THE LEGEND OF WYATT OUTLAW

THE LEGEND OF WYATT OUTLAW

FROM RECONSTRUCTION THROUGH BLACK LIVES MATTER

SYLVESTER ALLEN JR.
AND BELLE BOGGS

A Ferris and Ferris Book

The University of North Carolina Press
CHAPEL HILL

This book was published under the Marcie Cohen Ferris and William R. Ferris Imprint of the University of North Carolina Press.

Manufactured in the United States of America

Designed by Lindsay Starr
Set in Quadraat and Irby by Copperline Book Services, Inc.

Cover art: Wyatt Outlaw's Union League commission from 1867. Wyatt Outlaw Union League of America Commission, #00569-z, Southern Historical Collection, Wilson Library, University of North Carolina at Chapel Hill.

Library of Congress Cataloging-in-Publication Data
Names: Allen, Sylvester, Jr., author | Boggs, Belle author
Title: The legend of Wyatt Outlaw : from Reconstruction through Black Lives Matter / Sylvester Allen Jr. and Belle Boggs.
Other titles: From Reconstruction through Black Lives Matter
Description: Chapel Hill : The University of North Carolina Press, [2025] | "A Ferris and Ferris book." | Includes bibliographical references and index.
Identifiers: LCCN 2025029921 | ISBN 9781469689999 cloth alk. paper | ISBN 9781469686493 epub | ISBN 9781469690001 pdf
Subjects: LCSH: Outlaw, Wyatt, –1870 | Lynching—North Carolina—Alamance County—History—19th century | White supremacy movements—North Carolina—Alamance County—History—19th century | African Americans—North Carolina—Alamance County—History—19th century | Alamance County (N.C.)—Race relations | BISAC: HISTORY / United States / State & Local / South (AL, AR, FL, GA, KY, LA, MS, NC, SC, TN, VA, WV) | SOCIAL SCIENCE / Ethnic Studies / American / African American & Black Studies
Classification: LCC F262.A3 A45 2025 | DDC 305.896/07307565809034—dc23/eng/20250825
LC record available at https://lccn.loc.gov/2025029921

For product safety concerns under the European Union's General Product Safety Regulation (EU GPSR), please contact gpsr@mare-nostrum.co.uk or write to the University of North Carolina Press and Mare Nostrum Group B.V., Mauritskade 21D, 1091 GC Amsterdam, The Netherlands.

For Walter Boyd, my friend and educator.

For my mother and stepfather, my earliest teachers of right and wrong . . .
and of good and evil.

For the ancestors, the ones who died in an effort to make
this country what it was promised to be.

—SYLVESTER ALLEN JR.

• • • •

For the students and teachers of Alamance County, North Carolina.

—BELLE BOGGS

Q: Was it a dark night or a moonlight night?

A. A dark night.

Q: Cloudy?

A. Yes, sir, it was cloudy. It rained mightily the next day, and it had rained some that night. It was the 26th day of February.

—Testimony of Jemima Phillips
on March 1, 1871, the twenty-sixth
day of the impeachment trial
of North Carolina governor
William Holden

So wo were fi na wosan kofa a yenki.

(It is not taboo to go back and fetch what you forgot.)

—Akan proverb

CONTENTS

ILLUSTRATIONS

ACKNOWLEDGMENTS

A collaborative book like this one results in many debts of gratitude. We want to first thank everyone who shared stories, experiences, insights, and wisdom with us, especially Dr. Samuel Merritt, Thomas Holt Russell III, Jaki Shelton Green, Audra Faucette, Michael Harris, Kris Loy, Maurice Wells, Kathy Lee Erlandson Liston, Dreama Caldwell, Daniel Ayers, Ebony Pinnix, Dr. Nettie Baldwin, Beth Lavinder, Amy Cooper, Avery Harvey, Ricky Hurtado, Kevin Greene, Amanda Perry, Faith Cook, Walter Boyd, Shineece Sellars, James Shields, Omega Wilson, Brenda Wilson, Wade Harrison, Patsy Simpson, and the members of the Alamance County Community Remembrance Coalition. We are also grateful to artists and photographers whose work is included here, especially Nic L. Cassette, Carey Kirk, and Anthony Crider. Profound thanks go to the late Jane Sellars for her pioneering work collecting and showcasing African American history in Alamance County.

The National Humanities Center provided crucial research support, and the Culture Mill, Carolina Performing Arts, and the Weymouth Center for the Arts and Humanities provided residencies and creative inspiration. We could not have learned what we have without the important work of historians Carole W. Troxler (also a member of the Alamance Remembrance Coalition) and Scott Reynolds Nelson. A special thanks goes to writers Christina Sharpe and Kidada Williams for giving us useful frameworks for thinking about Wyatt and his time and to librarians Matt Turi, Joe Millilo, and Sarah Harris for their patient and generous assistance.

Our brilliant editor, Lucas Church, believed in and guided this project, and our appreciation goes to the many talented folks at the University of North Carolina Press who devote their working lives to shaping and sharing necessary stories, especially Thomas Bedenbaugh, Sonya Bonczek, Julie Bush, Erin Granville, Michelle Wallen, and Kim Bryant. We thank Lindsay Starr for the beautiful cover design and Kyle Villemain at *The Assembly* and Dan Kois at *Slate* for publishing early, connected work.

Thanks go to the activists, teachers, parents, grandparents, historians, artists, musicians, museum keepers, memory keepers, and justice-minded leaders—past, present, and future—of Alamance County.

Belle would like to express sincere love and gratitude to Richard Allen, who not only encouraged her to write this book with Sylvester but also invested countless hours in researching, reading, discussing, and reviewing the work they did (including its proofing and index). His volunteer work as a legal observer protects the rights of many protesters, and as a wonderful father he helps his and Belle's two children understand justice, fairness, and history. She also thanks Beatrice Boggs Allen, Harriet Boggs Allen, Cat Warren, and Buttons Boggs for listening, reading, and learning alongside her—and to Sylvester, of course, for his vision, courage, and teaching.

Sylvester would like to thank David Anthony Wright for first introducing him to the name Wyatt Outlaw with his wonderful theatrical work; Belle, for believing that he could help write this important story; and his partner, Karla, who endured with him the wonderful and arduous roller coaster of completing this book and who led with love and understanding every step of the way.

INTRODUCTION

WELCOME TO ALAMANCE COUNTY, NORTH CAROLINA

Late February in North Carolina's Piedmont can feel like springtime. Trees aren't yet in bud, but vibrantly green grasses carpet the riverbanks, and frogs sing in the creeks. The air is softer, and the extra minutes of daylight seem like a promise of good things to come.

On February 25, 2021, sunset in the small town of Saxapahaw, North Carolina, was at 6:09 p.m., and a group of thirty people, mostly longtime residents of Alamance County, had been invited to a short outdoor play, *The Spirit of Wyatt Outlaw: Final Peace*, scheduled to begin at dark to take advantage of projected light and shadows. The guest list was small because of the COVID-19 pandemic, and for most of the audience, it would be the first live performance they'd seen in a year.

The play had been rescheduled just days before—it was supposed to premiere on February 26, the 151st anniversary of Wyatt Outlaw's death, but that day called for steady rain. February 25, a Thursday, was clear, the high temperature nearing seventy degrees. By the time audience members began making their way into the riverside amphitheater at 5:30, it was starting to get cool, but the long cement benches still radiated the sun's warmth.

Most of the audience, a multiracial, multigenerational group, would have also been there in the rain. For eight months, these individuals had marched on freezing days, blazing days, and everything in between. After the January 6 insurrection, they had stood every night in the park they call Wyatt Outlaw Park, holding signs reading GOOGLE WYATT OUTLAW and TRUMP IS A TRAITOR and JUSTICE FOR GEORGE FLOYD in sleet and snow.

In many ways, they were like Black Lives Matter protesters across the country, bringing attention to national and local cases of police brutality as well as to the urgent need to remove Confederate monuments from public land. But they also had a secret weapon—emphasis on "secret"—which was the Reconstruction-era true story of Wyatt Outlaw, a voting rights crusader, education leader, and the first Black elected official in the small town of Graham. Both because he dared to oppose the growing terror of the Ku Klux Klan and because he was a prominent example of Black political power, Outlaw was kidnapped from his home by a group of white men, dragged down Main Street, and hung in the public square on February 26, 1870. The mob who lynched him pinned to his clothes a warning for all to see: *Beware you guilty, both white and black.* His death touched off what became known as the Kirk-Holden War and led to the first successful impeachment of a sitting American governor. Attempts to hold the Klan accountable were widely weaponized by the conservative press, precipitating vast Republican losses.

Outlaw's story doesn't appear in textbooks, and as of yet there is no public marker recognizing his accomplishments or the significance of his life. Few learn about him in public schools, though his story is one of the most historically important in the county.

The audience members who waited for the play to begin knew more than most, because they had learned about Outlaw at marches tracing his final steps and because they had repeated his name alongside recent victims of police killings and white supremacy. But there was plenty they didn't know, too—when, exactly, Outlaw was born (because his mother was enslaved, no such records were kept), whether he was born enslaved or free, and how he came to prominence and power.

What they knew, and why they identified with Outlaw, was more gut-level.

He was a Black political leader who cared deeply about voting rights and education. He founded a school and a church and encouraged voting and political participation by other Black men.

He was a coalition builder who worked with white and Black citizens and believed in justice and the rule of law. He discouraged citizens from taking up arms against the Klan and cautioned them to allow law enforcement to do its work.

His opposition to violent white supremacists was met with disproportionate force. Historical records show that about 100 men were present at his lynching, and armed guards blocked every exit to the town square.

His murder sparked a statewide battle, and sensational, incorrect stories printed by right-wing papers and spread by orators fanned the flames of racism and white supremacy.

The end result was the disenfranchisement of Black voters and the entrenchment of segregation.

All of that sounded familiar to the audience members waiting for the play to begin.

They cared deeply about voting rights and education.

They worked in multiracial, multiethnic, multigenerational coalitions.

They'd been met with disproportionate police force at marches, rallies, and protests. They'd been pepper-sprayed and arrested on their way to the polls. They'd been smeared by right-wing media. They'd been in shouting matches with neo-Confederates and shoved to the ground by police.

Their determination to learn and retell Outlaw's story reflects an outrage that is being felt across the country as communities reckon with untold BIPOC histories and, especially in the South, what to do about Jim Crow era "Lost Cause" iconography like the 1914 Confederate monument that stands outside the Alamance County Historical Courthouse. That statue was erected and dedicated by some of the same people who killed Wyatt Outlaw—but few in the county knew that, until they started digging deeper.

Many say that they have been robbed: of a full historical and cultural education, of a sense of pride in who they are and where they came from, and of a spark that might have invested them in further learning. "I felt cheated," Dreama Caldwell said about the experience of learning about the county's hidden histories, especially the story of Wyatt Outlaw.[1] It inspired her to run for a seat on the county's board of commissioners—a race she lost, even though she raised more money than any of the other candidates. Dreama would have been the first Black woman commissioner in county history. Instead, in 2021, the county commissioners, members of the Graham City Council, and the Alamance County sheriff—all elected officials—remained 100 percent white and Republican.

None of these elected officials sat in the audience, but Dreama was there, masked against COVID-19. Members of Forward Motion Alamance, a local activist group, stealthily monitored the play's perimeter, protecting the actors and audience from disruptors. Behind the scenes, actors drew deep breaths, paced back and forth, adjusted their costumes.

Chorus frogs called; geese honked across the sky as the light slowly faded. At full dark—nearly an hour after sunset—the play began.

A NOTE TO OUR READERS: We started working on *The Legend of Wyatt Outlaw* in early 2021, meeting regularly to talk, interview folks, and write side by side. At first, because of the pandemic, we met on Zoom and in parks and outdoor spaces in Alamance County, but later we moved inside to libraries, coffee shops, and the Culture Mill, an arts incubator in Saxapahaw. Most of the book has been written together, in a plural voice, but some sections (like what follows) is just Sylvester, or just Belle. Those sections are marked with the writer's name.

SYLVESTER

The idea to write the play came from my good friend Walter Boyd, a local historian. Walter had tracked Wyatt's story for some time, despite the attempt by locals in the Reconstruction era to bury and disown not only his murder but also his significant impact on the rebuilding of the Black community in Alamance County after slavery's end.

Walter—he saw something in me that I didn't, not yet. He urged me to write my own play about Wyatt. So I did.

Opening Night

In the darkness, and as the prelude music played, audience members, in their concrete seats, saw a noose hanging over a tree branch, displayed on a lit screen.

There was an atmosphere of solemnity and solace. As the lights on the noose faded and the final note of the recorded music played, I, as the narrator, came out onstage wearing a black dress coat, black slacks, and a blood-red cotton turtleneck.

Standing behind the podium, I stared down at my script in silence, as if in prayer. I took one more beat, one more breath. Finally, I looked up and recited the first line of the play: "You may have heard by now the legend of Wyatt Outlaw."

Right here. At this exact moment, time stopped. And everything that happened in the last year flashed before my eyes, right there on the stage.

The space between the first and second lines of my play could be its own story. I thought about everything that had happened to get us to this moment in time.

The police killing of Jaquyn Light on a Graham front porch on January 28, 2020.[2] The COVID-19 pandemic and the hundreds of unmasked white people who gathered at Ace Speedway, a local racetrack, in defiance of the governor's shutdown orders.[3] The murder of George Floyd by Minneapolis police on May 25, 2020. The peaceful but anguished protests that followed, circling the Confederate statue that stood in the middle of our county seat. The unconstitutional laws against protest in Graham. The threats by Proud Boys and KKK members, the doxing and harassment of activists. The threats against Black children, against disabled people. Good ol' boys parked outside my house. Buying a handgun for protection.

The hundreds of arrests, and hundreds of thousands of dollars spent on arrests, surveillance, and court cases. The sting of pepper fog in my eyes, the bitter taste of it in my mouth.

". . . the legend of Wyatt Outlaw." I realized the importance of those words only when I spoke them for the first time in front of an audience—in front of my fellow activists—in front of people who understood how the past and present were connected.

I wasn't even sure what it meant to me. But I knew that Wyatt Outlaw represented something bigger than any one of us. And I wanted to chase it.

BELLE

When I first met Sylvester, I was learning about Wyatt Outlaw. I'd been reporting on the Black Lives Matter movement in Alamance County and saw how many activists had taken his 150-year-old story as inspiration for their work.

"Wyatt's story is a microcosm of everything Alamance County has been," Sylvester told me. Idealistic, hardworking, faithful, patriotic. Racist, violent, anti-democratic.

More than four years later, I'm *still* learning about him, because a figure like Wyatt holds many secrets. The historical record is scanty. We don't have any writing by Wyatt, though his life was the inspiration for characters in two best-selling novels by the writer, judge, and carpetbagger Albion Tourgée, an ally and close associate of Wyatt's. There are no known photographs of Wyatt, and his burial site is still unknown.

In Alamance County, most nonhistorians have learned about Wyatt Outlaw from the activist movement or from news reports about lynching victims in North Carolina. Before meeting Sylvester I'd spoken to Alamance

County activists, pastors, politicians, historians, and teachers about Wyatt. Most discovered Wyatt Outlaw in adulthood, outside the classroom, and each person had a slightly different take on the man: a heroic figure, a formerly enslaved person who fought for the North, a victim of racist violence. A mixed-race freedman and skilled carpenter. A father, a son, a peacemaker. A freedom fighter. A troublemaker. One person I spoke to, a white Republican county commissioner, mused that "as much as Wyatt Outlaw went through, he probably made some bad decisions too."[4]

Sylvester had been writing his play for several months and was in rehearsals when we first talked about Wyatt. I told him how I'd gotten interested: I wanted to tell a story, longer than the reported stories I'd done, about education and untold, deliberately hidden histories. When I started interviewing people in 2020, Wyatt's name came up again and again as the historical story they wish they had learned in school. Few people were taught much about Reconstruction. They learned about the Civil War through a Lost Cause, states' rights lens—not as a fight over slavery versus freedom. They missed out, they told me. They were betrayed.

Sylvester said that he felt he'd spent his childhood *not* learning the most important stories about where he grew up. By the time he was in college, he said, "I felt like my time had been wasted. We were all sponges, but everything we learned was in a textbook, and it turned out that textbook left a lot of things out."

After talking to Sylvester and watching his play that unseasonably warm February night, I began to see that the interpretations and reverberations of Wyatt Outlaw's story—how his life's work and the meaning of his life and death were covered up, forgotten, misinterpreted, reinterpreted, and rediscovered—were just as important as the historical facts.

"It's one thing to hear about Dr. King," Sylvester often reminds me. "It's another to say, 'I have a legacy right here.'"

This book is the story of "right here": Alamance County, North Carolina, a battleground of ideas about who gets to tell historical stories, whose voices get heard at the ballot box and in the public square, and who gets to feel like they belong.

SYLVESTER

Wyatt was a ghost. Maybe an idea. They had tried to erase the man, erase the story, erase the heinous lynching that was perpetrated by the townspeople in 1870. His murderers were never punished. Descendants of that mob still lived in town. How many would go to great lengths to stifle the story—to silence the storytellers?

I knew I had to bring Wyatt back to life.

From the start of the evening, I could feel that the audience understood the importance of Wyatt's story. It would be easy to assume that what happened in the Reconstruction era couldn't and wouldn't happen today. It would be easy to assume that the chaos of 2020 was America out of character and that our identity is much sweeter, much more civilized.

But on the day before our performance, as I was working on the stage set with a friend, a white man in a blue pickup truck drove by and yelled "Nigger" out of the driver-side window.

"Did that guy say what I thought he just said?" my friend asked.

"Sure did. Not the first time; won't be the last," I said.

The legend of Wyatt Outlaw lived in the local activists. That's where the story is. And I wondered whether there were other Wyatt Outlaws from the Reconstruction era, in other towns across the United States.

I would get a chance to find out when Belle, whom I'd invited by letter to attend the play, came to me afterward about cowriting a book about Wyatt and about the work of local activists. About the lack of education surrounding local history. About the injustices committed toward the Black community in America's history. About the lack of acknowledgment of their contributions to society.

I knew this book had to be written and that our different life experiences and vantage points would likely be a strength. I also knew I could never do it alone.

Wyatt was murdered for his audacity. But to be inspired by Wyatt is to be inspired by his courage. It would be up to me to find that courage. And so we set course, Belle and I, to tell the story of this community together.

PART ONE

HOME

CHAPTER ONE

SMALL TOWNS AND WHAT MATTERS

BELLE

Saxapahaw wasn't Sylvester's first choice of staging venue for his play about Wyatt Outlaw. The town—small, predominantly white, and liberal-leaning—had never been a common destination for many Black activists, who didn't care for the drive through Southern Alamance County, where Confederate flags flew proudly and Trump signs lined the roads.

As far as we know, Wyatt never went to Saxapahaw, which during his lifetime consisted of one textile mill and a village for its workers. The railroad didn't cross through Saxapahaw, so it's unlikely he would have seen its trees, small houses, and riverbanks from the window of a passenger car.

Wyatt's life, what we know of it, was centered ten miles north, in the small city of Graham, and in the adjacent railroad repair community known then as Company Shops, today as Burlington. As Alamance's county seat, Graham is where Wyatt had a family and his own property, operated a carpentry workshop that sometimes functioned as a tavern, and patrolled the streets as an elected constable and commissioner.

Graham is also where Sylvester grew up and lives today and where—perhaps like Wyatt—he has felt sometimes at home but often like an unwelcome, even threatened, outsider.

At the center of this town is the Alamance County Historical Courthouse, ringed by a traffic circle and a collection of small shops. In front of the courthouse's entrance is a thirty-foot-high Confederate monument: A tall column carved with crossed Confederate flags rises from a square plinth; a marble soldier, facing north with his rifle at his side, stands on top of the column, one foot stepped forward as if he might walk off the precipice.

Locals know the marble soldier as "Conrad," though it is neither as unique nor as old as many of them think. The monument—plinth, marble, carvings—looks common because it was, of the type that was mass-manufactured, bought by local groups, often the United Daughters of the Confederacy, and installed throughout the South during the Jim Crow era of segregation and brutal disenfranchisement of Black people. Graham's monument was installed in 1914 by the United Daughters of the Confederacy, and Jacob Long, one of the architects of Wyatt Outlaw's murder, spoke at its unveiling.[1]

ON CONFEDERATE STATUES

Though some Confederate memorials were dedicated shortly after the Civil War ended, the two most significant periods of Confederate memorial building happened decades later, during the Jim Crow era, from around 1900 through the 1920s, and during the civil rights era, from the mid-1950s through the end of the 1960s. These monuments were often placed directly in front of courthouses or other public buildings and delivered a clear message to Black people: This is a white space.

According to the Southern Poverty Law Center, which tracks the more than 2,000 remaining public memorials to Confederate soldiers, most of these statues and monuments reflect a historically inaccurate "Lost Cause" mythology, venerating the Confederate dead while ignoring the brutal history of enslavement. It wasn't until the 2015 massacre of nine African Americans at Emanuel African Methodist Episcopal Church in Charleston, South Carolina, that significant numbers of monuments and Confederate flags began to be removed from public spaces. More were removed after the 2017 Unite the Right rally in Charlottesville, which killed one person, and still more were removed and toppled after the 2020 police murder of George Floyd.

In six Southern states, including North Carolina, Confederate monuments have been protected by Republican legislatures and governors, who signed new laws preventing their removal. A 2015 North Carolina law, enacted one month after the mass killing at Mother Emanuel, made it illegal to relocate a monument or memorial unless it proposes a threat to public safety.*

Though dozens of people have been arrested and injured by police in protests connected to the Confederate monument in Graham, county commissioners have refused community requests to relocate it, choosing instead to surround it with a $32,000 fence.† In 2021, the state and Alamance chapters of the NAACP filed a lawsuit claiming that the county violated the state constitution and exercised discriminatory intent by refusing to relocate the statue. Both a trial and appeals court judge ruled that Alamance County and its commissioners acted within the state law.‡

The statue remains on public property in North Carolina—as do 140 others.

---

* Monument Protection Act, sec. 100–2.1, "Protection of Monuments, Memorials, and Works of Art," North Carolina General Assembly website, accessed May 29, 2025. www.ncleg.gov/EnactedLegislation/Statutes/PDF/ByChapter/Chapter_100.pdf.

† Jessica Winters, "Why Is an 8-Foot-Tall Iron Fence Going Up around the Confederate Monument in Graham? We Got Answers," WFMYNews2, August 6, 2021, www.wfmynews2.com/article/news/local/why-is-an-8-foot-tall-iron-fence-going-up-around-the-confederate-monument-in-graham-we-got-answers/83-64254f7e-18e2-4552-bb90-53cfd2ea406e.

‡ Lisa Sorg, "Alamance County Can Allow Confederate Monument to Stand, NC Appeals Court Rules," NC *Newsline*, March 19, 2024, https://ncnewsline.com/2024/03/19/alamance-county-can-allow-confederate-monument-to-stand-nc-appeals-court-rules/.

On July 11, 2020, Sylvester sat outdoors at a nearby pub, in full view of the statue, and thought about Wyatt Outlaw, whose story had been told that day over the course of a protest march from Burlington, a town of 60,000 people, into Graham, a town of 18,000. (Burlington sits to the north and west of Graham, and its borders are contiguous.) The purpose of the march had been twofold: to demand the removal of the Confederate monument, and to draw attention to the police mistreatment of Black and Brown people in Alamance County. "No Chance Alamance"—that was the county's unofficial nickname from people in the know, a reference to Sheriff Terry Johnson's nearly two-decades-long practice of targeting Black and Latinx people for traffic stops and arrests. In 2012, Johnson's department had been sued by the US Department of Justice for "targeting Latinos for investigation, detention, and arrest, and conducting unreasonable seizures and other unlawful law enforcement actions."[2]

Graham's power structure, aided by the sheriff, was similarly hostile to Black people and antiracist groups. The city council was 100 percent white, 100 percent Republican. After the May 25 police murder of George Floyd in Minneapolis, many in Graham wanted to protest, but according to an obscure 1978 city ordinance, any demonstration of two or more people required a permit, and the town had issued a moratorium on permits.

But July 11 was different. Days before, the local chapter of the NAACP, along with the other plaintiffs, had challenged the city's ban on protests, claiming them unconstitutional, and sued the officials responsible for enforcing it. On July 6, all parties moved for a consent temporary restraining order regarding the ordinance, preventing its enforcement.[3]

Reluctantly, the city granted a permit for a march planned by local activists and a charismatic forty-year-old pastor, the Reverend Gregory Drumwright, who preached at the Citadel Church in Greensboro. Over the mile-long walk, Reverend Drumwright repeated the now-familiar names of victims of police brutality and white supremacy: George Floyd, Trayvon Martin, Breonna Taylor, Tamir Rice. And a less-familiar one: Wyatt Outlaw. He paused to tell people in the crowd of more than 600 marchers, "This is where Wyatt planned to build his church. . . . This is where Wyatt lived with his mother and children. . . . This is where Wyatt Outlaw was hung by white supremacists." No one at this protest got arrested. Nothing got broken, and no one tried to topple the statue. But young Black men, used to presenting a stoic face to the world, had cried—"profusely," Drumwright later remembered—while hearing Wyatt's story narrated to them as they marched.

Sylvester knew that story well, having learned it around 2016, when Dave Wright, a friend in the theater community, wrote and staged a play called *Wyatt Outlaw*. Wright's play sketched out the basic historical facts of Wyatt's life and death, focusing on the conflict between Republicans and the White Brotherhood and on the decision to murder Wyatt. That performance had happened in Burlington, inside the comfortable darkness of the Paramount Theater. But on this hot and sticky afternoon in July, with the memory of the successful march fresh in his mind, Sylvester began to consider what that play would feel like outdoors, in view of Wyatt's former place of work, of the home where he raised his children, of the courthouse he defended from Klan members—and also in view of the statue, which had been erected some forty-four years after his death and which Black and Brown residents had gritted their teeth and borne for more than a century now, walking past it for their own court dates, to file important papers, to go to work. Shouldn't everyone in Graham have a chance to hear the full story of this town?

THE PARTY OF LINCOLN?

Republicans these days like to claim Abraham Lincoln as one of their own, but in reality his party more closely resembled the modern Democratic Party. In the mid-nineteenth century, the Republican Party was the one more aligned with racial and economic equality, as well as "big government" programs like the income tax, federally funded education and transportation, and government oversight on behalf of citizens.

Like today's Democratic Party, nineteenth-century Republicanism also had moderate and progressive sides. Abraham Lincoln was a Republican whose views evolved from "antislavery" to abolitionist over the course of the Civil War. Radical Republicans wanted more than the abolition of slavery: They fought for civil rights and equality for Black men. This was the party faction that attracted Black voters to register to vote in droves in 1867. ("Radical ticket" referred to the more progressive, equal rights, working-class side of the Republican Party.)

Democrats, by contrast, were known as the conservative party. They championed "agrarian" values and opposed big government; they fought to maintain slavery. After the Civil War, they opposed the expansion of civil rights, including voting rights, to Black men. Most members of the first (Reconstruction era) and second (Jim Crow era) iterations of the Ku Klux Klan were Democrats. In the early twentieth century, Southern Democrats enacted Jim Crow laws that disenfranchised Black voters for decades.

After the 1964 Civil Rights Act signed into law by President Johnson, many anti-integration Southern Democrats became Republicans, and

(continued)

many Black voters—outraged by Republican opposition to protection of their civil rights—switched alliances to the Democratic Party. Republicans, who'd become powerfully pro-business and less invested in civil rights following Reconstruction, also gained conservative voters who opposed gay rights, women's rights, and social welfare programs.

SYLVESTER

Regularly, after an organized, peaceful demonstration in Graham, some of the local activists would sit at the picnic tables outside of the pub only yards from the Confederate statue, debriefing and decompressing. I always found it odd that our debriefing space was in such close proximity to the meeting spaces of the neo-Confederate counterprotesters, sometimes seen having a drink at the same pub at the same time. The police officer with the megaphone may have been the umpire for my high school baseball games. The Confederate sympathizer wielding the large red flag might be the clerk at the local store that rang up my groceries last week or a former high school classmate. And the angry man in the Trump bandanna, shouting racial slurs over the shoulder of a sheriff's deputy and pointing a finger in my face, may be the son of the owners of that barbecue place three stop signs down. In a small town like Graham, knowing who was who was not only important but inevitable.

NEO-CONFEDERATES

The Southern Poverty Law Center defines neo-Confederacy as "a reactionary, revisionist branch of American white nationalism typified by its predilection for symbols of the Confederate States of America."* In Southern towns and cities, neo-Confederates are most often roused toaction by perceived threats to Lost Cause memorials, like the Confederate statue that stands in front of the Alamance County Courthouse or the renaming of public roads and buildings.

In 2017, the local neo-Confederate group Alamance County Taking Back Alamance County (ACTBAC) organized a "Confederate Memorial Day Celebration" marking the 156th anniversary of North Carolina's secession from the Union. On the group's Facebook page,

ACTBAC described its purpose as "not just to support our precious Confederate Flag but to support oour rights as American Citizens," though it was unclear how those rights were being infringed. More than 100 supporters, many holding flags and signs, showed up at the courthouse that May. By May 2021, a rally commemorating the 160th anniversary of secession attracted only a couple of dozen people to the courthouse. It was outnumbered by the antiracist counterprotesters who stood in the park across the street.

This decrease in public neo-Confederate activism follows a national trend. After the deadly August 2017 Unite the Right rally in Charlottesville, Virginia, the number of neo-Confederate groups across the South began to decline, from sixteen groups in 2021 to five in 2023. But the impulse to venerate the Confederacy goes way back and is not easily excised. Groups like the United Daughters of the Confederacy (established 1894) and the Sons of Confederate Veterans (established 1896) began rewriting the history of the Civil War during the brutal period of Jim Crow segregation. They venerated the Ku Klux Klan, financed and installed statues of Confederate soldiers in public spaces, and maintained the fiction that the South seceded and fought the Civil War not to maintain slavery but for "the preservation of liberty and freedom."† Their mythology has influenced everything from history textbooks to the platform of today's Republican Party. Their influence on right-wing politics has been consistent, dating back to the civil rights era.

In 2009, historian Nancy MacLean wrote that "even into the twenty-first century mainstream conservative Republican politicians continued to associate themselves with issues, symbols, and organizations inspired by the neo-Confederate Right."‡ This trend continues. Recent examples include the January 6, 2021, insurrection, when pro-Trump insurrectionists, some carrying or wearing Confederate flags, violently attacked the US Capitol.

---

* "Neo-Confederate," Southern Poverty Law Center, accessed May 29, 2025, www.splcenter.org/resources/extremist-files/neo-confederate/.

† Home page of the Sons of Confederate Veterans, accessed May 29, 2025, scv.org.

‡ Nancy MacLean, "Neo-Confederacy against the New Deal: The Regional Utopia of the Modern American Right," in *The Myth of Southern Exceptionalism*, ed. Matthew D. Lassiter and Joseph Crespino (New York: Oxford University Press, 2009), 231.

Those counterprotesters? Their anger, pride, and ignorance were directly connected to the misinformation passed down to them about their home, their beloved Alamance County.

Just after a protest, baking in the hot sun, near the sidewalk where we were just being threatened by neo-Confederates (who were also still close by), I tried to visualize what it might look like to reenact the murder of Wyatt Outlaw at the actual murder scene, 150 years later. I thought about how powerful that would be. My overall purpose of such a reenactment—in the form of a play about Wyatt—would be to educate, not to anger. To spark the conversation about his life. To make the town face its harsh truths. To educate the locals, Black and white, on what led to the look and feel of today's Alamance County. To remind local police of the tragedy of their own fallen hero. To teach the kids the importance of accurate history. It was all perfect.

It was yet to be seen just how difficult that would be.

• • • •

I went home and sent Dave a message through Facebook: What if we staged your Wyatt Outlaw play in downtown Graham? Outside, there wouldn't be the same threats of COVID exposure, and being steps away from where Wyatt died would be powerful. They could even invite Samuel Merritt, Wyatt's great-great-grandson, who'd spoken a few words at a 2016 production of the play.

Despite my enthusiasm, Dave stalled and demurred, sending intermittent messages over the next few weeks. It was a good idea, but it wasn't the right time. It was too complicated, too risky with all the political unrest and fights over protest permits. Finally, in late August, Dave told me that he'd agreed to allow a staged reading of the play at Elon, a local private college that catered primarily to out-of-state students.

I was disappointed but responded with words of gratitude: "Thank you for using your play to educate the youth about WO," I wrote.

• • • •

"Why don't you write your own play?" Walter Boyd, another friend in the theater community, asked me a few days later. A white retired attorney and amateur historian, Walter had consulted on historical details for Dave Wright's play and thought that I could write one just as good, possibly stronger, from my vantage as a Black man who grew up just down the street from the courthouse.

I was flattered, of course—but also scared. The idea took hold of my mind over the next few days as I wrestled with my fears, not so much about what Alamance County's police and neo-Confederates might do to me but about whether I was up to writing it. I had acted in and directed many plays but had never written one myself. I didn't even know the whole history. Yet Walter's suggestion, his faith in me, was a challenge that I could not move past.

At first, I imagined a dramatic vigil staged in downtown Graham around Sesquicentennial Park, where Wyatt drew his last breath. Maybe we could call the play itself a protest. Because wouldn't it be a kind of protest—an objection to the violence of white supremacy? I pictured an actor dragged down Main Street, white-robed men on horseback, the audience seated on the same sidewalks where they'd walked, that spring and summer, in silent protest.

I asked around and was told to contact the Graham Police Department. Duane Flood, a lieutenant in Graham's police department, informed me I'd have to get the performance approved by the state and then by the City of Graham, where I'd need to go before the city council and give my name and address publicly. That gave me pause—my friends and I had been followed both by police and by neo-Confederates—so I turned next to the City of Burlington, envisioning a similar outdoor production where the old train depot stood. With Wyatt's connection to railroad labor organizing, this wasn't a bad second choice, but the parks department official I spoke to didn't like the idea of calling it a protest or vigil and suggested moving the date. I'd envisioned something in October, so the play might encourage voter turnout, but she advised something later—a lot later, she said. Let's wait until the smoke blows over.

Let's wait, not here, not now: This was what I heard, again and again, even from people who, on the surface, agreed with me.

BELLE

W. E. B. Du Bois wrote, in 1905, "Study the past then, if you would comprehend the present; read history if you would know how to vote intelligently, read history if you do not know what sound money is, read history if you cannot grasp the Negro problem."[4]

But it's hard to read the history of a town like Graham, where the only museums are privately run, where most people remember learning about the Civil War as a fight over states' rights, and where Reconstruction is barely discussed at all.

Graham is barely 175 years old, a small town sketched out in the same year that Alamance County split from Orange County to the east, but its history, of course, is much older. The earliest people to make their home in what we now call Alamance County were the Sissipahaw Indians, who lived along the Haw River watershed for thousands of years before Europeans arrived. They farmed, hunted, fished, and made pottery from the abundant clay. Their language was never recorded, and their population was decimated by diseases brought by encroaching European settlers. By the eighteenth century, most of the surviving Sissipahaw joined tribes to the north and south.

The Haw River, which takes its name from them, would remain important to the county's history. This rocky river is some 110 miles long and bordered by steeply eroded cliffs. Its waters can run at two feet or twenty feet, depending on how much it rains, but have an average depth below five feet. At low flow, the river shows its bones: jutting, gray-black igneous rock, formed hundreds of millions of years ago in what is now West Africa.

The earliest European settlers built dams and mill races along the Haw, using its power for grist mills to process grain and corn and eventually for textile mills. Enslaved people, escaping along the Underground Railroad, used the river's crossings as landmarks and as a way to cover their tracks as they fled.

Arriving in the 1700s, the area's first German, Scotch-Irish, and English settlers were mostly small farmers, growing apples and stone fruits, sweet potatoes and white potatoes and field peas, collards and corn and onions and tomatoes. But there were also slave-farmed plantations growing grain and tobacco and cotton and a merchant class selling goods to free workers. The nineteenth-century construction of dams and mill races on the Haw, as well as the invention of the cotton gin, led to a thriving textile manufacturing business that depended, before 1865, on slave labor not just to pick but also to process the raw cotton and run the machinery that turned it into cloth. Edwin Holt, manufacturer of dyed, woven cottons known as "Alamance Plaids," was the wealthiest man in North Carolina when he died in 1884. His son Thomas Holt later became governor—one of three governors from the same small town, Haw River, in this semirural county.[5]

Today, thanks to NAFTA, the textile business has mostly gone to Mexico and China, and the Piedmont is known for a knowledge economy driven by our dozens of universities, our four major hospital systems, and tech giants like IBM and Cisco. Alamance County doesn't have any of those businesses—its largest private employer is the clinical lab test company LabCorp—but nevertheless the town is changing, becoming a bedroom community for those larger employers and a retirement destination. Still, many older folks in Alamance, like Sylvester's mother, Patsy, are retirees who worked their whole lives in textiles or farming, the same as their ancestors did in the nineteenth century.

In Wyatt Outlaw's day, the Piedmont was connected by the Fayetteville and Western Plank Road, which stretched from Fayetteville to Bethania.

This 129-mile-long toll road, built from timber planks that sat flatly on top of the rutted dirt roads, was the longest of its kind when it was completed in 1854. It was soon replaced by railroads that connected the Piedmont with other parts of the state and with the rest of the country.[6]

Connection to the wider world via the railroads transformed the Piedmont, but it's not why Wyatt was there. Like many Black men of his time, Wyatt lived where he did because he was born there. His parents were Jemima Phillips and Chesley Faucett; both, like Wyatt, lived most or all of their lives in what became Alamance County when 429 square miles were carved out of Orange County in 1849. Unlike Wyatt, they would both see old age.

By luck of birth, Chesley Faucett was an exceptional American. A white man, a landowner as well as a slave owner, he was born in 1792 in what was then Orange County. His family had lived there since the beginning of the eighteenth century and must have seen the Battle of Alamance, a colonial uprising that predated the American Revolution. This legacy was his first, most significant privilege—his white family who came before him, farming the very land and making the connections that would later become his, smoothing the way for his considerable financial and political power. By the time he was sixty-eight, he was the sixth-wealthiest man in Alamance County, a merchant and a planter. His brick home, with ten rooms and eleven fireplaces, was one of the largest around, its barred-window basement used to hold prisoners before their transport to the county jail in Hillsborough.[7]

Chesley had rights that Jemima, Wyatt, and most of their neighbors did not have. He could testify in court, and no Black person could testify against him. That gave people like him considerable power over Black people, especially enslaved Black people. As a white person in the antebellum South, Chesley had the right to buy and sell people. He used this right, buying a dozen or more slaves who worked his land and produced goods for his store. Chesley could travel, hire a private educator for his children, and decide what his slaves could and could not learn, eat, wear.

Maybe the rarest of Chesley's rights was his right to vote—in North Carolina when he came of age, only about 6 percent of people had this right. One had to be a man, and white, and a landowner in order to choose one's elected representatives. This was true all the way until 1856, when North Carolina became the last American state to allow nonlanded gentry the vote. By this time Chesley was a leader of Union Ridge Christian Church, had helped to organize a college, had served in the state legislature, and was father of ten children born to his wife, Margaret. Though a slave owner, Chesley was a

Whig and an antisecessionist. More than loss of slaves and the wealth created by their labor, he feared the Confederacy, resented conscription, and preferred to stick with the Union.

Chesley followed the familiar path to significance in this country—inherit land, buy more, wield influence. But he was closely connected to others who did not have those privileges yet who became more historically consequential and who saw their own rights advance far more than his own. In fact, Chesley saw his rights diminish before he died, just a month after his eightieth birthday. After the war, he could no longer buy, sell, or own another person. After the Fourteenth Amendment was ratified in 1868, his freedom shrank further. Now if he harmed a Black or Indigenous person, he could be held accountable—they could testify against him in a court of law. We don't know if Chesley resented the loss of these brutal freedoms, but we do know that this was how a majority of former slaveholders felt. Their new accountability was an insult, as were the new freedoms of Black and Indigenous people.

Jemima Phillips, the mother of Chesley's first child, was exceptional in a different way—through her choices, actions, and fortitude rather than birth. As a Black woman in the antebellum South, she was born into a precarious identity that followed her everywhere she went. It's possible that Jemima was born into a free Black family, and if this is true, there's some good fortune at work in her story, as fewer than 5 percent of Black people in North Carolina were free in 1800. But scholars guess that Jemima was among these free people for a couple of reasons: Her last name, Phillips, connects her to free Black people living in Caswell County around the time she was born. We have no record of her enslavement. She also knew her birthdate—August 20, 1796—which would have been unusual for someone born enslaved. Slave owners intentionally kept these dates from the enslaved as a way of dehumanizing them.[8] Jemima's knowledge of this date suggests that she saw it written down, perhaps in a family Bible, or lived a life where a birthday could be marked in some way. Perhaps she could read it—learning to read was a right that enslaved people had taken away from them by the law in North Carolina in 1816.[9]

But even as a free person, Jemima's gender and skin color would have limited her freedoms at her time of birth and for most of her life. Travel was dangerous for free people of color—slave catchers might kidnap and sell Black people into slavery, and North Carolina was surrounded by slave states. Before the Fourteenth Amendment that gave people of color equal protection, a white person could have done anything to Jemima—stolen from her, threatened her, beaten her, or raped her—and Jemima would have had little legal recourse. Before 1868, her testimony against a white person would not have been admissible in court.

Given all of these limitations, her relationship to Chesley was almost certainly an extremely imbalanced one. He was a white man, a landowner, and a slave owner. She was a Black woman, possibly enslaved by Chesley, possibly free. No matter what, she lacked Chesley's considerable freedoms and resources. We don't know how they met, whether their relationship was consensual, or whether Wyatt was the product of rape or coercion. We do know that sometime around 1820, Jemima gave birth to a son she named Wyatt.

It's unclear whether Jemima lived with Wyatt when he was young or whether raising her own child was another freedom denied to her, as it was to many Black families in Southern states. Local historians think that Wyatt's last name came from Nancy and George Outlaw, a couple who owned a 100-acre tobacco farm just across the creek from the Faucetts. A mixed-race man named Wyatt, about the correct age, is mentioned in George's 1854 will in a note forbidding his sale: "My negro man Wyatt be hired yearly."[10] This limited though considerable freedom—the ability to hire oneself out for wages—was common among manumitted former slaves, people whose freedom had been bought by relatives or sometimes by Quaker abolitionists who allowed them to live as free people on their land.

But back to Jemima and her freedoms, which increased considerably after the war. Not only was she free from slavery and the shadow it cast over Black people's lives, but she was also legally protected in ways she had never been before. Though she could not vote, she could testify in court, a right that would become especially important before she died. If she didn't live with Wyatt when he was a child, she did live in his home in her later years, where she cared for his three young children after he was widowed. In this four-room home, we can imagine her doing things that she missed out on in Wyatt's young life: cooking meals and presiding over a Sunday dinner table, perhaps singing lullabies or teaching her grandchildren to read. We can imagine her mending clothes and making sure her son and grandchildren were well-dressed. We can imagine her attending worship services nearby, legally able to attend church for the first time without a white person present.

She may have felt safe in that house, at least for a time, and enormously proud of Wyatt. Her son was a prominent man. He ran a carpentry shop and was known and respected by Black and white people in town. For that reason, and for his skill as a political organizer, he was eventually appointed town constable and commissioner by the governor of North Carolina,

William Holden. Wyatt traveled to Raleigh to state conventions and later founded an Alamance County chapter of the Loyal League, a political group whose goal was to help Black men find the courage and confidence to vote.

This was not a life without sorrow or hardship—Wyatt was a widow, and Jemima's grandchildren must have missed their mother—but Jemima's golden years were a time of dignity, mobility, and freedom from servitude. Jemima never had rights equal to white people or to men, but at the end of her life her rights were on an upswing.

Perhaps even more significant were the rights Jemima saw conferred to her son. At birth, Wyatt did not have a last name or a birth certificate. There were no schools for Black children—in fact, if Wyatt had been enslaved, it would have been against the law for anyone to teach him to read and write. Even free, he couldn't own property or get married or hold office or vote.

But Jemima was able to see her son conquer all of these barriers to full citizenship and help others conquer them too. For a few years, living with Wyatt and his children, she experienced that version of the American dream that white families have almost always taken for granted: to imagine that life would only get better for one's children, and even better than that for one's grandchildren; to know that however humbly one started out in life, whatever sacrifices or struggles one had along the way, they were investments in a better future—a freer future, a more prosperous future.

This time period, known to us as the Reconstruction era, is the least-taught in American history. If we learn about it at all, we are taught that it was a failure, a time of turbulence and upheaval and things moving all too quickly.[11]

But imagine Jemima standing one morning just outside her home on Main Street in Graham. Maybe it's a summer morning, warm and humid, the time of year when you get your chores done early before the heat of the day. The crape myrtles are in bloom, and a breeze blows their magenta blossoms down the street. From her own front yard she can see the county courthouse, a place where her son does the work of protecting people and helping them access new rights and where a carpetbagger judge, Albion Tourgée, holds court to hear and settle disputes and endeavors to protect the rights, for the first time since the county's founding, of everyone who lives there.

Are there bitter, defeated Confederates, people who see Jemima's and Wyatt's gains as an affront, part of a zero-sum game in which the rights of people of color subtracted rights from white people? Is there fear, precarity, danger? A reckless right-wing media? Yes, yes, yes, yes, and yes. In that way, we'd learn, it was a time not so different from the one we live in now.

SYLVESTER

It had already occurred to me that part of my interest in the story of Wyatt Outlaw had a little, or a lot, to do with the absence of my own ancestral knowledge. I remember reading Marcus Garvey's words: "A people without a knowledge of their past history, origin and culture is like a tree without roots." I knew it was true, true on a community level and true on a personal one, because the absence of familial history has sometimes left me feeling like a boat out of water.

When Belle contacted me in the fall of 2020, I thought she'd mostly ask questions about the play that I was writing, but a lot of her questions were about me and what it was like to grow up in Alamance. Had I ever had any Black male teachers? (Only a PE teacher.) What did I learn in history class about slavery? About the Civil War? (The Civil War ended slavery. It was a long time ago. That's about all I learned.) Did I ever hear about Reconstruction in school? (The sense I had of the Reconstruction era was that it was to rebuild what was, not to build something new.) Who were my childhood heroes? (My stepfather, Willie, and Andruw Jones.) Who's Andruw Jones? (Wait, you don't know who Andruw Jones is?)

I told her that Andruw Jones was one of the greatest center fielders in history. At that time Alamance County, and North Carolina for that matter, was crawling with Atlanta Braves fans. But I wouldn't have learned about Andruw if it weren't for my stepfather's love of baseball. As a young kid sitting on the living room floor in front of our small television, I could have sworn it was Superman I was watching fly through the air to catch those line drives hit into center field at 104 mph. And how many home runs did he take away from disappointed opposing hitters as he climbed the wall to snatch the ball out of the air to keep the Braves in the lead? My stepfather used to say, "Been anybody else, that ball woulda dropped. Andruw so fast he standin' there waitin' on it."

We couldn't afford to go to the baseball games, but we had enough to keep the cable on. Legend has it that Willie never missed a day in forty years down at the old Cannon Culp weaving plant. His work ethic was legendary. Even as he became elderly and after recovering from a broken leg, baffled neighbors would watch Willie pushing a lawn mower in our small Graham yard with one hand and holding himself up on a walker with the other. Like Wyatt, he was willing to make the sacrifice for the betterment of people around him.

But that wasn't the only thing they had in common. During one of our midnight Facebook Messenger discussions about Wyatt, my historian friend

Walter started to talk about an old family Bible that he thought was in the possession of Wyatt's great-great-grandson Dr. Samuel Merritt. He revealed that Wyatt's speculated birthday was written toward the front of the Bible. This was a revelation to me, because up to that point, we didn't know of any record, official or otherwise, of Wyatt's birth. Finding even the most basic details about a Black man's life, even a man of such importance, was a chore. Family Bibles with personal records written in them were more common in those days, but the Outlaw family Bible dated decades after Wyatt's death.

Likewise Willie, whose great-grandparents were likely born in slavery, as possibly were his grandparents, could never be sure how old he was. The South Carolina birth certificate that was issued was said to have the wrong date and year, and his parents couldn't read or write. Yet a handwritten date, "February 6th 1935," made its way into the family Bible once kept in the possession of his late older sister. In my stepfather's struggle with record-keeping, I felt a connection to Wyatt and Dr. Merritt.

But there was something else. It was the image of Wyatt Outlaw. I mean literally.

As far as we know, there is no surviving photograph of him. He is said to have been light-skinned, with wavy hair and a forthright gaze. However, when I'd Google his name, an old black-and-white photograph of a dark-skinned older man in a black suit coat and cravat would pop up. The grainy, waist-up photo features his hands, folded one over the other, with what I believe is a walking cane under them. The man was Caswell Holt, formerly enslaved to the Holt family of Alamance, another brave historical figure whom Belle and I would learn much more about through our research over the next few years.

Caswell Holt's photo has been mistaken for Wyatt on several occasions. Even Alamance County law enforcement used what they thought was Wyatt's photo during a filmed fallen officer service in 2020 at the Alamance County Courthouse. It was a particularly awkward moment as they played a country song titled "If It Weren't for the Badge" over the part of the video showing Caswell's face beside Wyatt's name at the end of the service. Ironically, the words of the song at that very moment were "this can't be real."[12]

The very first time I saw this photo I thought, *My God, he looks just like my stepfather.* I meant that. Similar face, similar build, same expression. They could have been twins. I had to show my mother. The next time I saw her, I showed her the photo and got her opinion.

"Don't that look just like Willie, Mama," I said.

"Oh my God. Sho' does. Look just like him," she said, smiling.

To me, the hands were the most important thing about the photo. Main characters, so to speak. They were facing down, covering what were almost surely calluses from hard labor. I've always believed a person could write a song solely from the story their hands tell. His calluses were covered, just like his story was. Just like Wyatt's story.

They were all connected. We were all connected.

I also thought the photo was Wyatt the very first time I saw it. Because that was the story. "This is Wyatt Outlaw." When I learned the truth, it made me realize how easily we can get history wrong. That's why I hoped that somewhere along the way I would get to talk to Samuel Merritt, Wyatt's great-great-grandson, at length. I wanted to get a sense of what it's like to discover your ancestry as he'd done with Wyatt's story, unfolding piece by piece the heroics of someone who was a member of your family. What does it do for your life to set the record straight?

So, what was the draw? Was it the lack of my own ancestral knowledge? Was it the familiarity of an inaccurate photo? Or did Wyatt represent all that America misunderstood about its past?

I knew that for myself, and perhaps for the other activists in Alamance County, it runs deeper than a list of historical facts. Much deeper. But in order to really begin to understand the importance of the story of Wyatt Outlaw and Alamance County, I needed to dig into a memory that had been packed away for years, much like Wyatt's legacy. I knew I needed to go home again.

CHAPTER TWO
TESTIMONY

SYLVESTER

Home, for me, is a memory. Or should I say, home is a collection of memories. Everything that has uplifted me, that has taken on cherished meaning in my mind, is part of the feeling of home. Home is feeling grounded, safe, and like I belong.

As I was growing up, large parts of Alamance County didn't feel like home to me. Part of this is by design. I wasn't meant to feel at home in Graham's town square, where a Confederate statue still stands in front of our historic courthouse. I wasn't meant to feel at home in the shabby rentals that my parents struggled to afford and that our landlords barely kept up. I'm not even sure I was meant to feel at home in classrooms that were supposed to educate me: Hardly any of my teachers were Black, and we rarely learned about the accomplishments or significance of people who looked like me. The ones we talked about each February, like Martin Luther King Jr. and Harriet Tubman, were never people who'd grown up anywhere close to where I lived. I must have thought that no one important and Black ever came from Alamance County.

Home was also, of course, a physical structure: the roof over my head, the place where I lay down to sleep at night. The only home I ever lived in that was owned by my family was a small, one-story frame house at the end of a dirt road. This house was in Mebane, a small town in Alamance County founded in 1809 and close enough to Graham that some of Wyatt Outlaw's story spills into its streets and forests. Its motto today, printed in slanted letters on the green and blue town sign, is "Positively Charming."

The part of town where we lived was both in Mebane and not in Mebane. Our predominantly Black neighborhood was known as the West End, which was part of an "extraterritorial jurisdiction." That meant we had a Mebane address and paid Mebane taxes, but we didn't get any of the town services—no water or sewer—and my parents couldn't vote in town elections or run for office.

Not that they would have chosen to do that. They weren't activists, or what you might call political. They were quiet, hardworking, deeply religious Black Americans who'd gotten the short end of the stick almost all their lives. "Can't win for losin'," my stepfather, Willie, used to say. In South Carolina, he'd been pulled out of school to work in the fields in second grade. My mother, who grew up in Alamance County, made it to eighth grade. She worked in the fields too—both of them on farms sharecropped by their families and owned by white people. Eventually they both found jobs in the textile mills in Alamance County. They met, married, and raised three kids: my older sister, Carla; my younger brother, Timothy; and me. They taught us to listen to our elders, to be tidy and quiet, and to stay out of trouble.

The house in Mebane was small, bought by Willie in 1972 for a few thousand dollars. Carla and Timothy and I slept in the living room, and our parents slept in the only bedroom. There was no toilet, only a bare place in the yard where an outhouse used to sit. Our bathroom was a bucket that sat along the wall of the living room and had to be emptied at the end of the night, or we could go outside to the woods. We had options.

Yet I never thought much about safety, money, or hardship. The responsibilities that went along with those down times were not on me—not then.

My parents both worked long hours in the textile industry that still dominated Alamance when I was a kid: first or second shift for my mother, third shift for Willie. I can remember my stepfather coming home one day with a ball he had wound out of electrical tape. On his breaks at Cannon Culp weaving plant, he'd sat and wound the tape as tight as he could. He started with something in the center to give it weight and kept working on it every day for a couple of months until he had a basketball-sized toy to bring home to the kids. No, it didn't bounce, and I remember it being too heavy to actually play with. "Just pretend it works," I told Timothy, who must have been three years old at the time. So we played basketball in the dirt and grass in the yard with a makeshift goal and a ball that rumbled the rocks like an earthquake. The dirt would fly into our eyes as the ball hit the ground.

Mama would often pull a chair off the porch and find a shady tree, kick off her shoes to feel the ground under her feet, and read romance novels. With only an eighth-grade education, Mama's ability was a prized possession and a great source of pleasure.

Pulled out of school when he was, Willie never learned to read. His language of self-expression was working with his hands and capturing memories. He was always eager to snap Polaroids of ordinary happenings. I still have a fuzzy sunlit photo he took of me, Carla, and Timothy standing around the wooden hauling trailer that rarely moved from where it sat in our backyard. My sister is posing as a superhero, my brother is smiling and holding as still as a four-year-old can, and I'm standing inside the trailer wearing one of my favorite red shirts, one arm draped protectively over each of my siblings' shoulders. Behind us is the wood line.

In our rural landscape, you could see the stars on a clear night. I thought that the stars could testify to the history of the world, with each one overseeing a patch of earth and its collection of stories. No one could tear them down or move or replace them as they saw fit. These were the same stars that twinkled above Wyatt Outlaw in the previous century, but I didn't know about his story then. Would it have scared me? Wyatt was a courageous man, but he saw a lot of trouble in his life, and he died a violent death. Everything I'd been taught by Mama and Willie said to stay away from violence, stay away from trouble.

I think what would have spoken to me about his life, and probably to Mama and Willie too, was his faith in God. Wyatt was a religious man who, when he got a little money, used it to buy land for a church. That church land, bought for twenty dollars with four other men, eventually housed Wayman Chapel AME, a one-story brick church just four blocks from the courthouse. As a child I never attended Wayman Chapel or knew its history, but I loved being in church. I had a leather-bound Bible engraved with my name, given to me by the old folks at St. Luke Christian Church. I could still smell the newness of it. I couldn't wait to take it to the next Bible study.

That was the kind of kid I was: not an outlaw or a rule-breaker or a rabble-rouser. A dreamer, maybe. A quiet kid with a big imagination. A listener.

• • • •

The first place I heard the testimony of my elders was in the church, where my mother and stepfather sent me because they didn't want me testifying in the courthouse, before police and a judge and lawyers. In our small town, it was easy for young Black men to get caught up in the system. I heard this

Sylvester (*center*) with his siblings in the backyard of their house in Mebane, North Carolina, 1992.

phrase so often, "caught up in the system," that I imagined not court or jail but a vast, sticky web I needed to stay clear of.

I didn't know how the legal system that disproportionately punished people of color, and especially Black men, could be traced back to slavery. Nor did I know how the Black church was a refuge from all that or that the freedom for my people to go to church without white supervision was only a little more than a hundred years old. History influenced everything around me, was built into the very walls of my church, but I didn't know that then. I knew only that church felt safe, protected, and homelike. "Was it an escape from regular life?" Belle asked me once. "Church *was* regular life," I told her.

My brother and sister and I were always in church, about to go to church, or coming home from church, sometimes with our mother and stepfather, sometimes on our own. We went to white churches and Black churches, joining big congregations and small ones in Graham, Burlington, and Mebane. Wednesday nights were for Bible study, Saturdays were for choir practice, and entire Sundays were given over to worship. On Sundays we might visit five churches all around the county, getting home worn-out but well-fed long after dark. Our parents worked long shifts in the local mills, and they trusted church folk to look after us. On days that they were able to go with us, the church filled them up in a way that nothing else could.

More than school or sports, more than a job or where you lived, the church had a tight grasp on my whole community. Your sacred life had everything to do with your secular life, who you were, and how you presented yourself. If you didn't go, you were dogged about it: told that you were a heathen, that the devil got ahold of you, that you were bound to run these streets. But showing up meant you were on the straight and narrow—respectable, even if you were poor, which we definitely were.

By the time I was twelve years old, we'd moved eleven times, all within Alamance County. The reasons varied: rent hikes, shady landlords, money troubles, my mother and father's divorce. We lived in houses and apartments and mobile homes. In my stepfather's Mebane house, lead paint sickened my younger brother, and we went back to Graham to live with my grandmother and grandfather. But no matter what, we could always go to church and put a little something in the offering plate.

The white churches we attended, which my siblings and I traveled to by church van after school, were mostly in the town of Graham. We were usually the only Black kids there, and we were always on our best behavior. Other kids might run around in the fellowship hall, but not us—we knew the whuppin' we'd get if our mother found out we'd acted up. Despite the wildness of some of the kids in these white churches, the worship services there were highly regulated, sedate goings-on. There was no impromptu singing, no spoken testimony from random congregants. Nobody would clap. You found the song in the hymnbook and held it dutifully in your palms. They had the same choir every week, and only one piano player, the pastor's wife, whose textbook approach to playing kept the singers in steady rhythm. But the snacks were good, they had a big playground, and we were treated well there.

Our home church, where we went as a family on Sundays, was a Black church: St. Luke Christian in Mebane. Back then its congregation was housed within an old, red-brick building with narrow, Gothic windows inset with colorful stained glass. We'd leave the house early, stopping at the drive-through convenience store on Route 70 for a treat to tide us over until Sunday school and worship services were over. All the kids would get a pack of Nabs and a soda. We always looked good, my brother and me in clip-on ties, my sister in a dress and stockings. For a time I had a black three-piece suit that was especially sharp; it fit like it had been custom-tailored even though it was a thrift shop find. My mother, wearing a modest jewel-toned dress, would drive the family station wagon while my stepfather, in his suit and flat wool cap, would sit in the passenger seat and find gospel music or Joe Foust's radio show on the car stereo.

Stepping into St. Luke's sanctuary, we'd be greeted by the ushers, who'd hand out programs to everyone and paper fans to the women. Someone would already be playing piano. There would be fellowship, talking, perfume in the air. Most of the women wore their crowns, the elaborate, colorful hats they kept on throughout the service. My grandparents would be there. I remember feeling like I was covered by a sturdy roof at St. Luke, better than the one at home or school or anywhere else I went.

The joyful, raucous gospel music of St. Luke's Sunday service was my favorite part of the week—better than the Power Rangers, better than an Atlanta Braves game on television, better than roller skating with white youth groups. We had a talented congregation with a deep bench of piano players and singers. Every service featured a drummer, a lead guitarist, a bassist, and a tambourine player. I'd watch the keyboardist's fingers flying up and down the keyboard, trying to figure out how she did it. And of course there was singing. I'd look forward to a new choir performing each Sunday. We had a senior choir, a children's choir, a male chorus, and a women's choir. The whole congregation could harmonize to a song being made up on the spot.

Before the preaching started, usually after the choir finished their biggest number—"Standing in the Need of Prayer," "Mary Don't You Weep," or "Old Ship of Zion"—the testimony part of the service would begin. If the song didn't wring every bit of feeling out of the congregation, someone would stand up. Maybe it would be an old man in a flat wool cap and worn suit, wiping his face with his handkerchief. "I've got something I want to say," he'd begin. "The Lord's been good to me—"

"Amen!"

What he shared might seem inconsequential—a broken-down car fixed for an amount he could afford, a wrenched back straightened, someone home from the hospital. "But for the Lord, I'd be down and out, but I'm here with y'all now." Then he'd start singing. If you were a musician in the church, you'd know the song. The piano player would whisper, "That's F major, right?" The singer would look at the musicians, moving his shoulders to indicate the rhythm. He might start improvising, and we'd have a whole new song before long.

By the time his testimony ended, people would be shouting and women would be fanning themselves. No matter how commonplace the tale, the congregation embraced the teller, because they'd been there too: broke or broken down, caregiver to another sick person. These were experiences my stepfather and mother knew well as parents to three kids with large, complex, extended families. They rarely stood to testify, but they'd sing and clap and say "Amen." Willie was ordinarily a quiet man, towering in his three-piece suit, one hand resting on his polished wood cane, but when he felt something in church he'd wave his giant hand in the air, and his "Yeah" was the loudest I'd ever heard.

As the song wound down, some people would be standing up and clapping. "Go ahead! Tell that word! Say something." The music would swell to fill the rafters until it all came back down again with the final roll on the ride cymbal.

After the service was over, we'd often share a meal in the fellowship hall. There would be fried chicken, macaroni with thick yellow cheese, collard greens slicked with pot liquor, buttery biscuits and golden cornbread, pinto beans and sliced tomatoes. You'd go down the line of the folding table, heaping your choices onto sturdy Styrofoam plates. There'd be strong sweet tea and lemonade for the kids. The dessert table would have chocolate cake, carrot cake, pecan pie, apple pie, chocolate pie. We'd sit with family members, and I remember once asking my grandaddy to arm wrestle. "Grandaddy, you can't beat me!" I boasted. He took my small hand in his sandpaper grip and steered it firmly to the table. Stronger than my disappointment was the feeling of comfort that I was protected, surrounded by strength.

As soon as I was old enough, I joined the children's choir. Adults who could hear something in the tone and tenor of my voice had always asked if I could sing, and it turned out I could. I sang my first solo at eight years old. The song I sang was easy to learn, its only lyrics "Thank you, Lord," repeated over and over. My mother supported my musical ability, but it might be more accurate to say that she endured it. My singing and love of music worried her, bringing to mind my biological father, whose mental health crises had tested their relationship to the point of breakdown by the time I was five years old.

Already, I presented many reminders of him: I had his name and looked like him. I was quiet like him, able to spend long stretches of time alone, and sometimes moody. Now people would say I had his talent. Maybe they'd wonder what else I'd do with it. I never once heard Sylvester Allen Sr. sing, but it's what everyone remembered most about him—more than his drinking, his love of a good time, or his various stints in jail. Legend has it that he recorded a whole album in the penitentiary, but I never heard it or saw it.

This was part of what motivated my mother to get us back into church, once she met and married my stepfather. She wanted us on the respectable, straight-and-narrow path that she believed would help each of us avoid the hard, rocky detours her first husband had taken and that she'd refused to follow. So more than my singing, it meant something to my mother for me to accept Jesus Christ as my savior so that I could be baptized, fully immersed in the waters that represented a new life.

I was baptized in the brick-walled dunking pool behind St. Luke on the morning of my eighth birthday: July 25, 1993. Barefoot and wearing shorts and a T-shirt, I walked down the steep, narrow steps until the cool water lapped at my neck. I leaned back, arms crossed over my chest, as the pastor dipped my whole body beneath the water. Because I couldn't even swim and had never been in a pool, I was terrified, but that dip proved I didn't have to be. I was only under for a few seconds, but I remember waiting to take a breath was like waiting on a prayer to be answered—it felt like an eternity. Coming up, water streaming down my face, I was cleansed of sin, reborn a follower of Jesus Christ, as countless others had before me in that very pool.

The year I was baptized was also the church's centennial, as told by our many celebrations, as well as by the white marble cornerstone carved with elegant, old-fashioned letters:

St. Luke Christian Church
Built by their Pastor
Rev. M. D. Harden
November 3, 1893

It was all that was left of the original church building, a wooden structure replaced in the 1930s by the brick sanctuary and hand-carved wooden pews I knew. To people in our congregation, it didn't just mean that we'd stuck together that long, though that was important, a mark of distinction in our small town. Even though the building wasn't original, the land had been bought and kept by Black people in a place that made it hard for Black folks to hang on to anything.

One hundred years was a quantity of time that felt both abstract and immense. Nothing in my house was a hundred years old—only the tall oaks that sheltered our backyard. One hundred years was longer than anyone

I knew had been alive. But my church's land had been owned, tended, and defended by Black people for all that time.

One of those defenders was Mr. Omega R. Wilson, who was treasurer of St. Luke when I was a kid. Mr. Omega, as I call him still, traces his family all the way back to the church founders. Like me, he grew up in Alamance County, moved often as a child, and knew St. Luke as home.

Belle and I met Mr. Omega and his wife, Brenda A. Wilson, one August morning at the Chik-fil-A in Mebane. The Wilsons each had breakfast sandwiches on a tray, I had a decaf coffee, and Belle had her computer out, ready to take notes. Mr. Omega chuckled as we sat down. Nodding at me, he told Belle, "I remember when he was just a wiggler."

I'd already described myself as a quiet, well-behaved child—literally a choirboy—so she thought this was funny. "A wiggler?" I asked. "I remember trying so hard to be still."

"You were young," he said, unwrapping his sandwich with a shrug. The Wilsons, who raised three sons in the church, are retired now, but this morning they were dressed as they might have been during their working days: Ms. Brenda, who was a special education teacher, in a blouse, slacks, and pearls; Mr. Omega, who left a career in academia and radio production to sell insurance, in a button-down shirt and long pants. They're both still active in the community and travel regularly to speak about civil rights and environmental justice, work that grew out of their time as members of St. Luke.[1]

I'd called them up because I wanted to talk with someone about our shared history and how we remember the people and places that made it. I'd been thinking, more and more, about that first experience of religious life and shelter, how important St. Luke was to me and my family.

Mr. Omega began attending St. Luke as a young child in the 1950s. His maternal grandfather, Samuel Carr, was born the same year the first church was built, and his paternal great-great-uncle was one of its first deacons. Let me just pause there. The grandfather of an active, youthful seventy-two-year-old man in 2022 was born in the 1890s.

When Omega was a child, Black churches in our part of North Carolina operated through circuit preaching—pastors would travel from church to church, staying the weekend with families who stood in for the hotels, motels, and restaurants that wouldn't accommodate Black guests during Jim Crow segregation. Most families had a pastor they took special care of, in a practice known as "pounding the pastor." Omega's paternal and maternal grandparents, Ernest and Georgia Wilson and Samuel and Elizabeth

(Lizzie) Carr, looked after Reverend James Albright, who served as pastor of St. Luke for nearly forty years and preached at Hawfields Christian Church (the Carr family church).

They'd host Reverend Albright for meals or a weekend—a kind of "Black bed and breakfast," Mr. Omega said—then send him off with provisions that could last for a week of travel: a whole cured ham, sausage meat, home-canned green beans, peaches, honey collected from hives, watermelon rind pickles. Carrying the heavily packed wooden crates to Reverend Albright's car was a privilege entrusted to the most responsible children.

Reverend Albright was "a figure," Omega said: so light-skinned he appeared white, and equipped with a loud, sonorous voice that sounded the same in the pulpit as it did in the parlor. The children would gather around him during his visits, hoping to get a glimpse of him without his clerical collar. "Stop staring," Omega's grandmother Lizzie would scold, but he and his siblings couldn't help it. This larger-than-life man they saw most every Sunday behind the big wooden pulpit was sitting in a chair in their grandparents' home. It was a little like seeing your teacher at the grocery store, a collapsing of worlds.

Omega remembered one home visit, a little before Christmas. Reverend Albright wore a black suit, and his tall black shoes were newly shined and neatly laced. But as he crossed his legs, Omega could see that the leather soles were worn through, stuffed with newspaper to keep out the weather. His grandfather Sam saw this too, and without a word he got up, left the room, and returned with brand-new high-top black Christmas shoes from his closet. "Take off your shoes," Sam said, and he knelt to set his own pair of dress shoes next to Reverend Albright's feet.

"We're sitting there on the floor looking at all this magic going on," Omega remembered. "We're thinking, 'Wow, Granddaddy doesn't give anything away.'"

Even as a child, Omega understood that the pastor, and the church itself, not only supported his community but was representative of its place in the wider world. Sam did not want his pastor walking around with damp, cold feet, but he also didn't want others to see that he wasn't being cared for by his congregation.

Omega felt a sense of awe when he considered this line of history, which stretched back into the previous century. It was Reverend Albright who'd raised funds to erect the new brick church in 1938—his name was engraved on its cornerstone, and legend had it that he'd helped to teach some of the white workmen who delivered its bricks how to read. Within this same church building, Omega thought about history. Helping to sweep up after worship services, he'd leaf through the soft pages of an old Bible ruffled with notes from past preachers. He remembered the "big old wooden pulpit" that Reverend Albright would thunder behind. "I'd go up there, grab both sides of that wooden pulpit, and just imagine," he said. "You have chills with certain things."

I got chills hearing this story, even though I don't remember the wooden pulpit, which had been replaced by Reverend Rory Garrison with a modern Lucite model when I was young. The chills I felt came from knowing that the same way I was moved by the music of our church, Mr. Omega had been moved by his pastor's larger-than-life figure and his grandfather's sacrifice. He'd lived that same life of imagination and wonder within those same walls. He'd thought about that line of history that stretched back into a century when all our people's rights were new.

• • • •

As the linguist Geneva Smitherman describes it, the word "testimony" has multiple meanings, especially in the Black community: secular and spiritual, as well as legal. At its core, she writes, Black church testimony is "telling the truth through 'story'" so that "one's humanity is reaffirmed by the group and his or her feeling of isolation diminished."[2] No matter what happened during the week, the members of St. Luke Christian Church could show up and expect to hear and be heard by people who moved through the world as they did: with Black skin, Black dignity, and Black joy.

This was a hard-fought freedom, as precious to people like my mother and stepfather as the freedom to vote or testify in court. It's only a little older than those freedoms, dating back to 1865 and the Thirteenth Amendment that freed Black people from bondage. Before emancipation, enslaved people were expected to attend church with their masters, where they sat silently in a separate, cordoned-off section and often had to hear their own enslavement and punishments justified by white preachers. Even free Black people, like Wyatt, could not attend church unless a white person was present, and they were prevented by law from holding evening services. White people were afraid of Black spirituality, but they were even more afraid of the Black community represented by the church.

After emancipation, the first thing many free Black people across the South did was build churches. In Charleston, the first building constructed amid the charred ruins of the Civil War was a Black church on Calhoun Street; it opened its doors to 3,000 congregants. This was Mother Emanuel, a Black AME church that had been in operation since 1816 but had been forced to operate secretly after repeated targeting of its congregants and destruction of its buildings by white supremacists.[3] Ten more Black churches were erected nearby in the next year alone. Churches were raised in Atlanta, Charlotte, Richmond, New Orleans, Raleigh—and where churches could not be built in a hurry, Black people improvised, as they had during the days of the "invisible institution." They gathered in a railroad boxcar in Atlanta and in a "bush arbor" in Memphis. Sam Holt, a popular lay preacher who'd been born a slave at Locust Grove plantation in southern Alamance County, preached streamside before building a wooden church on land donated by his former enslaver. In 1868, Wyatt Outlaw led four other church trustees to buy an acre of land in downtown Graham—this was the first land that Outlaw purchased, even before a home for his family.

In places where existing Black congregations shared space with white churches, Black parishioners withdrew to create their own autonomous churches. They would be led by Black preachers and Black deacons; they'd hire Black carpenters and masons and, when possible, Black architects. In Chapel Hill, the University Baptist Church (then called the Baptist Church of Chapel Hill) was founded in 1854 and built, like most everything else in town at that time, with slave labor. The congregation included whites, free Black people, and enslaved Black people. But on September 3, 1865, the church minutes include this note: "On motion, it was unanimously voted that the colored patrons of this church be allowed to withdraw from the church and organize a church to themselves."[4] This became First Baptist Church, which is still in operation today.

A church to themselves—that's what was essential about these first houses of worship. Not only could Black people make decisions about how, when, and where to worship, but they could express themselves freely. As a child, and even a teenager, I didn't know about the 1832 North Carolina law that forbade free or enslaved Blacks from preaching and worshipping together without a white person present, nor did I know that this law was part of a wave of laws passed following Nat Turner's 1831 rebellion against enslavers.[5] It never occurred to me that what Black people might say and do in church was a threat, or even of special interest to white people. I can't remember ever seeing a white person inside St. Luke.

I also didn't think of my church as a fragile space or a target. I knew about the 1963 white supremacist bombing of the Sixteenth Street Baptist Church in Birmingham, which killed four young girls and brought worldwide attention to the violence suffered by Black people in the American South. But what I didn't know was that Sixteenth Street Baptist had been targeted long before the civil rights era. Birmingham was a young, Reconstruction-era city, and it had dozens of Black churches that sprang up around the time of its founding. But Sixteenth Street Baptist was the first, founded in 1873, and by 1880 it was also the grandest—a brick church that took up nearly a whole city block, with the tallest steeple in Birmingham. In 1908, the city condemned the church for what it deemed structural inadequacies and forced its demolition.[6]

Despite the widespread economic, educational, and legal discrimination enforced by Jim Crow segregation, the congregation of Sixteenth Street Baptist had raised funds and built a new church by 1911. This new church was designed by Wallace Rayfield, a prominent Black architect, and constructed by T. C. Windham, a Birmingham-based Black contractor.[7] The three-story Romanesque structure is the church we know today: red-brick, square, with two imposing towers flanking front steps so wide there's space for going up, going down, and standing and chatting in the center.

Three years—that's all it took to rebuild an enormous, expensive church in the same spot where Black people had to demolish their previous enormous, expensive church by order of white building inspectors and a white city government. These were Black professionals, doctors and teachers and businesspeople, but also blue-collar workers who must have had to sacrifice quite a lot to contribute to the rebuilding. Sixteenth Street was known, then and now, as everybody's church.

Humble or grand, the Black church was a spiritual home, but also much more than that—"the epicenter of Black life," as the Reverend Al Sharpton has said.[8] In the South, a new life for Black folks began with our first autonomous churches built during Reconstruction. By necessity, churches like Sixteenth Street Baptist were also schools, meeting places for Black businesspeople, and ground zero for civil rights advocacy rooted in the teachings and activism of Jesus. Black churches were mutual aid societies and a source of social outreach. They celebrated births and marriages and baptisms, and they mourned deaths. They were where Black people were encouraged to vote. The church was a source of spiritual, emotional, economic, cultural, and political power.

But the power of the Black church as meeting and gathering place is also what makes it a target. An even more common force that took down Black churches and divided and destroyed Black community wasn't the blatant white supremacy that attacked Sixteenth Street with sticks of dynamite. The action that demolished hundreds of Black churches in the twentieth century, and continues to threaten them in the twenty-first century, is the exercise of eminent domain.

Eminent domain is the sovereign right of governments or government agencies to take private property for public use. All governments use eminent domain to build roads and infrastructure, create national parks, protect the landscape, and preserve historically important places. The Fifth Amendment balances this need and the rights of landowners by stipulating that private land cannot be taken for public use "without just compensation."

Yet many Black Americans haven't been served by either the public-focused purpose of eminent domain or the legal protection of the Fifth Amendment. Our communities have gone without paved roads, clean water, and municipal sewage systems, without schools and public parks. Our history has been discounted as unimportant to the national story, and so our historic places, including our historic churches, have been razed to make way for shopping centers, highways, and "urban renewal." Again and again, Black landowners have not been paid a fair price—or sometimes even at all—for the land that has been taken from us.

In the mid-nineteenth century, the largest community of free landowning African Americans in New York state was Seneca Village, a forty-acre stretch of land around what is now Eighty-Fifth Street and Central Park. Seneca Village had private gardens, a spring-fed water supply, two schools, three churches, and two cemeteries. By 1855, more than 20 percent of the Black landowners in New York City lived there, attracted in part by the construction of an AME church and by the chance to buy land free from housing discrimination and overcrowding. More than half the residents owned land and were therefore eligible to vote. But the community's more than 200 residents were forced to leave in 1857 when the city began construction of Central Park, which became the country's first major landscaped park. Residents tried to fight eminent domain demolition, but they must have known it was an uphill battle—racism was what had caused them to found an independent community in the first place. They saw their middle-class, stable neighborhood described in the press and by politicians as a "shantytown" or "n—— village." Landowners in Seneca Village were paid an average of $700 per lot, and renters were paid nothing at all.[9]

Eminent domain's patterns of racism continued in the twentieth century, when communities devalued and underserved by racist redlining practices that began in the 1930s were further targeted for "urban renewal" or "slum clearance" to make way for a suburban, car-centric culture. This happened all across the country, in big cities and small towns. Whole communities of Black and minority residents were bulldozed to make way for roads, shopping malls, and office parks. In St. Louis, a neighborhood of 20,000 mostly Black families was destroyed in the early 1960s.[10] In Treme, Charlotte, Durham, Lansing, and Miami, Black neighborhoods were divided by highways to predominantly white suburbs. Vinegar Hill, a middle-class Black community in Charlottesville, Virginia, was knocked down for a road and shopping centers.[11]

Since World War II, between 3 and 4 million Americans, most of them people of color, have been displaced through eminent domain. Between 1949 and 1973—boom time for "urban renewal"—two-thirds of the more

ON REDLINING

During the New Deal of the 1930s, the American government invested millions of dollars in government-insured mortgages designed to promote homeownership and keep struggling homeowners from foreclosure. To allocate the loans, neighborhoods were rated A through D, according to their perceived risk. The D neighborhoods, least likely to receive funds, were outlined in red. Most of these "red-lined" neighborhoods were majority-Black or multiracial neighborhoods. This secret practice was discovered by historian Kenneth T. Jackson in 1976, but Black people and other people of color were well aware that they'd been discriminated against because they never received the loans they applied for or were offered unaffordable interest rates.

Today, the term "redlining" is often applied to other forms of racial discrimination, from racial covenants to the practice used by some realtors of "steering" Black homebuyers away from white neighborhoods. The Fair Housing Act of 1968 and the Home Mortgage Disclosure Act of 1975 improved housing and lending practices, but so much damage was already done. Redlining depressed homeownership among Black people and lowered the value of the homes they did own, contributing to a vast generational disparity in wealth. It reinforced segregation and affected nearly every service to families located in D-rated areas—from parks to schools to utilities. More than 60 percent of D-rated neighborhoods remain nonwhite, and these neighborhoods are disproportionately hotter (thanks to fewer trees) and more polluted.*

* Nadia Lathan, "50 Years after Being Outlawed, Redlining Still Drives Neighborhood Health Inequities," Berkeley Public Health, September 20, 2023, https://publichealth.berkeley.edu/news-media/research-highlights/50-years-after-being-outlawed-redlining-still-drives-neighborhood-health-inequities.

than 1 million people displaced by "urban renewal" projects and highways were Black.[12] They were also poorer and less educated, with less access to legal representation than their neighbors in surrounding communities. Because of redlining and gentrification, Black people had fewer options for new housing once their old neighborhoods were destroyed, and many were shuttled into high-rise housing projects.

In almost all of these so-called blighted neighborhoods, houses of worship were at the center—and were also destroyed, along with the small businesses, homes, schools, cultural centers, and gardens tended by people of color. Three churches in Seneca Village gone. Forty churches in St. Louis. One church in Vinegar Hill. Pittsburgh's oldest Black church, Bethel AME, was one of nine predominantly Black churches destroyed when the city's Lower Hill neighborhood was targeted as "urban blight." But Bethel, whose membership dated back to 1808, had a congregation of 3,000 and a rich history—the church was a stop on the Underground Railroad and served as Pittsburgh's first elementary school for Black children. Its congregation fought for voting rights for Black men and women, organized health and public service projects, and generally provided a place for Black excellence to thrive. Yet it was torn down to make way for a civic arena, displacing 8,000 mostly Black residents and 400 businesses.[13]

Though the loss of a historic church is incalculable, the redlining that devalued Black neighborhoods meant that congregations were not offered adequate compensation for their churches. Communities fractured. At Bethel AME, congregants suspected that the $240,000 compensation they received in 1958 for the destruction of a massive brick church in the city center was inadequate. They knew that their church's history was discounted because they were Black, but some also felt that they were targeted because their membership was progressive. The survival of an Irish Catholic church two blocks away just rubbed salt in their wounds. Bethel's congregation eventually rebuilt in a different part of town, but the loss of community—hundreds of Black-owned homes in a walkable, urban neighborhood were also demolished—meant that much of the old congregation was scattered.

In 2023, the Pittsburgh Penguins, a franchise of the National Hockey League, transferred to the church the ownership and development rights of a 1.5-acre parcel of land that includes the original church parcel. This "restorative redevelopment project" was celebrated by parishioners, who plan to build a mixed-used development serving the neighborhood, including affordable housing, and who would now have more than a sign to show where their church once stood.[14]

• • • •

St. Luke wasn't famous like Sixteenth Street or large like Mother Bethel AME. Our small church sat on the grassy side of a country road, surrounded by trees and a working-class neighborhood. We didn't have wealthy parishioners or famous visitors. W. E. B. Du Bois never spoke from our pulpit, and Paul Robeson and Mahalia Jackson never sang with our choir. Yet the church was historic because it had endured, even thrived, in times of turmoil and struggle for its people. This struggle didn't end with the lives of the people who founded it, some of whom had been born into slavery. Many of St. Luke's parishioners lived on dirt roads and without indoor plumbing, well into the 1990s. They lived "pillar to post," as Mr. Omega said, yet they had the resources to support a pastor, to form multiple choirs, to do charity work in the community. Gifts and service from the ordinary people who sat in the pews each Sunday were recognized by small brass plaques nailed beneath the modest stained-glass windows.

I was a child in the mid-1990s when the North Carolina Department of Transportation and the City of Mebane first targeted 200 parcels of land, including the land that had belonged to St. Luke since 1893, for a road expansion and the creation of an on-ramp. I heard rumors about this plan, rumblings from older folks who said that "if we can just make it to one hundred years we'll be OK." It was inconceivable to me that my mother's church, and my grandmother's church, could be knocked down to build something as ordinary as a road, so I didn't worry too much about it.

But behind the scenes, things were happening. Reverend Rory Garrison, our pastor, asked Omega Wilson, who served as the church's treasurer, to look into the matter. Omega had returned to Mebane just a few years earlier, in 1987, leaving a fulfilling career and a good life in Jackson, Mississippi, to take care of his ill mother, father, aunt, and grandmother Lizzie. In Jackson, Omega had been a professor of communications and director of a Black community radio station, WMPR-FM.[15] He and Brenda, a special education teacher, lived with their three sons in a "nice three-bedroom home in North Jackson among a lot of other Black business leaders and professors," he said. But when he got a call from his mother saying that his father was forgetting things and could no longer drive safely, they "packed it all up."

Back in Mebane, they had to make do—Omega got a job selling insurance, and Brenda taught at Efland Cheek Elementary, in a rural community in Orange County. They bought a century-old small millhouse, which had been renovated and upgraded, close to Omega's family. They began attending St. Luke again, where many of Omega's family members, including his parents, still worshipped. When word about the government letter got around the church, many in the congregation looked to him for answers. Why was this happening? What could be done?

"I was the guy who'd been away and come back," Omega explained. "Plus, there was the matter of my formal education. But a lot of it was 'You Jesse's boy, and we love Jesse. We love Ms. Georgia.'"

The proposed bypass and one-mile overpass cut right through the historic Black community of West End, identifying not just St. Luke but also another Black church, more than seventy homes, a Black-owned Masonic lodge, and a historic Black cemetery.[16] At church meetings to discuss the plan, people began to understand the enormity of the loss: "They're thinking, 'I'm gonna lose my house, my sister's house, my mother's house, the cemetery where my people are buried, *and* the church I'm sitting in?'" Omega said.

He and Brenda began writing letters, holding meetings, and digging into federal civil rights law. They learned that the Mebane City Council had held private meetings about the plan with the North Carolina Department of Transportation, where they approved the construction of a four-lane highway and overpass without notifying or consulting anyone in its path. There were no plans to adequately compensate or assist homeowners or residents, no plans to assist elderly or frail residents with moving, no plans to address or even assess the environmental impact of the road. There was no plan to pay anything at all for St. Luke or the Masonic lodge.

The plans, as well as the ongoing discrimination and redlining experienced by the majority-Black West End residents, violated both Title VI of the Civil Rights Act of 1964, signed into law by President Lyndon Johnson, who was motivated by Rev. Martin Luther King's marches, and President Bill Clinton's Environmental Justice Executive Order 12898 of 1994. The Wilsons documented these violations and brought them back to the church in a thick binder, where they explained how the church members could fight back.

For Brenda, it wasn't even the first time she'd been involved in a campaign against redlining and eminent domain. As a young woman in Philadelphia, she'd watched her grandparents, Luther and Mamie Borroughs, and other church elders successfully fight against attempts to tear down *their* historic church, Mother Bethel AME, with its 1794 cornerstone—the first African Methodist Episcopal church in the United States. Just a couple of years after Mother Bethel was saved from demolition and designated a national landmark, in September 1974, Brenda and Omega were married there. Brenda expected a long fight for St. Luke too, a lot of paperwork and meetings with lawyers and government officials. But she wasn't prepared for what she and Omega found in Alamance County: bitter resignation and, behind that, generational fear.

Reverend Garrison prayed about it, but he declined to draw the church into a fight. Maybe this was God's plan for them after all. Many of the old-timers in church said the same thing: "Leave it alone. White folks gonna do what white folks gonna do." There was no point in fighting only to lose—or even to lose one's job, as many who worked for white people or for UNC Medical Center, feared would happen if they spoke up. Some older folks remembered the days of night-riding Klansmen, who'd dragged family members and ancestors out into the woods. "You're gonna make them mad, and then they're gonna come down here and kill us all," Omega remembered people saying. "They're gonna burn your house down."

But a few parishioners were willing to join him, and four families—the Wilson family, the Graves family, the Holt family, the Snipes family, and the Martin family—started attending city council meetings, taking turns presenting so no one person bore the brunt of the pushback alone. They wanted to know why no one in the community had been consulted and—while they were at it—why so many Black residents had been redlined out of basic services enjoyed by Mebane's majority-white communities, like paved roads, sewer and water service, sidewalks, and streetlights. Was this road construction a way of getting rid of Black residents once and for all?

Once they took their grievances public, people began to speak privately with the Wilsons, especially with Omega. A wealthy white businessman who identified himself as a distant cousin stopped by Omega's insurance office repeatedly, asking him not to "let them tear down that church." Two North Carolina Department of Transportation officials, both people of color, came to his home to warn him to be careful.

But not many people wanted to speak publicly. The white people feared a loss of status among other whites. People of color feared reprisal from white people. The Wilsons cofounded the West End Revitalization Association (WERA), a nonprofit organization that in 1996 became the first community development corporation in Alamance. They continued attending city council meetings, repeatedly asking the council to apply for federal grants to remedy their community's contaminated well water and failing septic tanks. The city council repeatedly declined, refusing to even sign a HUD grant application written by WERA. In 1998, City Manager Robert Wilson (not related to Omega) interrupted WERA's annual dinner at the Mebane Arts and Community Center to demand that the group "stop interfering with Mebane's progress."

Finally, in 1999, Charles Graves and Omega Wilson, along with eight co-signers, filed a formal administrative complaint with the Civil Rights Division of the United States Department of Justice. They alleged that the planning of the new road was part of a pattern of discrimination against the town's Black residents, who'd long been underserved by county and city services and left out of community planning. The harm from this discrimination included illness from drinking contaminated water, lack of access to parks and other community spaces, and lower property values for homeowners.[17]

In February 1999, less than a month after WERA filed the complaint, an official from the Civil Rights Office of the Federal Highway Administration in Washington, DC, met with officials from Mebane, Alamance County, and North Carolina's Department of Transportation and Federal Highway Administration. The bypass project was placed on hold for at least four years, pending compliance with the Civil Rights Act of 1964 and the Environmental Justice Executive Order 12898.[18]

Eventually, a compromise rerouted the bypass, saving the Masonic lodge, Mebane First Presbyterian Church (freedpeople founded this church a few months after slavery ended), the historic cemetery, and more than seventy homes. But St. Luke could not be saved—its property was too close to the bypass on-ramp. By this time my family had moved several times and were attending Children's Chapel, a historic Black church in Graham that dates to 1875. Omega and Brenda Wilson left St. Luke for Melfield United Church of Christ, in Haw River, where Brenda serves as a deaconess and food pantry volunteer. "A lot of people left," Omega said, shaking his head over the divide that emerged between those who wanted to fight for the church and those who were afraid.

St. Luke was bulldozed by the North Carolina Department of Transportation in 2016.[19] Though it had been years since he attended St. Luke, Omega was there to witness the demolition.

"I woke up that morning, and something told me to go by the church," he said. "There were no church members there. Nobody was in the yard. Just a guy on a yellow machine, doing what guys on yellow machines do."

Omega watched from the side as the bulldozer crashed through walls and windows, pushing the debris toward a waiting dump truck. Beneath a maple tree along the still-standing brick wall, an empty bassinet rested in the shade. The bulldozer operator had taken the time to remove it during the safety check.

In one of the photos Omega took, the baptismal pool where I'd been dunked was dug up out of the ground, sitting there like a child's toy in Fred

Sanford's junkyard. What happened to that pool? He shrugged. What happened to the bronze bell that sat outside the church, or the great wooden pulpit he used to grip in imitation of Reverend Albright?

"No one knows," he said. Omega and Brenda Wilson have traveled the country talking about their work. They've had doctoral dissertations written about them, have received numerous awards and commendations from powerful people, including President Barack Obama and President Joe Biden. But there were some questions they still couldn't answer.

Omega told us he felt "sad, tearful, disgusted, defeated—just about every emotion you can imagine" as he watched the bulldozer flatten his home church, crushing the bronze name plates of his grandparents Ernest and Georgia Wilson. I noticed that he didn't say *afraid*. Trump was running for president then, and it seemed that, in addition to the MAGA signs, there were even more Confederate flags flying in our county than usual. There was even one flying directly next to the small, half-brick new building that housed St. Luke—a provocation. A warning.

• • • •

No marker at all stands where St. Luke Christian once was—just a weedy lot near a newly built highway bypass. I decided to go back to look at it one hot July afternoon. So many landmarks were familiar—the old water tower, the railroad tracks, the long, straight expanse of Route 70. I hadn't seen the empty lot, nor had I been to the new church, which had been constructed not far away with funds from the state—far less, Omega told me, than what the original land and building were worth.

Dark clouds were crowding up the sky, and the trees were starting to sway. I felt a sense of urgency to reach the site and walk around before the storm. But I barely recognized the land that had been home to my church for 123 years. I saw the highway on-ramp, its black pavement painted with still-sharp yellow and white lines. Beside this road was an empty, weedy lot that looked large and small at the same time. I circled the block and then slowed in front of a small cream-colored house surrounded by a chain-link fence. An old white man sat on the front porch, watching the weather change.

I rolled down my window and pointed to the unkempt land next to his. "Excuse me, sir," I said. "Was this where St. Luke Christian Church used to be?"

"Yep," he said. "They knocked it down a few years ago. It's over there now." He pointed across the street to a gravel road that ran through a pine forest. I thanked him and drove slowly down the short cut-through.

The gravel road opened onto a paved lot. I parked my car next to a small, unassuming building that I recognized from St. Luke's Facebook page. The lot was empty, and I stepped out into the humid, storm-charged air as the first raindrops began to fall. Walking all the way around the building, I saw that it was brick on two sides—the west side, facing Route 70, and the south side, facing the parking lot. North and east, facing the pine woods, were corrugated tin, like the siding on a garage or an outbuilding. Two small, plain windows faced the road, and an overhang on the parking lot side provided a little shelter where older folks could wait for cars to pull around. It could have been any kind of building—a funeral home, maybe, or a dentist's office. Only two things revealed the building's actual purpose: a flimsy sign out front listing the Sunday school and worship service hours, and a narrow white steeple, already showing wear.

The rain was falling faster. I walked around to the porch area and peered inside the glass windows. I didn't see much, just a floral carpet and a couple of chairs in the small vestibule and some signs about COVID safety taped on the doors to the sanctuary. I closed my eyes and imagined, into the silence, the sounds of fellowship: talking, laughing, singing. Nowhere else would I have felt comfortable looking inside the windows of a locked, empty building. Only a Black church, even one I'd never set foot inside, could give me that sense of safety and familiarity. That feeling of home.

Before I left, I stepped back to get a quick photo and inadvertently stepped into the past—a bare-dirt plot planted with names and dates carved onto smooth granite blocks: M. Harden 1893–1917, A. A. Hazel 1917–1921, J. W. Albright 1921–1959, F. Curry 1959–1966, W. O. Howard 1967–1990, R. H. Garrison 1992–2019, Jerome Henry 2019–. These were the names and dates of service of all of the church's pastors, going back 129 years. Above them, leaning against two squat brick pillars, were the church's original marble cornerstones. The oldest one was dated November 3, 1893. The cornerstones were jagged at the edges, where they'd been pried away from the old building, and they weren't secured to anything, as if to do so would just invite another move, another disruption.

I wondered what testimony those marble slabs could offer, the same way I'd wondered about the trees surrounding our house in Mebane, just a few blocks away. What songs had these cornerstones heard, what sorrows and joys? How many baptisms had taken place just behind that old building; how many weddings inside its sanctuary? I knew enough about Alamance County's history to know that there'd be darker testimony too—about the slavery endured by some of the church's first founders and the racism and discrimination that still dogged the steps of so many members of the church. I knew that the end of slavery was not the end of terror for Black people—for some, like Wyatt Outlaw, it was just the beginning.

Loose cornerstones are all that remain of the original St. Luke Christian Church in Mebane. (Photo by Carey Kirk.)

But I had no idea that what happened to Wyatt Outlaw could stretch all the way across the twentieth century, shadowing and dividing my childhood church into people who wanted to fight for its survival and people who were willing to accept what we'd always gotten, which was less than what we'd invested. I understood both perspectives—the first one about rights and the second one about survival—because I'd heard them both reflected inside the walls of St. Luke.

CHAPTER THREE
PRIVILEGE

BELLE

Sometimes while writing this book, Sylvester and I would text each other to say, "Jimmy Carter is still alive!" It was a sign of God's favor, we both thought, even though only one of us believes in God. The idea that the ninety-nine-, then one-hundred-year-old former president and Nobel Peace Prize winner could enter hospice, lose his wife of seventy-seven years, and stay alive twenty-one months into care at their family home in Georgia—long enough to fulfill his wish of casting a ballot for Kamala Harris—felt comforting to us, a reminder of the persistence of good in the rural South. You have to be able to believe that good persists in order to stay here, in order to keep fighting for a better South.

I'm nine years older than Sylvester, born the same year Carter was elected. I grew up in King William, Virginia, a county more rural than Alamance and just as conservative. My family wasn't from there; my parents moved to King William from Richmond before I was born because they both had jobs at Kings Dominion, a 700-acre amusement park that sits just east of I-95. My dad was a carpenter who helped build the massive wooden roller coasters the park was known for—one of them, the Rebel Yell, was still running when I worked there as a teenager (the Confederate-referencing name wasn't changed to Racer 75 until long after that, in 2018). My mom was an artist for the park, sculpting and painting displays for the kiddie tunnel coaster, Magic Mountain: a hammerhead shark, psychedelic groupers and angelfish, a giant pair of feet.

Until I was fifteen, my family lived in poorly insulated rented houses with no heat, save for woodstoves that had to be fed all winter with trees my dad and his buddies cut and split. I suppose we were poor; I once heard my grandmother tell my uncle that my parents didn't have a pot to piss in. My brother had severe asthma, and my mom was always on the phone, fighting to get hospital and doctor bills paid by our crummy insurance. She wrote checks to "Shittybank," which, she pointed out, the credit card company always cashed. But like Sylvester, I didn't feel deprived. I loved to be outside under the canopy of trees or by the river or lake near our log cabin. As in Sylvester's family, my mom loved to read, and my dad could fix anything.

I had the sense that we didn't fit in—not in the way we lived, not in the things we believed. My elementary school best friend was sure I was going to hell because my family didn't go to church. My dad didn't hunt or own a gun, and I remember casting the only vote for Walter Mondale in my second-grade class mock election. My mom made Black Santas and Black baby Jesuses for our Christmas trees. My dad taught me and my younger brother not to trust the police or ever let them search our cars.

But I never felt afraid—not of getting arrested, going to jail, or winding up in the sticky web of "the system" that Sylvester writes about. I didn't like the police or trust them, but I didn't think they'd hurt me. I never felt *not at home*.

I was at home in my car, a lime-green 1975 Volkswagen Bug my mom and I painted with yellow sunflowers, which I drove without fear from the day I turned sixteen. My first year on the road, I was pulled over in my hippie VW more than a dozen times, until my dad called the county sheriffs to complain. Then it stopped.

I was at home in classrooms, where my teachers showed kindness to me that they didn't always show to other kids: Black kids and Native kids, fat kids, disabled kids, queer kids. My strengths were recognized instead of overlooked, as they were for so many others: I was in a gifted program and invited to do extracurriculars.

But like Sylvester, I went to underfunded schools, where I learned history from outdated textbooks and from teachers who believed the Civil War was about states' rights. And we spent a *lot* of time in middle school on the Civil War—its battles and generals, who were presented as either deeply conflicted, genteel lovers of the land (Lee and the Confederates) or else as violent, mercenary marauders (Grant and the Yankees). I knew what I was learning was wrong—like Sylvester, I watched *Roots* alongside my parents when it was rebroadcast on local channels. Like Sylvester, I'd learned about Harriet Tubman and Frederick Douglass. How could the Civil War not be about slavery?

But I'd never read a novel set in the South during the time period just after the Civil War. I never learned about a single Black hero or Black victim of Reconstruction, so I had nothing in my mind to counter the dominant narrative: It was a chaotic time, a political and social failure. A time when the South was taken advantage of by greedy, opportunistic carpetbaggers who exploited an economy devastated by war. Like a lot of kids, I mostly believed that Reconstruction was about the literal rebuilding of burned and wrecked cities, but it's not like we spent much time on it: a couple of days in sixth grade are all I remember.

RECONSTRUCTION IN AMERICAN SCHOOLS

In *Lies My Teacher Told Me*, American sociologist and historian James Loewen describes a discussion he had in 1970 with freshmen at Tougaloo College, a historically Black college in Mississippi. Though the school, founded in 1869, was itself one of Reconstruction's many remarkable success stories, the students shared a misguided understanding of this important American time period. Their understanding closely matched the story that white supremacists wrote into our history books: Reconstruction was a time when African Americans took over Southern governments but were "too soon out of slavery, so they messed up and reigned corruptly, and whites had to take back control."*

Loewen found their misunderstanding tragic, writing that "it invited them to doubt their own capability" as well as to conclude that white-dominated government was correct and inevitable. But he knew where the lies came from: the same textbooks, history books, and misguided teachers he'd had as a student. These books and ideas were largely influenced by the "Dunning School" of thought established by William Dunning in the early twentieth century. Dunning empathized with Southern slaveholders and vilified "carpetbaggers" (Northern

(continued)

Republicans allied with Black voters), "scalawags" (Southern white Republicans allied with Black voters), and especially Black political leaders. It was William Dunning's work that inspired W. E. B. Du Bois to comment, "One cannot study Reconstruction without first frankly facing the facts of universal lying."†

Though the Dunning School is widely seen by contemporary historians as racist and reactionary, its influence has been lasting. Reconstruction is still undertaught, mistaught, and poorly understood by many K–12 teachers, even those with good intentions. As of this writing, forty-four states have also introduced bills or taken other steps to limit the way teachers teach racism and its history. We recommend that teachers and school systems consult the Zinn Education Project's report *Erasing the Black Freedom Struggle* for suggestions about teaching Reconstruction fully and accurately.‡

---

* James Loewen, *Lies My Teacher Told Me*, 2nd ed. (New York: Simon and Schuster, 2007), 157.

† W. E. B. Du Bois, *Black Reconstruction in America* (New York: Free Press, 1998), 347.

‡ See Ana Rosado, Gideon Cohn-Postar, and Mimi Eisen, with the Zinn Education Project team, *Erasing the Black Freedom Struggle: How State Standards Fail to Teach the Truth about Reconstruction*, 2022, www.teachreconstruction report.org/#findings.

I assumed that I'd learn more about the South's history later, when I was in high school. But high school classes were barely more critical of the Lost Cause narrative—Virginia still celebrated Lee-Jackson-King Day when I was in school, and everyone in my senior English class was assigned to write a college scholarship essay about Robert E. Lee, sponsored by the Daughters of the American Confederacy. I wrote a critical essay, based on the single book I could find in our school library that argued Lee was not such a great general after all, and was surprised when I didn't win.

• • • •

When my husband and I moved to North Carolina in 2005, I was twenty-nine years old and had two graduate degrees—one in teaching and one in creative writing. I'd taught in elementary schools in Southern California and New York City and began working for a literacy center in Durham, teaching writing and GED prep to adults.

By the time I came to Alamance County, I had a decade of teaching experience and certification to teach elementary school as well as middle and high school English. I considered myself a good teacher, but there was so much I didn't know. This is so often the condition of being white, which most of us don't acknowledge, or realize only when it's too late. We have only a small part of the information, a narrow window that, most of the time, serves to keep us comfortable and maintain our privilege. It isn't the size of our window that's the greatest problem but our belief that it offers a complete view.

My place of comfort and privilege in Alamance County started with a small charter school housed in a converted textile mill on the banks of the Haw River. I heard about the Hawbridge School through an advertisement on public radio. I needed a job, inquired, and was invited to visit the next day.

After a twenty-minute interview with the school's director, I was hired. No background check. No transcripts or review of my credentials. I don't think anyone called my references. I was given an AP English class that the principal no longer had time to teach and assigned to a supply area near the building's entrance. In the doorless and windowless nook, a few old wooden desks sat in a circle. I had five students—all girls, all white. In fact, most of the school's students—there were only about seventy at the time—appeared to be white. All of the teachers and staff at the time, except for an Indian Kiwi art teacher who'd been hired away from a school in Harlem, were white.

I didn't think much about the lack of diversity, though I noted it. I'd taught in three schools before this one, and all of my previous principals and school leaders had been Black, along with many of my colleagues. In the last school where I taught, a middle school in DC, all of our students were Black, and the hiring process was intensive. That school had no art teacher at all, and PE took place in an empty lot across from the school.

On my first day of class in Saxapahaw, the principal gave me a cardboard box of materials the AP students were using in an oral history and documentation project: old photos and newspaper articles about the cotton mill and the history of the Jordan family, who owned the building that leased space to the school. Descendants of Senator B. Everett Jordan, the Jordan family took an active role in the town of Saxapahaw and envisioned a community museum that would include memories of life and work in the mill village. John Jordan, the grandson of B. Everett, hoped that our oral histories could become part of the museum.

Most of the mill workers we interviewed were white, and you had to look past their platitudes—"We were all friends; it was like one big family"—to see that there was poverty and exploitation, mothers and fathers working six and seven days a week while children fended for themselves at home. But one morning we had an interview with a Black man who'd been employed by the mill doing custodial work. One of the students asked whether he'd experienced discrimination there, and he looked surprised by the question. "Well," he said, "I had to use the bathroom outdoors." "Outdoors?" she asked. "Yes," he said flatly. "An outhouse."

I don't remember the man's name or age or the years he worked in the mill, but the interview took place in early 2010. It's possible he was referring to a time as far back as the 1950s but more likely that he worked there around the same time my neighbor David worked at Saxapahaw Cotton, in the 1960s. Public schools in Alamance County didn't integrate until the late 1960s. Parts of the county still feel segregated.

Halfway through the spring semester, my students and I were asked to stop our project. Word had gotten around town that the memories that workers were sharing were not all of the one-big-family variety, and John Jordan, who was then our landlord, asked the principal to discontinue it. We moved on to studying for the AP exam.

The next year, I was given a real classroom and a full-time schedule teaching tenth-, eleventh-, and twelfth-grade English. I'd inherited a shelf of Ayn Rand's *The Fountainhead*, which the previous American lit teacher had ordered for free from the Ayn Rand Institute. I threw those out. We had no textbooks and were supposed to study American literature alongside the American history class my students were also taking. I cobbled together a small library, and we read *The Scarlet Letter*, *The Adventures of Huckleberry Finn*, *The Autobiography of Frederick Douglass*, *The Great Gatsby*, *Sula*, and *Who's Afraid of Virginia Woolf?*

Classics, all of these. (Though a colleague expressed surprise at my choice of *Sula*, it was everybody's favorite.) But we were missing something, too—where was the literature that expressed something about where these students were from? Where was the literature about their history?

Had the American history teacher at my school and I been better informed, we might have learned about Wyatt Outlaw, might have taken our classes on field trips, just ten minutes away, to Graham. We could have read excerpts of the impeachment trial of North Carolina governor William Holden—ultimately removed from office for his aggressive actions to suppress the Klan in Alamance and surrounding counties—which includes testimony about Outlaw's life and death. We could have assigned selections from Albion Winegar Tourgée's *A Fool's Errand* and *Bricks without Straw*, two Reconstruction-era novels that include characters inspired by Outlaw.

But I didn't know about Wyatt Outlaw or the centrality of Alamance County to the history of Reconstruction in North Carolina. I imagine that our history teacher, a white recent graduate of Elon University, didn't know these facts either.

ALBION TOURGÉE

Born in Ohio in 1838, Albion Winegar Tourgée wore many hats throughout his long and distinguished career: Union soldier, editor, lawyer, judge, journalist, novelist, politician, and diplomat. Democrats in North Carolina knew him as a carpetbagger, which Tourgée defines through the eyes of Southerners in his bestselling novel, *A Fool's Errand: By One of the Fools*, as "a man of Northern birth + an abolitionist (according to the Southern definition) + incarnation of Northern hate, envy, spleen, greed, hypocrisy, and all uncleanness."*

Published in 1879, *A Fool's Errand* was the first novel by a white man, and only the second American novel, to depict the gruesome phenomenon of lynching. It was also unusual in its depiction of the Reconstruction South from the point of view of freedmen and their white allies. In this novel, Tourgée based the character Uncle Jerry at least partially on Wyatt Outlaw, a Republican colleague who worked alongside Tourgée, then a Greensboro-based judge, to resist Klan violence and encourage Black men to vote.

In the book, Uncle Jerry's lynching was closely modeled on accounts of Wyatt's. Uncle Jerry's body hung from a "low-branching oak not more than forty steps from the Temple of Justice." As everyone feared the Klan, no one would cut him down until "some colored men were found, and a little party made up, who went out and saw the body cut down, and laid upon a box to await the coming of the coroner, who had already been notified. The inquest developed only these facts, and the sworn jurors solemnly and honestly found the cause of death unknown."†

The irony of that passage—"the sworn jurors solemnly and honestly found the cause of death unknown"—reflects the deep frustration and anger Tourgée felt for many years after Wyatt's lynching and

(*continued*)

the dismantling of Reconstruction-era progress. He did not give up easily, and in 1873 he helped bring sixty-three white men under felony indictment for the murder of Wyatt Outlaw. However, the Democratic-controlled legislature repealed the laws used to bring the charges, and no one faced consequences for Wyatt's murder.

Tourgée was also a close associate of Caswell County's John W. Stephens, a state senator, magistrate, and Radical Republican ally of African American voters. At great risk to his own safety, he pursued an investigation of Stephens's lynching and provided names of Klan members to the investigating congressional committee.

In acknowledgment of his unending fight against lynching, segregation, white supremacy, and disenfranchisement, Tourgée was selected by Black political leaders in New Orleans as the lead attorney for the test case that became *Plessy v. Ferguson*. Tourgée lost this case, its outcome the basis for the infamous "separate but equal" legal doctrine, which would remain in place until 1954's *Brown v. Board of Education*.

To read more about Albion Tourgée, we suggest starting with *A Fool's Errand*, which is freely accessible through public domain, as well as *A Refugee from His Race: Albion W. Tourgée and His Fight against White Supremacy* by Carolyn L. Karcher (University of North Carolina Press, 2016).

---

* Albion W. Tourgée, *A Fool's Errand: A Novel of the South during Reconstruction*, John Harvard Library ed. (Prospect Heights, IL: Waveland Press, 1961), 189.

† Tourgée, *Fool's Errand*, 231.

In the summer of 2022, more than a year into working on this book, Sylvester and I often met at the Culture Mill, a performance space and arts incubator in Saxapahaw, where he was in residence as a writer and musician. The Culture Mill isn't a mill at all but an office inside a red-brick general store sort of building on a hill in the center of town. Rocking chairs perched on the building's porch look out over mill buildings along the riverfront. Inside our borrowed office we sat on worn, side-by-side sofas and wrote; occasionally Sylvester played piano. We interviewed people in person and on Zoom: parents and activists, school board members and pastors, historians and ex-cons. People told us surprising things, as well as things we knew, by now, to expect: No, they'd never learned about the local history of their community. No, they were never taught about Reconstruction and Black people's inspiring fight for voting and economic freedom. But now that they knew, they wanted to make sure this history wasn't forgotten.

Sometimes we took walks along the Haw River, which sported a newly cleared trail. Other times we strolled around town, past the coffee shop and fancy butcher, the eco-friendly boutique where our friend and fellow activist Carey Kirk worked, the coworking space and bike shop and new entrance to the Hawbridge School.

One afternoon we walked to the museum, which was closed for the day. We stood on the porch, and I pointed out Morrow Grove School—Morrow Grove had once been a one-room African American schoolhouse and had been purchased by the Jordans. I had left the school in 2013 to be a writer-in-residence at a small college in nearby Hickory, but my class at Hawbridge had attempted an oral history project based on Morrow Grove, which fizzled due to lack of interest. Morrow Grove was also closed and locked but renovated and freshly painted. I peered into the new windows and saw ordinary-looking tables and chairs, empty bulletin boards. There was nothing about the school, aside from brick markers reading "1929–1949," that indicated its history.

Sylvester didn't want to trespass. He'd worked with Nettie Baldwin on the Alamance County Community Remembrance Coalition but hadn't heard much about the school or its restoration. I looked back at him from where I was squinting into the darkened building, my hands cupped to the glass, and saw that he wasn't comfortable here. I felt a little surprised, at first, maybe even mild annoyance—it was *fine*, what was he worried about?

But then I remembered my window and how small it is. How limited.

I didn't grow up in Alamance County, and I've never lived there.

I drive a car—often out of registration, to Sylvester's dismay—to the same downtown Graham protests without ever worrying about getting pulled over.

I'm a cross-country runner, hiker, and wild foods forager, and I probably trespass once a day without thinking about it.

I've never considered owning a gun.

I am often racing ahead, trying to see everything I can, while Sylvester hangs back, watching, thinking, mulling things over. He is steeped in this place, its problems as well as its promise.

I'm late to the story of Wyatt Outlaw, late to the history and present-day terror and injustice of Graham and Alamance County. I was poorly educated about Reconstruction and Black history and in that way underprepared to be an educator. But like Sylvester, I don't want another teacher, another student, another person to miss their chance to hear about Wyatt Outlaw or the people who have taken his story as inspiration for the lives they live and the work that they do.

Sylvester is one of those people, walking a difficult, uphill path—sometimes literally—for many years now. I met him through activism and because some of the things that had been happening to him for years—police brutality, neo-Confederate threats—happened to me too. I met him again through his writing about Wyatt Outlaw and his work as a performer, musician, and interpreter of history that is so often buried, neglected, or minimized.

Sylvester's story is as inspiring to me as Wyatt's is, and it's an honor to walk beside him as we tell it.

CHAPTER FOUR

STORIES WE HEARD

SYLVESTER

“They’re gonna burn your house down.” That’s what Mr. Omega Wilson remembered people telling him, when he started organizing his community to stop eminent domain land seizures. “They’re gonna come down here and kill us all.”

I’d hear this kind of talk when I’d want to look through the store glass to window-shop or to cross a field when we weren’t sure who owned the land. *Stay in your lane, don’t get curious* was the internalized message echoed by my friends and cousins in our upbringing.

The fear goes back to Wyatt, but it wasn’t only his fate that had people in Alamance County scared of white folks. Jim Crow segregation—the time of separate schools, hospitals, and drinking fountains—was a direct response to the gains of Reconstruction. Its aim was not just to halt the progress of Black leadership and political participation but to prevent Black and white working people from building political power together. Instead of allies, as they were during Wyatt’s time, poor and middle-class whites saw Black people, and especially Black men, as threats. Black people, in turn, accurately perceived the danger of white people, who could respond to any suggestion or accusation with vigilante attacks and murders.

In 1920, John Jeffress was an eighteen-year-old Black man accused of raping a seven-year-old white girl near Elon College. A mob of some twenty-five white men, including the president of Elon, went on a manhunt for Jeffress. They delivered him to Alamance County Courthouse, where he was expected to stand trial on August 23. Before a trial could happen, an even larger group of white men kidnapped him from sheriff's custody and took him to nearby woods, where he was shot to death, his body left alongside the road for spectators. The sheriff later claimed he couldn't identify a single member of the unmasked, daytime crowd that kidnapped Jeffress, and no one stood trial for the lynching.[1]

This kind of extrajudicial killing was common during the Jim Crow era, when Black men were demonized as sexual predators and frequently accused of rape or assault on the basis of scanty or no evidence. Due process was deemed "too good" for Black men like Jeffress, who were subject to gruesome public murders across the South. Between 1877 and 1950, more than 4,000 men, women, and children were lynched in acts of domestic terrorism like the kidnapping and murder of John Jeffress.[2]

It's not surprising that these atrocities, plus the daily reality of racism and economic subjugation, would have a long-term effect on Alamance County. "Leave it alone"—that's what Mr. Omega was told, which has meant everything from suppressing the vote to keeping stories buried so new generations didn't hear them, or heard only a warped version of what happened. It even caused some people to believe things that weren't true.

One such story was of an accomplished Black doctor, Charles Richard Drew, who was a pioneering medical professional. Driving through Alamance, Drew—who was the first African American to receive a doctor of science in medicine degree, among many other firsts—flipped his car into a field, crashing due to fatigue. His injuries were grievous, and though he received the best treatment available, he died at Alamance General Hospital.

A small town in the segregated Jim Crow South. A famous and important Black doctor. A tragic accident.

The rumors started, as Spencie Love writes in *One Blood: The Death and Resurrection of Charles R. Drew*, "within hours" that Dr. Drew was denied medical care, turned away because there were no "Negro beds" available in the segregated hospital. He was sent to the Black hospital and died along the way. The pioneer of the modern blood bank was denied a blood transfusion, all because of the color of his skin.[3]

Despite attempts by his colleagues and family to correct the record, the rumor became myth and was entered into written history with a 1964 newspaper column about segregated health care by civil rights leader Whitney

Young. Though well-meaning and "true" in spirit—segregated hospitals and refusal to treat patients of color cost many lives in the South—Dr. Drew's life was not taken by racist medical negligence.

Stories withheld, stories untold. Stories *incorrectly told* that nevertheless express an unacknowledged but commonly experienced truth. It's no wonder people feel adrift, afraid, cheated, and angry.

But how do you turn that anger into positive action? How do you tell accurate stories to the people who most need to hear them? When we're hungry we search for food. When we're thirsty we search for water. I may not have the perfect answer, but one thing I'm learning is not only to encourage people to tell the stories but to encourage those who can to become storytellers. If there's an acoustic guitar on every corner, you can't help but hear the music. And with great storytelling comes the potential for great enlightenment. My play *The Spirit of Wyatt Outlaw* attempted to do just that, enlighten, charge, inspire to celebrate, to mourn, to learn.

Sometimes those stories come in the form of songs like Jess Klein's "The Ballad of Wyatt Outlaw" or Kenneth Russell's "We Don't Want to Die No More." Sometimes it's a historical marker on the corner of Court Square. The only useful thing to do with the anger and betrayal that we feel is to channel it into action.

Stories mend. Stories quench. Stories can begin to mend. If you can get these stories to the children, no matter how ugly and how atrocious, how shameful, defenseless, and unjaded, they will learn the truth and learn *from* the truth long before finding their allegiance to one side or the other.

We may have learned later than we should have, but that doesn't have to be true for the next generation.

PART TWO

FAMILY LEGACIES

CHAPTER FIVE

COUSINS

Thomas Holt Russell III and Jaki Shelton Green are cousins who discovered their connection online, through Black genealogy websites. Though Thomas was born in the Bronx, New York, and Jaki in Alamance County, they both trace their families to Caswell Holt, a former slave who became important to Alamance County and US history when he testified before the North Carolina Senate and the US House of Representatives about the terrorism of the Ku Klux Klan.

Thomas Holt Russell III is an educator and cybersecurity analyst who works to introduce more young people, particularly young people of color, to careers in technology and cybersecurity and then train them. Jaki Shelton Green is also an educator, as well as the first African American poet laureate of North Carolina, and the author of eight books of poetry. They met in person in the summer of 2022 and have remained in touch. You can read more about their ancestors in chapter 9. What follows is an essay from Thomas and a poem from Jaki.

"DIGGING THROUGH MY FAMILY ROOTS" BY THOMAS HOLT RUSSELL III

My name is Thomas Holt Russell Jr., but I am not technically a Jr. I should be the III because my father was Thomas Holt Russell Jr. When my mother tried to name me the III, a hospital employee told her that those designations are only for white people and royalty. Because of that bit of false information, two Thomas Holt Russell Jr.'s can be found in my family tree. That is just one of the abnormalities found on this important historic document.

Before mail-in DNA tests and ancestry websites became common, I used a pencil and paper and sometimes a phone and the post office to find and gather information. Since Ancestry.com is a great way to trace family roots, my search into my family history has been an obsession. I traced my family name back to a little house in Alamance County, North Carolina.

As an African American researching history, I already knew that some of the things I might uncover would tax my emotions. I want to think things have changed, but two things happened on my trip to Alamance that reminded me we still have a long way to go. First, on the day that I made this trip, Kyle Rittenhouse, murderer of two in Kenosha, Wisconsin, during the August 2020 protests following the police shooting of Jacob Blake, was found not guilty. Second, when I visited downtown Graham, North Carolina, I noticed the enormous Confederate statue in front of the courthouse. A tall iron gate protects the figure, protected even from the touch of a human hand. I am not used to those monuments. Any time an African American visits former slave states, they have to be prepared to encounter unpleasant reminders of the past.

My research into my ancestry led me to the living room of the Oak Grove Plantation in Alamance County. The formal plantation is now the Alamance County Historical Museum, full of documents, photos, old furniture, paintings, sketches, silverware, and hand-crafted dinnerware. A middle-aged white man took my wife and me on a personalized tour of the plantation home and went about his business in a matter-of-fact but detailed way. This home belonged to the Holts, who were originally from Bavaria and settled in Alamance in the 1740s.

An industrious lot, those Holts were. By 1853, their Alamance Cotton Factory was producing woven fabrics known as the Alamance Plaids. This material had the distinction of being the first colored cotton cloth produced in the South. By 1900 the Holt family owned twenty-four cotton mills in the county. Fast-forward many years later: These mills were consolidated and formed the core of Burlington Industries, a diversified fabric maker with over 8,000 employees and offices all around the world. The Holt family produced doctors, lawyers, and businesspeople, and they married into other families like theirs and retained those family riches until this very day. The other side to this American success story is about the other Holts, the

African Holts. They were the slaves owned by the European Holts. The African Holts date back to the 1770s with the first recorded Africans at the Oak Grove Plantation, a couple by the name of Charles and Pattie, who are my fifth great-grandfather and grandmother.

It did not take a genius to figure out where my name, Holt, originated. Like many African families after the Civil War, the slaves adopted the names of their enslavers. The Holts were no exception. Before Reconstruction, slaves did not have last names, as proven by all of the slave-era documents that list only the first names of slaves. When slaves were free, they adopted the names of prior slavers for practical reasons. It was easy to be identified, the government was in a hurry requesting names for all former slaves, and they had to register to vote. Those names also identified where a person was from.

This actually answered some of my questions from my family tree. It seems that a lot of Holts were marrying other Holts. This was for two reasons. First, all of the slaves who adopted the name Holt were not blood relatives. They only took the name out of convenience, as noted above. Second, Holts and Russells remained at the plantation for multiple generations, long after the Civil War and Reconstruction, producing more Russells and Holts and making tracing family origins a little tricky.

Several families have either the middle or last names of Russell and Holt. Additionally, census records show that the Russell and Holt families also shared the same dwellings for many years. At graveyards such as Woods Chapel, Linwood Cemetery, and Springdale Church Cemetery, I found several family plots with Russells in the Holt plots and Holts in the Russell plots.

Two brothers were born on the plantation who made a significant mark on North Carolina history, and these are the type of stories you will not find in history books. Caswell Holt Jr. and Sam Holt were brothers born to Oak Grove slaves Caswell Sr. and Rhena. The Holt brothers grew up with Thomas Holt, a future governor of North Carolina.

Both brothers worked at the dye house for Thomas, producing the first indigo dyes used to make the famous Alamance Plaids. The plantation home has an oil painting by Mort Kunstler, titled *Alamance Plaids*. The picture depicts Thomas showing off his company products to visitors with his wife, while Sam is working on the left side and Caswell is depicted on the right.

Sam went on to be a prominent preacher in the area. In 1832, North Carolina passed a law stating that "any free negro, slave, or person of color" could not preach in public or private. But Sam preached so well that the

European Holts would sometimes attend the informal services. E. M. Holt deeded one acre of land to Sam for the sole purpose of developing a church for the Black population.

It would soon become a school where emancipated slaves were taught how to read and write. The school, the only one of its kind in the county, is credited with training the first Black teachers, who spread around the states teaching others. In one of the first generations of African American teachers was my great-grandaunt Eliza Holt, who opened the Pattillo School in the area. The church was later named the Springdale Church and is still in operation today.

As for Caswell Holt, he was a tough man. Besides helping with the dyeing process that made his owners millions, Caswell was the first Black deputy in Alamance County. He teamed with Wyatt Outlaw, an African American political activist, and established patrols to curb Klan violence and to enforce curfew regulations during Reconstruction. This put them in the crosshairs of the KKK. First, the Klansmen attacked Outlaw and dragged him to the courthouse, where they hung him from a tree and left his body until the next day to send a message to anyone who would go against them. Caswell was next on the list. The Klan attacked him several times. He was shot seven times, whipped, hung, and bucked (horrible torture that was widespread during the Civil War that I am not even going to explain here). No matter the physical pain he endured, Caswell never gave in to the demands of the Klan. He denounced them in the face of danger and would rather lose his life than admit to a crime he never committed.

Working against the wishes of his ex-owner, E. M. Holt, Caswell traveled to Washington, DC, and testified before the US Senate. The brutal Klan terrorism in Alamance prompted North Carolina governor William Holden to declare an insurrection in the county, which was basically a war against the Ku Klux Klan. Governor Holden put martial law into effect and occupied Alamance and Caswell Counties. On July 6, Colonel George W. Kirk was in charge of troops, and eighty-three Klansmen were arrested. This was known as the Kirk-Holden War. Scrimmages broke out all over the county, and the federal troops were accused of hanging two Klan members in an effort to get information from them. The people of North Carolina were incensed at the government's pursuit of the Ku Klux Klan, and it cost Holden politically. After the Kirk-Holden War ended, he was the first US governor to be impeached and removed from office.

As I wrote earlier, history can sometimes put you in a funky mood, especially if you are Black. Tracing my family history for a couple of years and finally visiting the plantation where my relatives lived in bondage for almost 100 years was an emotional experience. I knew what to expect. Though I did learn a few things, my research was so thorough before I arrived that I found no great surprises once I was there.

Oak Grove is a melancholy place. It is definitely not Tara of *Gone with the Wind*. Oak Grove is not palatial and glamorous. Slavery is not a technicolor dream; it was a dirty, grimy life. I do not know how many visitors the museum receives, but I suspect tourists do not overrun the Oak Grove Plantation. The main walkway was blocked with an elaborate and symmetrical spider web. I walked around the web because destroying this type of nature seemed too much for a short visit. The Holt graveyard on the property was scrubbed and tidy, unlike the unmarked and washed-out headstones found in the place where the slaves were buried. The gravesite for the slaves of the plantation is about a mile from the plantation in the rear of Springdale Church, separated, even in death. This is the church that Sam Holt started.

Though most of the slaves were not related to the slave owners, it is also just as accurate that many of the slaves were blood relatives of the owners. My own DNA says so. Slaver E. M. Holt gave land to both Sam and Caswell for a church and school and attended Sam's Sunday sermons, but he did little to stop the harassment and beating of someone he looked upon favorably, albeit paternalistically. Slavery and the relationship between master and slave have always been complicated.

My uncle Caswell wasn't having any of that paternalistic crap. He went his own way and paid a substantial physical and emotional toll. But he had resiliency. This is why I am so proud of him. He had it much worse than any of us today and lived to a ripe old age with his dignity intact. Now that's admirable!

Before I left the plantation, I stood near the historical marker and took a deep breath. I did my best to imagine what it was like being here 200 years ago. And I knew I would never return.

"I WANTED TO ASK THE TREES" BY JAKI SHELTON GREEN

I wanted to ask the trees. do you remember. were you there. did you shudder. did your skin cry out against the skin of my great uncle's skin. was the smell of bark a different smell from the smell of meat flesh. human meat flesh. beloved father husband lover friend man flesh. could the air discern burning tongue from burning arm. does the neck bone stay intact or grizzle like the shaft of toes fingers ears.

• • • •

I wanted to ask the trees. were you there. did you shudder. are you an elder that wailed out loud when they strung him up on your youngest branch. no mercy even for the lynching of new sprawling birch limbs just learning themselves how to crawl towards an un-emancipated sky. are you a grandchild or great grandchild of the tree that drank his blood. the tree that cried tears into the rope around his neck. his arms. his legs.

• • • •

I wanted to ask the trees. but the ground spoke first. annoying perfectly manicured azaleas. annoying perfect graves of perfect skeletons. whose blood-stained hands are forever etched on the hearts of my ancestors who cry out to me. plantation ground scratches the soles of my feet. ancestors beg me to lie down. be still. they waited so long for this day. when someone would come and dance with their spirits. they are everywhere whispering. holding up this house that dares to ignore them. holding up a sanitized history and herstory. one for the trees. one for us.

• • • •

I wanted to ask the trees. do you remember. did you refuse to hold his weight. did your branches crackle. did you refuse to hold him. did you feed his blood to your roots. who are these new trees. look how they glisten against an unshackled firmament. did you tell them that his blood was the only nourishment you could provide that entire season. did you tell them it was a winter of blood. no rain. no snow. blood storms. lightning and thunder lifting other names onto the wind's tongue. so many names for the wind to carry. so much hair teeth bones for the ground to gather.

• • • •

I wanted to ask the trees. who will carry your stories. who are your historians. who will measure the rings of ropes that wrapped around your waists. your shoulders. under your arms. beneath your head. I wanted to ask the trees. did you forget to breathe when the red thunder inside you painted everything the color of love.

• • • •

I want to ask the trees. do you remember. do your branches still crackle with his weight. do you shudder. do you know mercy.

CHAPTER SIX

PASSED DOWN

"FAMILY TREE" BY AUDRA FAUCETTE

Audra Faucette is a physical therapist who lives in Burlington and serves with Sylvester on the Alamance County Community Remembrance Coalition. She met Belle and her daughter Beatrice on a bus tour for community members, which Belle writes about in chapter 16.

I was thirteen years old and in the eighth grade when I was required to create a family tree. This was how I learned about my great-great-grandfather "One Arm Bill," a Confederate hero in the Civil War, a.k.a. "The War of Northern Aggression" or "The War of States' Rights," as my dad likes to call it. This is what was written about him by General John B. Gordon, Confederate States of America:

> At Big Falls, North Carolina, there lived in 1897 a one-armed soldier whose heroism will be cited by orators and poets as long as heroism is cherished by men. He was the color-bearer of his regiment, the Thirteenth North Carolina. In the charge during the first day's battle at Gettysburg, his right arm, with which he bore the colors, was shivered and almost torn from its socket. Without halting or hesitating, he seized the falling flag in his left hand, and, with his blood spouting from the

> severed arteries and his right arm dangling in shreds at his side, he still rushed to the front, shouting to his comrades: "Forward, forward!" The name of that modest and gallant soldier is W. F. Faucette.[1]

Based on his great-grandfather's act of courage, my dad was inducted into the Sons of Confederate Veterans. We visited the North Carolina Museum of History to see the battle flag that Bill carried, we were given a photo of the bones of his severed arm from a medical museum in Washington, DC, and our next family trip will likely be to Gettysburg, Pennsylvania, to see where he was injured and taken captive. He was and still is a hero in the Faucette family—despite the rest of his story. The first part of the story was told to me with pride; the second part was just a "matter of fact."

During Reconstruction, "One Arm Bill" became involved with the White Brotherhood of Alamance County, and one night they lynched a Black man. The reason I was given: "He raped a white woman." To avoid prosecution, Bill fled to Texas and stayed with family until things involving the lynching in North Carolina settled down. He returned to Alamance County to the family farm. He lived there until he passed away in 1902. This was the story passed down through the family and then told to me when I was writing my genealogy report.

Twenty-one years later, I attended the Global Leadership Summit in Chicago, Illinois, where I heard Bryan Stevenson, lawyer, activist, and founder of the Equal Justice Initiative, speak for the first time. I listened as he explained the connections between lynching and mass incarceration and how systemic racism has been used to continue to subjugate racial minorities. I bought and began to read *Just Mercy*, which also described how the fear of interracial sex and marriage was used to justify lynching and killing as punishment if "racial integrity" was not upheld. I immediately thought about the lynching my great-great-grandfather was a part of, and something in me said, "There is more to this story." When I returned home, I began researching lynching in Alamance County during Reconstruction.

This was when I learned about Wyatt Outlaw, his ties to the Faucett/Faucette family, and the true motivation behind his murder. His death was an act of domestic terrorism meant to subjugate the free Black community, and a lie was told to justify it to the rest of the family. It was this revelation that opened my eyes to so many other things, including the fact that this pattern of fear and subjugation continues today. His lynching likely changed the course of history for Alamance County and is the undercurrent for many of the beliefs, attitudes, and behaviors in our community. I knew I couldn't live in those beliefs any longer; I knew the true story needed to be told, and the community needed to begin to change. This was the catalyst for me to learn more about the mission of the Equal Justice Initiative and to join the Alamance County Community Remembrance Coalition in its work toward community reckoning and healing.

There is sorrow and a definite tension in my identity as a Faucette. How do I reconcile being a direct descendent of a rebel Confederate soldier who participated in a public murder *and* a distant cousin to a former slave who fought for the unity of the United States, went on to fight for the flourishing of his community, and was killed for it? When you are a white Southerner, there is an expectation to be loyal to your "family and heritage." But which family and which heritage? Wyatt is also, very likely, a part of that family and heritage. Am I forced to choose which part of the family I am loyal to? Do I disown one to claim the other? Can I claim both, the good and the bad, the beautiful and the ugly? Can I be a bridge between the two and live between the tension of each side?

Both parts are true: Without acknowledging the reality of Bill Faucette, I would be ignoring the attitudes and beliefs that shaped my upbringing and neglecting the work of disentangling from them in order to model a different way. Without the truth of Wyatt, I would be whitewashing history and denying the hope that the future can be more unified, loving, equal, just, and full of dignity for every human being.

In Dr. Martin Luther King Jr.'s "Letter from Birmingham Jail," he wrote, "One day the South will recognize its real heroes." I reread the letter two days before Martin Luther King Jr. Day in 2025, and this stood out to me. I thought about who Southern "heritage" prefers to honor and who it chooses to ignore. Wyatt is the real hero.

SOME VETERANS

Dr. Samuel Merritt is Wyatt Outlaw's great-great-grandson. Born in Vance County, North Carolina, he now lives in Raleigh and is a retired epidemiologist. He is a US Army veteran and was the director of the North Carolina State Laboratory of Public Health.

"Your great-great-grandfather is in the history books," Samuel Merritt's mother, Lucy Williams Merritt, told him growing up.[2] The story came down from his grandmother Nancy Outlaw Williams Green, the daughter of Lucretia Scott Outlaw and Oscar Outlaw, Wyatt's youngest son. Lucy and Nancy believed that their famous ancestor had been a blacksmith and inventor of a new kind of horseshoe, one that muffled the noise made by horses' hooves as they traveled.

ALAMANCE COUNTY COMMUNITY REMEMBRANCE COALITION

Formed in 2019, the Alamance County Community Remembrance Coalition was inspired by a glass jar of soil, printed with the following:

> John Jeffress
> Graham, North Carolina
> August 20, 1920

Early coalition members saw this memorial to a Black man lynched in their community at the Equal Justice Initiative's Legacy Museum and National Memorial for Peace and Justice in Montgomery, Alabama. They returned to Alamance County determined to bring EJI projects to their community. The multiracial, multigenerational group includes historians, educators, musicians, pastors, and community members from across Alamance County. Many are allied with other local organizations, including Elon University, the Alamance NAACP, Alamance Agents for Change, the African American Cultural Arts and History Center, Benevolence Farm, Down Home, the Saxapahaw Social Justice Exchange, the West End Revitalization Association, and Whites Against White Supremacy. They receive support, guidance, and educational materials from the EJI.

In September 2021, thirty members of the Alamance Remembrance Coalition gathered in Graham and Haw River to memorialize the three known victims of lynching in Alamance: John Jeffress, Wyatt Outlaw, and William Puryear. The solemn ceremonies included *djembe* drumming, readings about each man's life and history, prayers, hymns, and soil collection from the approximate death sites into two jars each: one for Alamance, and one for the EJI Legacy Museum, where members traveled again in April 2022.

To find out more about the EJI's community remembrance work across the country, including soil collection, historical markers, community engagement and education, and an essay contest for high schoolers, see its website: https://eji.org/projects/community-remembrance-project/.

Obtaining a patent as a Black man in the nineteenth century would have been an impressive accomplishment, but there were no history books with this specific record, or even with the true story of the father-in-law Lucretia never met. Oscar, who grew up without a father or mother, had moved about seventy miles away to Henderson, the county seat of Vance. There he opened a successful barbershop, where he served a white clientele. Oscar and Lucretia owned a home on South Hall Street, and Lucretia had a horse-drawn surrey, which she used to take food and medicine to the poor. The Outlaw home had a wraparound porch, a handsome family Bible, and a piano, which daughter Nancy learned to play for company.

Perhaps the family didn't want to talk about the violence that Oscar had been witness to as a five-year-old, or about his own words—"Oh, Daddy! Oh, Daddy!" he'd cried as his father was abducted—which are also part of state history. "Some veterans don't talk about a lot of things that happen to them in war," Dr. Merritt noted.

In the Jim Crow South that Dr. Merritt himself was raised in, "there was nothing to be gained from talking about that." His parents were educated, middle-class Black people. His father was a teacher and then a high school assistant principal; his mother, a substitute teacher and librarian. The family settled in Warrenton but spent every Sunday in Henderson, where they visited with Nancy, affectionately known as "Laylay." She liked to sing and cook and was a "jolly, good person," Dr. Merritt remembered. "She was a lovable, warm person who could endure things but keep it to herself."

Dr. Merritt seems a little like this himself—warm and open but disinclined to dwell on difficulties he faced as a Black man growing up in the Jim Crow South. After graduating from the Henderson Institute, a historic "colored" school founded in 1865, he attended Virginia State College, where he played in the band and became interested in microbiology. He remembered the date—September 2, 1966—when he received what he ruefully called his "McNamara fellowship," or draft notice for service in Vietnam. Returning home after the Tet Offensive, a detail he mentioned without elaboration, he attended Michigan State and the University of Michigan, where he received a master's in microbiology, a master's in public health, and a doctoral degree in epidemiology laboratory practice.

It wasn't until decades later, when Dr. Merritt was practicing as an epidemiologist studying public health, that he learned a little more about his family. His great-uncle Oscar Outlaw Jr. wrote to him from his home in Philadelphia to share some of the family story. His great-great-grandfather—Oscar Jr.'s grandfather—was not a blacksmith but a carpenter and political leader. He was killed, Great-Uncle Oscar told him, by the Klan.

Sylvester and Dr. Samuel Merritt (*left*) were first introduced by Walter Boyd at a presentation of the play *Wyatt Outlaw*. (Photo by Walter Boyd.)

This news came to Dr. Merritt in the early 1980s, long before Carole Troxler or Scott Reynolds Nelson had published scholarly articles and books with details about Wyatt Outlaw. Dr. Merritt had a busy life, raising his family, working, and eventually becoming director of the state's public health laboratory. It wasn't until he retired in 2016 that he was able to dig deeper into Wyatt's story. He found articles online, met Sylvester's friend Walter Boyd, and even wrote to Graham's mayor, Jerry Peterman, to find out if anything had been done in town to commemorate Wyatt's life or mark what happened to him.

He did not receive a reply but did get an invitation from Dave Wright to see a screening of his Wyatt Outlaw play; this is where he met Sylvester. Dr. Merritt is regularly invited to commemorations of Wyatt's brave life and tragic death and will usually say a few words to encourage others who are also inspired by Wyatt's example.

"I think for some reason, his spirit lives on," he said. "All of this came into being without any push from me."

CHAPTER SEVEN

HEART OF DOWNTOWN

"NO REGRETS" BY KRIS LOY

Kris Loy is an activist, student, and one of the marchers who got pepper-sprayed at the October 31 I Am Change Legacy March to the Polls in 2020. He was a founding member of Occupy Graham, a protest movement that met for months in the town square after January 6, 2021.

I was born in Durham hospital, but I've lived for about fourteen years in Alamance County. I moved here when I was seven, but my family is from here going all the way back to my ancestor Martin Loy, who was one of the first settlers of Snow Camp, down south of the county, along with the Albrights. From what I understand, he was part of the wave of Quakers who came into central North Carolina. The Piedmont, Greensboro to Alamance, is all historical Quaker country.

So, I grew up attending Alamance schools. When I was in the third or fourth grade at South Graham Elementary, I remember taking a field trip downtown to learn about the local government or something. We were standing in what we now call Wyatt Outlaw Park, and the teacher pointed up at the top corner of the courthouse.

"That's where the Klan hung a man," she said.

It wasn't until years later, as an adult, I actually learned any of the other details surrounding the lynching. I didn't even know Outlaw's name. All I knew was that I lived in a town where a man was hung for the color of his skin, and it was public knowledge, but no one seemed willing to do much about it besides point, all the while standing a few feet from a statue built to honor the men who did it.

The first time I remember protesting injustice was the time my high school teacher got fired unfairly and was basically shamed and run out of the county for things people made up about him. We protested, but we were kids, and I basically feel like we didn't change anything. But I think that's what sparked my life as an activist.

By the time 2020 rolled around my dad had passed, and I was pretty much on my own. The murder of George Floyd had a massive national impact, and for the first time I felt that something was being done about police violence and racism. I always knew that the American system was egregiously wrong, and something was finally being done.

I started out going to Raleigh for what was happening there around George Floyd. There were these giant crowds. I was just sort of a face, another face. I was in the square and saw the Confederate statue brought down in Raleigh. Those statues directly represent white supremacist power in the South. And they represent the perpetuation of it.

So, then I got involved with the actions happening down in Saxapahaw. They were champions, protesting for something like 250 days in a row. And that led to me getting involved in Graham.

Occupy Graham was a movement that Carey Kirk, Avery Harvey, and I started in January 2021. We all recognized the need for continued action in Graham, especially after the January 6 riot. It was partially spawned out of Black Lives Matter, but our main messaging goal was one tying into the antifascism movement. Ted Budd, who had represented Alamance County in the state legislature, had just been elected as our senator. He voted not to certify the presidential election. We stood on the sidewalk next to the park where Wyatt was killed, just across from the Confederate statue. We held signs; we talked to people about that long-ago history and the things that were happening now.

It was an attempt to try to orient the conversation toward how the far right was working on a hyperlocal level and to demonstrate that our efforts to counter the rise of rightist populist movements must be met by leftist populist movements in those same arenas.

I don't know if we had much success. Eventually it got to the point where I felt like I was staging a one-man protest. There were nights I was out at

Kris Loy cofounded Occupy Graham, a democracy-focused protest, after the January 6 insurrection. “We held signs; we talked to people about that long-ago history and the things that were happening now,” said Kris. (Photo by Anthony Crider.)

Wyatt Outlaw Park completely on my own. There were also nights that Avery was out there on his own.

As far as the backlash—I mean, it's been difficult. It's been difficult. Getting a job around here after 2020 has been really tough. I remember I tried applying down at the library here in Burlington. I went for this interview, and the librarians were really impressed with me. That entire staff is basically telling me I got the job. And then they take it to HR. And HR looks into my activism. And they tell the library I'm a no-go. And that really impacted me.

Quakerism has really influenced my activism as I've grown up and made my own identity. Returning to the Quaker roots of my family has been really important to me, doing a lot to solidify my activist ethics. I guess I just thought of myself as doing something right and good. I thought of myself as living within my best moral and spiritual ethics, more so than I've ever done. And the "powers" around here decide to punish me for it. I've still got that case hanging over my head for when I got arrested for peacefully protesting. Still, with all the obstacles being an "Outlaw" has created, I have no regrets.

QUAKERS AND MANUMISSION

The Quaker community, also known as the Society of Friends, established itself in North Carolina, Pennsylvania, and Maryland in the 1600s after a migration from England and the Anglican Church, where the Quakers had been persecuted for their strong beliefs. The first Quaker community in North Carolina's Piedmont was the Cane Creek Friends Meeting in Alamance County, established in 1751. Though influential in early colonial politics, Quaker political leverage waned over the years with adherents' belief in the pacifist approach to conflict resolution, leaving them neutral in the violent battles with the French and in the American Revolution. Their pacifism and refusal to bear false witness also made their abolitionist principles difficult to practice—Quakers hiding enslaved people could not fight back or even lie to slave catchers or police.

Though many Quakers who lived in the region eventually migrated northwest over the next hundred years due to their opposition to slavery in North Carolina, some stayed and remained instrumental in the orchestration of escape routes for the enslaved. In 1816, Quakers in

North Carolina founded the Manumission Society, which worked to manumit, or free, individual enslaved people. Local Manumission Society groups would purchase enslaved people and then treat them as "trustees," cared for and educated until they could be officially freed. Levi Coffin, an active member of the Manumission Society and one of the founders of the Underground Railroad, helped thousands to freedom from his home in Guilford County and even after he moved with his wife to Indiana in 1826.

In Alamance County, the small Quaker community of Snow Camp, home to the Cane Creek Friends Meeting, was an important stop on the Underground Railroad; after the Civil War, the community founded a school for emancipated children. A play produced by the Snow Camp Theatre for decades, *Pathway to Freedom* (1994), told the story of local Quaker involvement in the Underground Railroad.

Kris Loy is only a recent member of a long legacy of Friends dedicated to activism and dissent, helping to extend the core Quaker beliefs of nonviolence, equality, and restorative justice to the new millennium.

But an important distinction in Kris's activism is how he draws part of this motivation from early Quaker settlers and their core principles, with a memory of his ancestors' relocation and political involvement over the last hundred years, locally. This is something that Alamance County attempted to strip from Black people, withholding knowledge of the Reconstruction efforts of Wyatt Outlaw and his comrades.

PART THREE

OUTRAGES, OUTLAWS, AND ACCOUNTABILITY

CHAPTER EIGHT

SEARCHING FOR HIDDEN TRUTHS

BELLE

If you're not a university student or a visiting scholar, it isn't easy to see some of the original documents that will help you feel and understand the weight of a deliberately hidden past. At the University of North Carolina's Wilson Library, which houses the world's largest collection of documents about the American South, you'll need a special, scholarly registration—given readily by a helpful library staff, and for free, but an extra step requiring knowledge and advance planning. You'll have to know how to search for the things you want, how to look for the hidden voices, the hidden truths.

"Go stand at the bell tower and spin around; look at the names on the surrounding buildings," manuscripts research librarian Matthew Turi told us at our library orientation. He was referring to the Teagues, the Kenans, the Hills—all wealthy white families, many with some connection to North Carolina's history of enslavement and white supremacy. "The people who counted, we have their papers."[1]

Many of the documents held by Wilson Library's Southern Historical Collection, where we hoped to get closer to Wyatt Outlaw's life, were first collected by J. G. de Roulhac Hamilton, a professor and head of UNC's

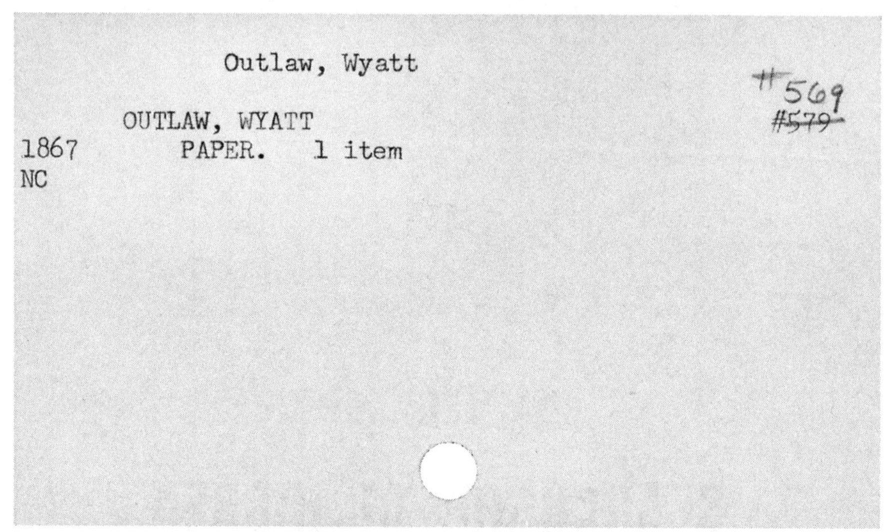
Outlaw, Wyatt

OUTLAW, WYATT

1867 PAPER. 1 item

NC

#569

#579

Catalog card for Wyatt Outlaw, drawer 53, "Oregon to Peace Troops (U.S.),"
former Manuscripts Department catalog, Wilson Library,
University of North Carolina at Chapel Hill.

history department from 1908 to 1930. Hamilton was born in 1878 and was the son of a Confederate army officer and former slave owner. He studied at Columbia University under William Archibald Dunning, a leading Reconstruction historian committed to racist, Lost Cause ideologies. Hamilton's own research on the Reconstruction era was pro-Klan, arguing that white supremacists saved the state of North Carolina from the political influence of Black men and carpetbaggers—he published more than 100 papers and eleven books, including a young reader's biography of Robert E. Lee—but his most influential academic role was as an archivist. Beginning in about 1915 and for the next several decades, he traveled around the South collecting thousands of primary source documents, mostly from the homes of white people.

"He *did* collect so expansively that things can be read in other ways," Turi told us. "Direct Black voices are often hidden, just like the voices of women."[2]

On the day of our first visit together to the Special Collections Reading Room, we each parked in the paid deck, about a half mile from Wilson Library. We walked past the George Watts Hill Alumni Center, past Kenan Memorial Stadium and Carmichael Residence Hall and Avery, Parker, and Teague Halls, all buildings and streets named after long-dead white men (until 2021, the building housing the history department was named after J. G. Hamilton). Under the shade of oak and pine trees whose roots push up against the brick sidewalk, we walked past the bell tower, across South Road, and around the other side, where wide stone steps led down to a lawn buzzing with insects.

The Special Collections Reading Room isn't grand. There's a wall of metal lockers for stashing bags and wallets, because visitors aren't allowed to bring in anything more than a computer, a phone or camera, a pencil, and looseleaf paper or notecards. We stopped at the desk staffed by librarians, who asked us to open our computers, then identified our station and handed us weighted "book snakes," which look like thick white shoelaces (for holding down stiff pages while we read). We collected a few other reading aids—magnifying loops, gray foam book supports, gray felt, and looseleaf paper and pencils marked with the UNC logo—and headed to our table, which would seat six comfortably, eight closely. The floor is covered in a brown carpet, warped in places, which hushes footfalls. All the glossy-topped tables and scratched wooden desks in the room are mismatched—some cherry, some oak—and the chairs have cracked leather seats. The items we requested—everything from Wyatt Outlaw's original Union League commission to a 2020 graphic pamphlet illustrating his life—looked paltry lined up on their metal cart.

The time we spent here went fast. The bell tower seemed to chime every ten minutes instead of every thirty, and construction trucks beeped on South Street. Sylvester, who had a music class to teach in Burlington at four that day, put on noise-canceling headphones and settled before the foam book blocks to read a time-yellowed 1930s scrapbook devoted to stories about Klan activity. Next to him, I carefully paged through an 1870 Union League of America handbook barely larger than a smartphone, its cover lost to time. I told him about the items suggested for setting up a meeting space and how it recommended a Bible, a flag, and "small anvil, sickle, and shuttle" to represent workingmen. I whisper-read some of the booklet's contents to Sylvester: "Aid and assist the government in so fixing the foundations thereof, that peace, happiness, truth, liberty, justice, and brotherly love may prevail for all time. . . . Unite us in love for our common country. . . . Worthy Sons of America! We bid you welcome. This circle of freedom and equal rights now encircling you must never be broken by treachery."[3]

We looked together at a full-page newspaper story from the *Raleigh Daily Standard* dated July 30, 1870, in which James Boyd, then a twenty-five-year-old lawyer, describes his participation in Alamance County's White Brotherhood, also known as the Klan, beginning in 1868. He writes that he "was informed that this organization was in the interests of the Conservative party, and intended to defeat entirely the reconstruction acts, and to deprive the negro of all privileges as a citizen of this country, and in the obligation was a section which bound the members thereof never to support any man for office who was in favor of the civil or political advancement of the colored race." Black voter disenfranchisement, to Boyd, was all well and good. But the "outrages"—burning schools and churches, whipping and killing people—these actions "did not agree with [his] feelings." Boyd explains, "I immediately put my foot upon it as far as I possibly could, occupying the position which I did. I made no public exposition of it at that time for the reason that my life would not have been safe for one moment, if I had." A "large majority of the Conservative party" in Alamance was involved in Klan activity, Boyd claims. This is why he was afraid, though most of the "outrages" had targeted Black men, women, and children—not wealthy white men like himself.[4]

I turned to Governor Holden's correspondence at that time—escalating pleas to the president, to Congress, for assistance quashing what was surely an insurrection of Klan activity. He explains that he can't call up local militia because "in the localities in which these outrages occur, white militia of the proper character cannot be obtained, and it would but aggravate the evil to employ colored militia."[5]

The clock struck two—how had four hours passed so quickly? Sylvester was reading a manuscript titled "Jacob A. Long Recollections," a sheaf of pencil-scrawled claims about the Klan, typed sometime after its collection in 1915. It's possible that Jacob Long, one year after speaking as master of ceremonies at the Confederate monument in Graham, handed the sheaf of papers to J. G. Hamilton himself.

The items before us were few, but they were speaking to us as plainly as the anvil, the sickle, the Bible, and the flag spoke to the men assembled at Wyatt Outlaw's weekly Union League meetings. They spoke to the connections between a man known to some as the "free nigro son of Ches. Faucett" and the highest offices in the state and the country: the president, the governor, North Carolina senators. They spoke to the terror of living in Graham in 1870 and to the truth about Black people and what voting had meant to them. "These outrages," Holden wrote, "are almost invariably committed on persons, white and colored, who are most devoted in their feelings and conduct to the government of the United States."[6]

They spoke to the lies—Sylvester was reading them now, in Long's recollections—that would replace the truth for many years and would set us up for the divided, violent, insurrectionist times we lived through recently and are still enduring.

"Can I read that when you're done?" I whispered to Sylvester, who was still bent over the folder.

"Oh, I'll never be done," he said.

SYLVESTER

The manila folder the library provided held a blue sheet of paper in the front that said the following documents were "submitted by Jacob A. Long, 1915." This information alone gave me pause. It was an eerie and strange feeling, personally touching the papers of Jacob A. Long, leader of the Reconstruction-era Ku Klux Klan in Alamance County, on his account of the events surrounding Wyatt's murder. We had been chasing Outlaw's story for some time, and this was like sitting in the interrogation room with the suspect.

After that first piece of paper, several old pages produced by a typewriter provided a legible version of the handwritten account, which was in Long's chicken-scratch cursive and placed in the back of the folder. It is unclear who did the typing, but the handwritten recollection in the back was on the same sheets used by Long himself.

Again, I paused. Hesitant. Looking for distraction.

I looked up at a focused Belle as her fingers moved rapidly across her laptop keyboard. I surveyed the room and the quiet researchers, noticing how precisely measured was the distance between each research table—a regimented positioning like soldiers standing at attention in formation.

I wiggled in my seat to loosen my tightened lower back, having been completely oblivious to the pain to this point, engulfed with the materials I had read so far. But also, I was stalling. I knew that once I got started, I would read things I could never unread.

This was why we were there. It was time. My eyes finally went back to the page.

Long's recollection opens with the ratification of the North Carolina Constitution in 1868 and the election of Henry M. Ray to the legislature, a soldier who Long says switched sides from the Confederacy to the Union in the middle of the war. And he seems to blame the "negroes" for Ray's election, stating they were "anxious to vote for him."[7]

But he very quickly moves to justify the presence of the Ku Klux Klan in Alamance County, claiming that its establishment was only in response to the "secret" group called the ULA. "I do not believe that these organizations would have even existed but for the existence of the Union League of America," he writes.

Long talks about his election as chief of Alamance County's KKK, having started with six members in September 1868. They selected the name "The White Brotherhood." He recalls, also, two other groups being formulated in 1869 called the Constitutional Union Guard and the Invisible Empire. "The object of all of them was the same—mutual protection for all we loved and held dear." *Mutual protection for all we loved and held dear* is underlined both in the typewriter copy and in the original handwritten copy.

He seems to loathe the fact that Governor Holden was head of the Union League in North Carolina, and in multiple spots in his writings he accuses the Union League of arson and whipping "persons they did not like for real or imaginary wrong" under disguise.

Long then goes into a description of an 1869 incident where Allen Paisley, a Black preacher, led a group of men who in disguise whipped two or three persons but were recognized and put into the penitentiary after capture. He tells how, while in jail, Paisley accused Wyatt of being "head of the order having these things arranged." He describes Paisley as a "reliable negro," explaining away his and others' hastiness to believe his story about Wyatt.

He talks about the townspeople's "intense and bitter" resentment caused by armed guards put on the streets. "Most of the guards were negroes and each one carried guns," Long writes.

I suspect that it wasn't so much the armed guard part that caused resentment but the "negro" part. Many white Southerners already felt intense and bitter anger following the loss of their "slaves" and their defeat in the war. And Alamance County had many slaves. In 1860, 33 percent of the population of the county was enslaved. And now, in 1869, twenty-four-year-old Jacob Long was being patrolled by them.

He tells about a night when the Klan raided the town to scare off the armed guards. Warning shots were fired by Henry Holt, one of the Black guards on duty. Long claims that Wyatt also fired a shot, though Belle and I had learned that most eyewitnesses told another story. The KKK, or the White Brotherhood, fired return shots, but no one was hit on either side.

He talks later in his account about a separate night where he claims multiple houses in different parts of southeastern Alamance were burned at the same time, accusing the Union League of a "concert of action." He writes, "The names of the perpetrators of these crimes was soon found out and they were hung as soon as the Klan could find them." He does not give the names of these supposed "perpetrators." And he seems to be referring to separate lynchings, before they got to Wyatt. This part of the statement was a true surprise to me, as I had only learned for certain about the murders of Wyatt and William Puryear. But these hangings I did not know about until reading them at this moment.

In the original papers, multiple places have words that are crossed out, as if Long were writing with a pencil without an eraser. I imagined him sitting at a desk with a notepad, in a black string necktie, as I had seen in an online photo of him, writing with a Dixon pencil and completely ignoring the ledger lines, often writing over them instead of in the spaces. I imagined him feeling prideful and justified in the actions he was writing about. He must have thought himself to be on the right side of history, sometimes exclaiming, even boasting the actions of his camp.

"Swiftly-Surely-and-fearfully was the punishment inflicted," he writes, after telling about a Black man they drowned in a mill pond (whom we knew to be William Puryear) shortly after they hung Wyatt in February 1870. Yet, after mentioning the murder of John Stephens, a state senator from Caswell County, and discussing the presence of Colonel Kirk and his troops in both counties, initiated by Governor Holden's Declaration of Insurrection, he reflects on the actions of both sides.

"I would not have you judge the parties to these matters on either side too harshly. War is a fearful thing and these are many things that then seemed to the actors right and proper that to us now appear to be cruel and unjustifiable." He then refers to the Civil War: "Our flag had been furled forever in defeat. We could not bear patiently the wrongs that the victors chose to put upon us and we sometimes may have magnified in our minds the burdens we had to bear."

Just then, as I read that last passage, some unexpected questions popped into my head. Could a leader of the KKK be feeling remorse later in his life for his actions? Was he admitting wrongdoing? Was he seeking redemption in this recollection? Maybe not.

He goes on to tell a story of a man he calls a mulatto who was formerly enslaved by the widow of a Confederate soldier and still worked for the widow and her daughter after the war. The man was accused of asking the daughter to marry him (which she is said to have rejected) and then threatened to kill both the daughter and widow if she told anyone. Long states that the daughter told her uncle what happened at church one Sunday.

The next sentence sent chills down my spine: "He and some others celebrated the close of that Sabbath day by lifting up a serpent in the wilderness."

I showed Belle the sentence, and we discussed the possible meanings.

"Was this another lynching?" she asked.

"Well, it was either yet another hanging or they were snake-handling in the woods," I responded.

Throughout his recollection, Long often refers to Black people like children, using language like "not docile" or "behaved very well" or "many of them went to the bad" when explaining his actions toward them. This immediately made me think about my home church, Children's Chapel, and how Jacob Long's brother Daniel was partly responsible for its paternalistic name. Though I'm sure the more recent members of the church think of the name as more of a reference to *God's* children, I now understood its origins. Long's own writings suggest his refusal to see recently freed people as anything other than escaped "slaves" that needed disciplinary action.

But there is no evidence that most of what Long accuses the Union League of was committed by that group or even happened in the first place. And just like in today's small-town South, lies and exaggerations seem to be the go-to methods used to justify suppression of what little rights Black people did have, often by way of Klan violence.

The UNC bell tower tolled again. But this time it wasn't the sounds of a traditional church bell. Belle and I looked up from the materials that gripped our attention since we sat down.

It took me a second to realize that it was the Tar Heel alma mater being played over the bell tower. It was August, and I had seen students moving in as we crossed through parking lots to get to Wilson Library. I wondered whether it was being played as a welcome to the new students or whether it was something that the bell tower played on a regular basis. It made me wonder for a bit how many new students were going to take the time to learn about how UNC–Chapel Hill was built and the hands that built it. I think about what I didn't know in college and the perspective that was lost in not knowing. Nonetheless, I enjoyed the short serenade, a welcome break from the chilling recollections of a Reconstruction-era KKK leader. But I had to press on.

Long displayed pride in Alamance when he writes, "On her soil was the first fight for American independence and a splendid granite shaft marks the spot." He is referring to the two-hour battle (which Alamance lost) near Great Alamance Creek against Royal Governor William Tryon and his militia over taxes and other disagreements in 1771. He is also referring to the monument dedicated to that battle in 1880.

I recognized that same deep pride in those defending the monument at Graham's Court Square back in 2020. I recognized that same deep pride in my friend John, a white man who lives in Alamance and has a Confederate family history. I recognized that same prideful talk in the newspaper clippings I had examined with a magnifying glass at this very table only twenty minutes earlier, cut out by a woman named Ellis and now being preserved in the Southern Historical Collection here at Wilson Library. In one of the clippings, darkened partly by the dried glue, are lyrics from the Civil War era song "Wait for the Wagon":

> To rising generation,
> With pleasure we will tell,
> How brave our Fisher
> And gallant Johnston fell

With lyrics like that, memorized and sung with gusto by Confederate soldiers and sympathizers, it's no wonder that the Lost Cause movement had such an effect on today's Confederate apologists. The main point was not to tell the true history of the Civil War but to make sure that by the end of that story, the South's soldiers and leaders were viewed in the same light as the soldiers in the American Revolutionary War, that both wars were fought virtually on the same principles, and that the leaders of the Confederacy could be seen as American heroes.

Because the actual spark of the Civil War was a true embarrassment. Alexander Stephens, vice president of the Confederacy, spoke very clearly about the cause for the war and about his view on the "proper status of the negro in our form of civilization. This was the immediate cause of the late rupture and present revolution," Stephens said in his Cornerstone Speech just a few weeks before the Civil War started.[8] The name of the newspaper had been cut out, so I couldn't tell who published the lyrics, but surrounding them were all pro-Confederacy stories and expressions of sympathy for the South and what it lost in the war.

Long's recollection echoes the accounts in the newspaper clippings: sympathy for the South. The pages bleed with an angst for the spoils of the Civil War. Like many Southerners postwar, he felt that he had been robbed of a way of life, that he now had to fight for a sense of superiority. He even says in the last few paragraphs, "The anglo-saxon never in all ages appears the inferior race."

Wyatt Outlaw's murder was not only a statement but a scare tactic. That's why his body was left hanging in the middle of Court Square until noon the next day. It was a "get in line or suffer the same consequences" hanging. You can hear a hero complex in Long's writings, as if the Klan was some necessary evil in response to another evil. This sounded similar to how Gregory McMichael sounded after his son killed Ahmaud Arbery in 2020: a "we did what we had to" kind of sentiment.

In 1914, Jacob A. Long gave a speech at the dedication of the Confederate monument in Graham in which he stated the purpose of the statue: "To recall the achievements of the great and good of our own race and blood."[9] One year later, his recollections of the Reconstruction era's violence in Alamance and Caswell were being submitted for preservation. The statue *and* his writings serve the same purposes: Control the narrative, bury an accurate account of history, and reestablish the stronghold of white supremacy.

I'd seen enough for one day. As I closed the folder and stacked it back on the Wilson Library shelf, I reflected on how evil triumphed in the Holden case and how Wyatt's murderers were never punished. And here we had one of those people, who should have been locked away, writing boldly about his actions. Like the Tulsa and Wilmington massacres that came later, everything that could have been built during Reconstruction was torn down instead. And so many people in Alamance still have yet to be made aware. So much of the struggle of the Black community back at home was directly impacted by the destruction of our progress. Over and over.

We hadn't gotten through all of the items in the cart. I realized what time it was, and my stint in the military has made me afraid to be late to anything. I began to pack quickly, anticipating the traffic on my way to teach my music class. But there was one more thing I needed to see.

"I have to go," I said.

"Well, do you want to see Wyatt's commission to the Union League before you leave?" Belle asked.

"I don't have a lot of time," I told her, still packing.

"You really should see it," she said. Belle is nothing if not persistent.

"Well . . . OK."

She handed me a single, fragile page. It was the original document from 1867, solidifying Wyatt Outlaw's deputy appointment to the Grand State Council of the Union League of America, representing Alamance County. I got chills again, but this time for a different reason. I grabbed a magnifying glass to see the cursive closely, noticing Governor Holden's frantic signature. It looked as though ink had spilled on the page while the document was being signed. There were some very defined creases and some of the lines had mirror reflections of ink, as if the paper had been folded before the ink had a chance to dry. Belle suggested the possibility that Wyatt could have folded it and put it in his coat pocket, before traveling back to Alamance.[10]

To all whom it may Concern:

Know ye, By this Commission that by virtue of the power vested in us by the Grand National Council of U. L. of A., we hereby constitute and appoint Wyatt Outlaw of Alamance a deputy member of the Grand State Council, and confer upon him full authority to initiate proper persons into the secrets of the U. L. of A., and install Officers of Councils within and for the State of North Carolina; to supervise and instruct the same, and to do such other and further acts as may be necessary for the advancement and good of the League, and in accordance with its Laws and Regulations, hereby requiring the said Wyatt Outlaw to promptly report to this Grand Council all of his doings by virtue of this dispensation.

Given under our Hands and the seal of the Grand State Council, at the City of Raleigh, N. C., this 5th day of July 1867.

W. W. Holden
Gr. President.

W. R. Richardson
Gr. Recording Secretary.

Wyatt Outlaw's Union League commission from 1867. Wyatt Outlaw Union League of America Commission, #00569-z, Southern Historical Collection, Wilson Library, University of North Carolina at Chapel Hill.

I saw not only inked dates and signatures on the page but also Wyatt's distinguishment. His distinction was what the Klan feared the most. He was their biggest threat in Alamance. He was courageous and intelligent and could bring white and Black people together. This was *really* why he was killed. And even though I never knew Wyatt, it made me proud to know that he was the man that he was—that Alamance County once had a leader of such stature and bravery and sophistication. This was what a true hero looked like—willing to stand up for his people and for what is right, even under the threat of injustice or death. He was far more than the narrow presentation of *Blackness* some throughout my life had tried to impose upon me. He was much, much more. I closed the commission and put it back on the shelf, handling it carefully, like it was made of the thinnest glass.

Belle and I began packing again. I felt both informed and curious at the same time after reading Wyatt's commission and Jacob A. Long's recollections, wondering what was still to be uncovered. So much history, so many lies, and so much truth still to be told. Maybe we would never truly be done.

• • • •

Later in the evening, teaching a voice lesson in Burlington, I mentioned to my student that I was coauthoring a book.

"What's the book about?" she asked.

"Black history, right here in Alamance County."

She jumped out of her seat.

This was a Black woman in her mid-fifties who started playing piano and singing for her gospel church choir after retiring from the US Army.

"Finally, a book about us, Black folks here in town," she said excitedly. "'Cause you *know* we need that."

We both laughed.

"True. That is true," I said under my breath.

"Well, you have to let me know when it comes out, 'cause I'm about to tell everybody," she said exuberantly.

"I definitely will," I replied, right before playing the first chord of the song we've been working on together: "Bridge over Troubled Water."

CHAPTER NINE

OUTLAWS

The word "outlaw" comes from the Old Norse word *ūtlagr*, which combines *ut* (out) and *lög* (law). In premodern society, an *ūtlagi* was a person who was outside the protection of the law—a punishment of exile, akin to the death penalty. Outlaws could not own property and could be injured or killed with impunity. In ancient Rome, outlaws lived under an "interdiction of fire and water."[1] This meant they could not access what Romans believed to be the two most life-giving elements.

In American society, when we think of a person who is an outlaw, we think most often of someone who has made a choice to live outside the law. We might conjure Billy the Kid, Jesse James, Butch Cassidy—robbers and gunslingers who lived fugitive lives and cultivated lawless personas, posing for photos with their six-shooters. *Outlaw*, in Wild West lore, is both a chosen identity and a condition of no protection—an outlaw is the cocky visage on the poster, the criminal wanted dead or alive.

Wyatt Outlaw, who got his surname from neither his mother nor his father, makes for an interesting study of that word and its meaning. Before the Thirteenth, Fourteenth, and Fifteenth Amendments, it was fair to say that every Black person in the South was a kind of outlaw. Black people, free or enslaved, lived outside the law that governed and defended the lives of white people. Free Black men, even those who owned property and businesses, had few protections against being maimed, killed, or cheated. A Black person couldn't testify against a white person in court, which meant that a white person could make or deny any claim of violence or other crimes. Black people could not legally marry, vote, or form their own church congregations. Enslaved Black people had even fewer rights—they could not legally learn to read, own property, buy goods, or visit the homes of free people of any race. Even after emancipation and the end of the Civil War, the racially discriminatory Black Codes, written into North Carolina law in 1866, outlawed voting by Black men. The Black Codes prevented Black men from serving on juries or testifying against whites; instituted capital punishment for Black men convicted of raping white women; and attempted to prevent Black men from owning firearms and other weapons or traveling out of state.

"Outlaw" is an Old English name, dating back to the Norman Conquest of 1066, connected to families who had once been considered outlaws and had no other name. The surname traveled across the Atlantic; the first US census, taken in 1790, records several Outlaw families in the Carolinas. By then the name had been wiped clean from association with crime or exile: A George Outlaw, born in 1771, and a David Outlaw, born in 1806, each served in the North Carolina state legislature.[2] North Carolina still has the largest number of Outlaws in the United States.

Some historians believe that Wyatt was born free; others, that he lived as a free man before emancipation. Wyatt had no birth certificate; according to historian Scott Reynolds Nelson, Wyatt was "almost invisible to county records."[3] He is believed to have lived with Nancy and George Outlaw, two prosperous neighbors of Chesley Faucett who moved to the area from Eastern North Carolina, buying property from Chesley's brother in 1831. On their hundred-acre tobacco farm, still known as the "Faucette place," Wyatt may have learned to read alongside the Outlaws' close-in-age children, and he may have developed his skill as a carpenter under the tutelage of well-known African American craftsman Thomas Day, who is believed to have carved the newel posts, mantels, and front door of Chesley Faucett's home—though even this is a guess, a story passed down. The best records connecting Wyatt with the Outlaws are two documents from later in his life: George Outlaw's 1854 will specified that "my negro man Wyatt be hired yearly," suggesting a manumitted status.[4] And in 1860, a biracial Black man of forty years, Wyatt's approximate age, was listed as living on the Outlaw farm.

Historians' accounts of Wyatt's life are filled with phrases like "the best candidate" and "may have," along with caveats that it is "impossible to determine" certain facts. Some historians have written that Wyatt escaped from slavery to become a Union soldier and fight in the Civil War. *Klan War: Ulysses S. Grant and the Battle to Save Reconstruction*, the 2023 history by Fergus Bordewich, opens and closes its story of the battle between the Klan and Reconstruction not with the Union general and president but with Wyatt Outlaw, the carpenter and small-town constable. Bordewich writes that Wyatt "had escaped slavery in 1864, made his way to Union lines and enlisted in the cavalry, and served with it through the end of the Civil War and a while after."[5]

Though Bordewich lists his sources for this information as being from Governor Holden's trial, such details cannot be found there. Instead, it is likely that this information was gathered from the earlier work of fellow historians Carole Troxler and Scott Reynolds Nelson, whose first publications on Wyatt Outlaw date to the late 1990s. Both Troxler and Nelson write that Outlaw was likely a Union soldier, based on the listing of a "Wright Outlaw," a possible misspelling, in the Second Regiment of the United States Colored Calvary. Neither Troxler nor Nelson claim that Wyatt escaped from slavery, leaning instead on correspondence suggesting a prewar free or manumitted status. A free status "helps to explain why [Wyatt Outlaw] had resources to draw on," Nelson told Belle in a 2021 interview. "No one in the Holden trial testimony said that he was enslaved."

"History is disciplined imagination," Nelson noted. "The discipline is the sources. You try to imagine what happened, then you test it by looking at more sources."[6]

But what happens when the few sources one can find disagree, or when new information emerges? Most local historians, including Carole Troxler and other members of the Alamance County Community Remembrance Coalition, now believe that "Wright Outlaw" was a different man named Outlaw, a soldier from coastal North Carolina, based on a muster card discovered by fellow coalition member Wade Harrison.[7] Wyatt's birth year is estimated by historians to be around 1820, but an Outlaw family Bible, later inscribed, records the date as January 26, 1816. That we have to do so much digging and guessing points to the outside-the-law life that a man like Wyatt lived, for most of his life.

Wyatt had no legal connection to his father, to his eleven half-siblings, or to the Outlaw family. He had no way to inherit or benefit from their prosperity, no way to prosper at all other than by his own labor—and it's likely, living in a manumitted status, that he could not build wealth until moving off the Outlaws' farm. He was outside the law in nearly every way until Reconstruction.

Unlike some free Black men who chose to change their names after the war, Wyatt kept the one he was given by white people. Still, the name evokes a contradiction to the way he lived his life. Like so many other Black men, Wyatt embraced the legal system newly opened to his people during Reconstruction. He was appointed and then elected as a constable—literally a man of the law. He bonded Black couples in marriage and built coffins for paupers, ensuring a dignified end for all his community's citizens. He encouraged Black people to register to vote, held Loyal League meetings with a decidedly patriotic bent, and traveled the state inducting and instructing other members and leaders. He bought land for a church and a school. He lived spitting distance from the courthouse, and for his school and church he chose an acre of land that was an easy walk from both his home and the courthouse. He operated a tavern, attracting Black and white Republican men who wouldn't choose the other nearby watering hole, known for its hot-tempered Democratic owner.[8]

From this perch—central to Graham and its legal and social power—Wyatt became both well-known and well-respected by his community. Wyatt kept the peace, patrolling the streets with Henry and Caswell Holt, the town's other Black deputies, to protect citizens from night-riding members of the White Brotherhood. This work put them at considerable risk, but it was arguably Wyatt Outlaw's work as a Union League leader, encouraging Black men to vote and consolidating the electoral and economic power of white and Black workingmen, that was most dangerous.

Living outside the law is perilous—who helps you when you're threatened? Who guarantees that you are paid for your labor? Who protects your family, your property, your interests?

But Wyatt's story shows how trying to live within the law—staking his place as a voter, a political leader, and an ally of the Republican governor—was the most dangerous, most consequential choice for an Outlaw like him.

• • • •

As a free Black man living in Graham, North Carolina, before emancipation, Wyatt Outlaw had important but limited privileges. He could work for himself, earning a living at a skilled trade—he was a mechanic and carpenter. He could learn to read and teach other free Black people the same. He could be head of household, living with family members who, if also free, could not be separated from him by force, the fate of so many enslaved Black families.

But these freedoms, before the Fourteenth Amendment, were limited by the noncitizen status of Black people in the South, as well as by the fact that free Blacks were the minority in North Carolina, making up just 10 percent of the Black population. Outside of his own community, how could Outlaw prove that he was part of this small, privileged group? He did not have a passport or identification, could not open a bank account, could not legally be married. Any travel risked capture by slave catchers or violence he could not address legally. He couldn't teach enslaved people the things that he knew, could not worship in a white church without permission. Organized worship with other Black people could not happen lawfully without a white person present. He couldn't vote or hold office and could not testify against a white person in a court of law.

Not having the right to testify was a significant barrier to freedom and security for workingmen like Outlaw. If a customer at his carpentry shop cheated him or a railroad boss refused to pay his wages or a client his bills, he had no way of recovering what was his. If he was stolen from by a white man, there was little he could do under the law. His children, wife, and mother were also unprotected when apart from him.

During Reconstruction, men like Wyatt Outlaw saw precious new rights emerge. After the Fourteenth Amendment, they could vote and could run for and hold public office. Black travelers no longer risked capture and enslavement (though travel wasn't without risk of violence). They could testify in a court of law about rights abridged by any other citizen—including white men. They could marry and could invest their earnings in one of the Freedman's Banks that opened across the state, starting in 1866. They could open schools for their children and churches for their community.

Like many others, Wyatt Outlaw valued and guarded these rights, which he saw as unalienable, emanating not from a changeable state government but from the higher authority of the federal government. Though it's unclear whether Wyatt fought for the Union—he would have been older than forty when North Carolina seceded—Black soldiers, including many from the South, made up 10 percent of Union soldiers and were crucial to preserving the Union.[9]

Understanding all that had been sacrificed to obtain them, Outlaw also saw that these rights would be most powerful when they were understood and exercised collectively by the many thousands of Black people, as well as by working white people, who had suffered under the Confederate and antebellum periods.

New citizens like Outlaw were encouraged—sometimes by fellow members, other times by Republican politicians—to join a semisecret Republican organization called the Union League of America. Founded in New York as a patriotic club for Black men in 1862, the league spread south after the Civil War and by 1867 had thousands of members, mostly newly free

Black men. These clubs, which typically met once a week, served as a place where Black men could discuss the issues of the day; make political, educational, and business contacts; and be encouraged to vote. "We just went there and we talked a little; made speeches on one question and another," remembered Henry Holt in 1871, after the league "broke up."[10] The purpose of the league, he said, had been to "instruct colored people that never knew anything." These men had never voted, and most had not bought property or had the opportunity to attend or send their children to school. Yet they wanted to learn—education, political power, and economic security were all highly prized by these new citizens. In *Reconstruction: America's Unfinished Revolution*, Eric Foner muses that "by the end of 1867, it seemed, virtually every black voter in the South had enrolled in the Union League or some equivalent local organization."[11]

Outlaw was no exception. In October 1866, he was one of two men to travel from Alamance County to Raleigh to attend the annual Freedmen's Convention, where he was elected to the five-member state board of what was then called the "Equal Rights League" and met former governor and Republican convert William Woods Holden.

Holden had some significant personal history in common with Outlaw. They were close in age—Holden's forty-eight to Outlaw's forty-seven. Holden was born in Orange County, less than twenty miles from the town of Graham. Like Outlaw, Holden was also born out of wedlock—he was mostly raised by his father and stepmother—and was ambitious and varied in his career, which included work as a printer's apprentice, a journalist and newspaper editor, and a self-taught lawyer. But until the beginning of Reconstruction, Holden had been a Democrat and a supporter of slavery. After the Civil War, influenced by the reforms promised in Washington, he became a Radical Republican, invested in the powers of the federal government to reconstruct North Carolina. Though his own newspaper had once argued against Black suffrage, Holden must have realized that without Black men's vote, he had little chance of winning elections, and he began to court the power of freedmen.

Holden was one of the few white dignitaries to attend the Freedmen's Convention, and his words of support were warmly received. According to convention minutes, "he spoke with plainness and feeling," He gave general advice, telling the men to invest in homes, "no matter how cheap or small"; to educate their children ("knowledge is power," he told them); and to keep out of politics, at least for the present. Politics, he counseled, represented a "weariness to the flesh" among whites in the state, who had not demonstrated their own capacity for self-government.[12]

But the Leaguers, including Outlaw, were already invested in politics—almost everything they did or planned to do, from buying homes to building schools to representing their counties at statewide conventions, had a political goal. As a member of the Equal Rights League board, Outlaw would be expected to go when needed to Raleigh and to travel around the state coordinating "agents" and "lecturers." These men, and all members of the league, would report back on the violence and "outrages" that threatened the equal rights of Black men across the state, which could then be reported in newspapers and speeches. It was all political work.

After returning home, Outlaw organized a group called the Loyal League, which had both white and Black workingmen as members. The group set as its first goal the construction of a church and school in downtown Graham. The next year, Outlaw accepted a commission from Holden to serve as a deputy member of the Union League, which Holden was organizing on a statewide level as he planned to run again for governor.

Though the names for the organizations vary—Union League, Loyal League, Equal Rights League—each one points to the shared values of the men who joined them. *Union*: the federal government and its inviolability, but also a "club, society, or association formed by people with a common interest or purpose."[13] *Loyal*: men who had supported the Union but who also gave "firm and constant support and allegiance." *Equal rights*: "equal protection of the laws," in the words of the Fourteenth Amendment.

The date of Outlaw's Union League commission—July 5, 1867, just one day after Independence Day—is significant. Union Leagues were known for parading on July 4, sometimes in Union army uniforms worn by veterans of the war. Only fifteen years after Frederick Douglass gave his famous speech "What to the Slave is the Fourth of July?," many now kept the once-exclusionary date as a sacred holiday. It's possible that Outlaw obtained his commission just a day after watching a Union League procession in Raleigh or after hearing inspirational speeches by Black and white leaders.

The commission paper now resides in the Southern Historical Collection at Wilson Library. It's a thin, age-faded sheet of parchment, signed by the governor, whose pen left multiple ink splotches across the page. Outlaw was commissioned to "supervise" and "instruct" new Union League members and to "do such other and farther acts as may be necessary for the advancement and good of the League." He had agency, power, and a formal document inscribed—twice—with his name.[14]

The commission is folded, unevenly but firmly, into eighths. Outlaw's name—the swoop of the *W* in "Wyatt," the low round of the *O* in "Outlaw"—is impressed in stray ink marks above the formal "Know ye, by this commission," as if the paper had been hastily folded, before the ink was even dry, tucked into Outlaw's jacket pocket or into a book he was carrying, perhaps even the pocket-sized *Ritual, Constitution, and By-Laws of the National Council, U. L. of A.*, which Outlaw would have been given, as a new commissioner, by the former governor whose fate would now be entwined with his own.

Wyatt would have returned home by train, which in 1867 was not racially segregated. He might have taken his seat wherever he liked, perhaps by a window, enjoying the experience of seeing his state at some leisure, the flat green fields surrounding Raleigh gradually turning to rolling hills, blue-green in the humid distance.

That two-hour train trip would have afforded a busy man a chance to rest and also to read over the materials he'd just been given. Maybe he'd have first reexamined the commission, hurriedly inscribed so that he could make this evening train, noticing that the ink had smeared against the unabsorbent parchment. Holden wrote "Carolina" as "Carole," a mistake—or maybe that was just his quick and loopy handwriting. There were dots of black ink scattered across the page.

Wyatt wasn't one to dwell on small imperfections, things that couldn't be changed. One could still read his name, handsomely inscribed near the top and again at the end of the document. It said that Wyatt had responsibilities—to instruct others, to supervise them, and to report back to Governor Holden. The small, bound book, a constitution of sorts, explained how he would supervise them.

He needed first to find a place to hold meetings—the back room of his shop would have to do until his community could build a church and school. It made sense to keep the meetings in a stable place, easy to get to. Somewhere people knew. The constitution started with details about where people should stand—the president, vice president, and so on. The second section detailed "emblems," the symbols of freedom and patriotism that would unite the league members. Wyatt would need a flag and a Bible. For symbols of industry, a wooden weaving shuttle for the mill workers, a sickle for the farmers, and a hammer for the rail workers would all do nicely.

After calling roll, the marshal was instructed to say, "Mr. President! All present are true and worthy." And Wyatt was to respond, "So may they ever continue!" The exclamatory nature, the formality, evoked the seriousness and importance of the meetings and their work. A prayer asked that the inductee "aid and assist the government in so fixing the foundations thereof, that peace, happiness, truth, liberty, justice, and brotherly love may prevail for all time."[15]

Peace, happiness, truth, liberty, justice, and brotherly love. Who can argue with that?

Initiates were called "Worthy Sons of America!" The president was to orate, "We bid you welcome. This circle of freedom and equal rights now encircling you must never be broken by treachery." Picture the faces of workingmen from the community of Company Shops, the railway men and carpenters at the end of a long day, and how it would feel to them to be called *Worthy Sons of America*.[16]

The book contained an oral obligation, which Wyatt was to read out in small pieces for the new members to recite:

> I, ______, with an uplifted hand, in the presence of God and these witnesses, do solemnly swear, without reservation of any kind, that I will support, protect, and defend the Constitution and Government of the United States of America, one and indivisible, and the flag thereof, against all enemies, foreign and domestic; that I will vote only for those who advocate and support the great principles set forth by this League, to fill any office of honor.
>
> I will aid and defend the working men of the nation, and in all lawful methods endeavor to secure them the right to labor and enjoy the full fruit of their labor, and that I will not countenance or employ anyone who is in any manner hostile to the working men of the nation.[17]

Then Wyatt, as president of the league, was to say: "Take your place in this sacred circle. Formed to perpetuate freedom and good government, we trust every added link will make stronger the chain which binds us together."[18]

A sacred circle. Like the road that wound around the courthouse, or a choir singing. Or a nail head, driven clean and true.

• • • •

In that hopeful time, Wyatt Outlaw accomplished a great deal. Before getting involved at the state level, he already *had* accomplished a great deal within his community for the betterment of working people like himself. Prior to 1867, Outlaw had founded a local chapter of the Loyal League, a political organization that was somewhat more activist and independent than the Union League. As its leader, Outlaw worked with other Black community members to found an AME Zion church that held daytime services and nighttime meetings. Alamance's Loyal League petitioned the railroad for land and money for a school and teachers for Black children; when the league was refused, members began making plans to build their own. Leaguers tested their strength in other areas of public and civic life, attempting to integrate a white Methodist church (the land was owned by the Northern-based United Methodists, who opposed segregation). League members helped elect T. M. Shoffner, a white blacksmith friendly to their cause, to the state senate.[19]

Wyatt had a home on Main Street, just down the street from the courthouse. His four-room house also served as his workshop, where he built coffins for the town's paupers and did mechanical repair work. He had three young sons but was widowed; his youngest was two years old in 1867, when Wyatt was appointed deputy of the Union League by the ambitious Holden.

In the evenings, his shop was a tavern for white and Black railroad workers who passed through town on their way to or from Company Shops. We can imagine that the tavern served two functions—as a place to congregate and to share stories and experiences, and a place for them to learn more about the Union League, which also likely met in Wyatt's shop.

Back then, it wasn't uncommon for homes to serve more than one function—Wyatt's father, Chesley Faucett, operated a shop as well as a jail out of the mansion where he lived with his large family. But for Wyatt, and Black men like him, having a home where one could also work, socialize, and organize the community—independently, and without interference—was a new and valuable freedom. Though Wyatt didn't own his house—he rented it from a white Republican named William Albright—people in Graham knew it as "Wyatt's house." Wyatt was well-known in town, respected by white and Black people.

Wyatt had certainly heard William Holden's advice—invest in a house, no matter how cheap or small. But he'd also heard Holden say that it was important to educate his children and, by extension, the children of one's community. His first large purchase was therefore not a home for his own family but a parcel of land he hoped could be put to just that use—one acre in downtown Graham where he and four other trustees planned to build a church and school. It was a little more than a half-mile walk to the county courthouse, less than that to Wyatt's place. It's easy to imagine that Wyatt intended his children to attend that school; certainly, his family would worship at the church.

None of the work Wyatt endeavored to do was easy. Political activism, voter education of brand-new citizens, and community protection—all of that was on top of Wyatt's main work as a carpenter and mechanic. His identity as a skilled tradesman was common among Southern-born Black activists after the war. According to historian Eric Foner, "Artisans were men whose skill and independence set them apart from ordinary laborers, but who remained deeply embedded in the life of the freedmen's community." These were men of standing and influence with both white and Black citizens.[20]

But this political significance also made men like Wyatt targets of Conservative white men who preferred to think of Black people only as laborers. Josiah Turner, a former slave owner and Confederate veteran, born to a wealthy Hillsborough family, was one such man. Turner took over the North Carolina Railroad office in Company Shops in 1867 and immediately identified Republican workingmen, white and Black, as threats to his Conservative goals. As railroad president, he fired white workers born in the North, pitting them against what he called the "pride and manhood" of Southerners.[21] He targeted Loyal League members specifically, falsely claiming that they were insurrectionists whose secret society threatened the community. The league protested its members' firings to the general assembly, which passed a law protecting workers from being fired for political reasons. But the law did not stop Josiah Turner, who responded by firing Solomon Lunsford, a Black shopman who was a member of the Loyal League.

Turner traveled around the state by rail, making speeches about the culture wars of the day and using the sharp tongue and argumentative nature he'd developed over two decades as a lawyer. He claimed that Southern landowners and farmers were unfairly taxed and mistreated by the federal government, playing into the grievances of financially struggling whites. He warned his large audiences about upcoming radical threats to their way of life: interracial schools, interracial militias. He particularly warned of a life under the thumb of "negro commissioners" and politicians.[22]

Wyatt became one of these commissioners in July 1868, one year after accepting his role as Union League leader. He was recommended for the post by Shoffner, the blacksmith he and other Leaguers had helped elect to the state senate, and appointed by William Holden, who had been inaugurated as governor on July 4.

Holden also appointed a new railroad president, William A. Smith, who used the office to advance Republican politics. In *Iron Confederacies: Southern Railways, Klan Violence, and Reconstruction*, Scott Reynolds Nelson details how the shift in power meant payback: The new leadership fired Democratic workers and gave free rail passes to Republican electors and friends of the governor.

The loss of railroad power didn't quiet Josiah Turner, Nelson writes. Backed by wealthy friends of his family and with a loan from conservative railroad lobbyist George Swepson, Turner bought the *Raleigh Sentinel* and took over as editor. He could now use print media, as well as his extensive speaking circuit, to rile up disgruntled whites. Turner slammed the Republican-run railroad and emerging Black leadership as the undoing of the old ways and a threat to white authority. Nelson writes that his "attacks . . . joined images of railroad lobbying with images of black men in positions of power." Turner referred to the railroad as a political "machine" and claimed that the judiciary and state legislature were now dominated by carpetbaggers, deceivers, and "gibbering Africans."[23]

Into this primed space, the Ku Klux Klan emerged. Originally formed on Christmas Eve, 1865, in Pulaski, Tennessee, the first Klan was made up of Confederate veterans united in their white supremacist beliefs and determination to resist Black rights. The Klan did not become widespread until 1867, when violent former slave trader and Confederate general Nathan Beford Forrest was elected its first Grand Wizard.

Nelson writes that the Alamance Klan, also known as the White Brotherhood, was first formed by former Confederates from F and K Companies of the Sixth North Carolina Regiment, mostly low-level enlisted men who'd spent a year as prisoners of war in southern Maryland. There, he notes, they were likely under the supervision and control of Black Union soldiers. They also would have certainly fought against Black soldiers on the battlefield—by the end of the war, Black men accounted for around 10 percent of the Union army. By early 1868, the White Brotherhood had organized into dozens of "camps" around Alamance County. Each camp had at least six men but often more than twenty. Their ranks included shopkeepers, farmers, police, and the sons of some of Alamance's wealthiest families.

Unlike Loyal and Union Leagues, Klan camps held their meetings outdoors and at night, in fields and woods that separated their activities from their respectable daytime identities as patriarchs, shopkeepers, and preachers. Instead of displaying symbols of patriotism and industry, they wore costumes evoking devils. Members swore a blood oath never to reveal their fellow members' names, suggesting that they knew what they were doing was covert and illegal. And rather than operating according to principle and with an ethic of equality, they had a strictly hierarchical system. Initiates promised to obey the violent directives of camp leaders, called "chiefs," without question or hesitation and were asked to be "suitably disguised and ready for all occasions."[24]

Their goal was not enforcing laws but evading them. These were men who could not abide living in equality with Black people and who swore to resist any system or group that would "elevate the Negro with the white man." What such elevation meant was the conferral of basic rights, like the right to own property, work for a wage, vote, and hold office. These rights, in Klansmen's eyes, degraded their own rights. The idea that they could not punish a Black man for a rumored theft but had to use the legal system and follow due process? The notion that a Black person could choose to work for them, or not, and could demand payment for their labor? The thought that a Black man could earn a decent income as a railroad worker and therefore *his* wife and children would not be in service to *their* wives and children? The idea that a Black man might run for office and hold power in the community? All of this was deeply offensive to Klan members, who saw their secret society as a way of returning, covertly and using tactics of fear and terrorism, to the old slave-master dynamic. The message they would send, through break-ins, beatings, whippings, and other acts of terror and violence, was that Black men and Black families did not truly own or have dominion over anything in the community—not their homes and land and fields, not their churches and schools, not even their own lives.

• • • •

The attacks happened almost always at night, often on Saturdays, in or outside the private homes of Black people, and began in Alamance County in 1868. They were made in force—usually between five and twenty horse-riding men, but sometimes as many as eighty or a hundred turned out. They carried clubs, sticks, rifles, knives, swords, pistols, and whips and disguised themselves in long white gowns that obscured their bodies. They hid their faces with pointed white hoods bearing horns, mule ears, fearsome red and black features, and beards made of horsehair. Sometimes their horses were also disguised. The goal was to appear, to supposedly superstitious freedmen, as the avenging ghosts of dead Confederates.

These paramilitary groups were known as the White Brotherhood, the Ku Klux Klan, the Invisible Empire, and the Constitutional Union Guard, but they most often went by Ku Klux and would refer to themselves that way as they interrogated and terrorized their victims.[25] Their signs, signals, and initiation rites were first invented by Confederate soldiers captured and imprisoned in Union jails during the war.[26] They brought these invented rituals back down South, along with bitterness over the loss of the war and a deep resentment for newly enfranchised Black people and any white people aligned with Black political or economic power.

They broke into peoples' homes, sometimes pounding the door first and sometimes just "bursting" the latch or breaking down the door. These were mostly modest homes—one or two rooms—and as many Klansmen would crowd inside as would fit. Usually, they sought a specific person—most often a man—but their collateral victims could and did include women,

Ku Klux Klan hood/mask, c. 1870–72.
(Courtesy of the North Carolina Museum of History.)

children, and even infants. The family was often forced to hide under the house, in the woods, or under floorboards. The Klansmen stole weapons, if they could find any, and demanded rope. Commonly, the only rope inside the house was a bed cord, a twisted hemp rope strung between headboard and sideboard that supported their victims' mattresses. So they'd turn over the mattress, cut the bed cord, and haul their target, often half-dressed or in bedclothes, into the unprotected night. Threatening to hang victims with their own bed cord told Black people that they could find no easy rest or comfort, not even in their own homes.

One of the early Alamance County victims of Klan violence was Caswell Holt, a man who would survive two separate, near-fatal Klan attacks and live to tell his story before the North Carolina Senate and the US Congress.

Despite this bravery and notoriety, as well as a lack of physical resemblance, his photograph would be regularly mislabeled as that of Wyatt Outlaw for more than 150 years.

Caswell Holt was born enslaved by the white Holt family, owners of Alamance Plaids, a Haw River factory producing cotton gingham fabrics. Along with his brother Samuel Holt, Caswell helped to create the colorfast dye that made the white Holts financially successful and politically powerful; Holt scion Thomas Holt, one of Caswell's white contemporaries, went on to become governor of North Carolina and a founder of North Carolina State University. (Caswell and Samuel Holt's descendants Thomas Holt Russell III and Jaki Shelton Green write about them in chapter 5.)

Both Caswell and Samuel—a popular preacher and educator—were smart, educated, well-respected members of their community. In 1868, at age thirty-four, Caswell became the first Black deputy in Graham. He was a farmer, was married, and was father to six children.

It's hard to say what prompted the Klan's attack, though it seems likely that it was connected to the perceived audacity Holt showed when he became a law enforcement officer. How could a Black man, someone so recently outside the law, enforce the law? What did that mean for white men used to committing crime with impunity?

So, the tack the Klan took the first time they broke into his home was to accuse Caswell Holt of theft. They grabbed his arms and dragged him out of bed, carrying him outside. One Klansman put his hands around Holt's throat and choked him. Holt begged him to stop, and another struck him in the eye. They threw him to the ground and tied his hands. When they let him stand, they asked whether Holt knew anything about some missing chickens, some stolen wheat or corn?

"I don't, sir, nothing but my own," Holt responded, his customary deference edged with pride. "I have got plenty of wheat and corn of my own. I don't know anything about any other but that."[27]

The Klansmen took him farther into the woods, stopping at an oak tree with a limb that ran perpendicular from the trunk. They questioned Holt about the thefts, and after he again denied it, the "one who talked"—having only one speaker made it harder to identify members—asked him, "Do you know how near your time is?"

"I don't, sir," Holt answered.

"This is your last moment," the Klansman warned.

But Holt was not going to confess to something he didn't do, and he wasn't going to cry or beg these disguised men. "If it is," he said, "I can't help it."[28]

The Klansmen threw the rope over the oak limb and tied the other end around Holt's neck. "Draw him up," the Klansman commanded, and Holt was lifted until he dangled, only his toes touching the ground. They let him down after a time and asked him again, "Do you recollect anything about it now?"

Holt remained polite but stalwart: "I don't, sir; just as I told you at first. I say I don't know anything about it, and I can't tell you anything about it."

He maintained his innocence through two more near-hangings, a common act of terror by Klansmen who wanted their victims to believe that every moment was their last. Frustrated by Holt's steadfast denials, the Klansmen decided on another common, brutal form of torture: Holt was to be "bucked."

Bucking meant that Holt's wrists were crossed and tied, his arms looped over his knees, and a straight stick was run through the space between his knees and arms. This tight confinement meant no escape or movement and exposed the victim's back to lashings. The speaking Klansman ordered the other men—there were sixteen—to form a line and deliver three licks apiece, spreading among the group both the culpability and the violent dominance over a Black man who refused to confess. They hit with the intention of causing pain and injury, rubbing a stick into his back so that the skin tore.

After forty-eight lashings, Caswell Holt was unable to work for three weeks. This was another common tactic—if a victim wasn't killed, he'd be beaten until he was almost dead, until he couldn't look after his crops, his family, or his occupation. The Klan's brutality served as a warning to the victim—*We might return*—as well as to anyone who knew him—*You might be next.*

If a victim was allowed to live, Klansmen often demanded to know whether he would report them. Did he know anything? Would he say anything? The victim usually said of course, he wouldn't report them—how could he, anyway, when the men were disguised in their fearsome costumes?

"Who are you going to tell this to when you get away from here?" the Klansman asked Holt, who answered that he didn't think he'd tell anyone. They made him swear that he wouldn't tell it and told him to "be off," leaving his home within ten days.[29]

Like many newly free people, Caswell Holt had few options for seeking justice, and after the first attack, he summoned his former enslaver, Colonel Jerry Holt. Despite the disguises and the fact that only one of the attackers spoke, Holt could identify them just from being in their proximity. He knew the size of their bodies, the way they moved. He knew their violent natures and the party they belonged to: the Democratic Party, which opposed the rights of men like him.

Holt could name the primary perpetrators of his attack—including George Holt, Jerry Holt's son. He knew them because, he later reflected, "I have always been close by them, all my life. I was raised within three miles of them," he said. "I lived within a mile of them."[30]

Caswell would continue to live on Jerry Holt's land another year. He asked Edwin Holt, his "old master," for advice. Holt replied that the best thing to do was to "go along and say nothing about it." He'd receive no real protection from the man whose family his labor had enriched.[31]

• • • •

Though Alamance and Caswell Counties were the epicenter of Reconstruction-era Klan activity in North Carolina, Klan terror and violence was not confined to those places. Attacks and murders happened across the state and across the South, increasing as Union soldiers departed and as Republicans, aided by new Black voters, made significant political gains. Any kind of Radical Republican political participation could attract Klan violence—from political and militia organizing to voting.

In McDuffie County, Georgia, Klansmen learned that Perry Jeffreys was planning to vote for Ulysses S. Grant in November 1868. They massacred his entire family, including Jeffreys, his wife, and four sons.[32]

In Charlotte County, Virginia, in 1869 shoemaker Joseph R. Holmes was lynched on the courthouse steps, where he'd gone to obtain a warrant against Klan members. Holmes had been a state representative and Radical Republican, helping to rewrite Virginia's constitution to include the freedmen.[33]

That same year, in Columbia County, Florida, a Black man named Lisher Johnson was abducted and never seen again. His only crime was political activism.[34]

In York County, South Carolina, Captain James Williams—a formerly enslaved man who served in the Union army—became an active civil rights leader, encouraging other Black people to vote and serving as captain of an all-Black militia raised to protect citizens from the Klan. Williams refused to give up his post when the governor disbanded militias in January 1871. He was abducted and hanged by the Klan in March.[35]

In North Carolina, Black men, women, and children were subject to violence not only in the Piedmont counties of Alamance and Caswell but were attacked in Wake, Sanford, Rutherford, Chatham, Duplin, Moore, Johnston, Pender, Brunswick, Columbus, Northampton, Halifax, Vance,

BLACK MILITARY PERSONNEL AND THE AMERICAN CIVIL WAR

General Order 143, per the War Department, established the United States Colored Troops in 1863.* However, Black troops had served in the military in previous conflicts, particularly the American Revolution, when an estimated 20,000 Black troops fought for the British under the promise of freedom. Some 9,000 Black soldiers fought for the Continental army.†

A 1792 federal law prohibited Black soldiers from serving further in the army, a law that lasted until Abraham Lincoln's Emancipation Proclamation on January 1, 1863, allowed slaves from most seceded states to fight for the Union. Nearly 200,000 Black troops fought for the Union in the army and navy in the Civil War. The myth of the large numbers of Black men having fought on the side of the Confederacy during the Civil War gained steam generations later.‡ Adherents of the "Lost Cause" narrative of the Civil War—the idea that the war was about states' rights and independence, not slavery—liked to tell stories of enslaved men who fought willingly alongside their masters. Today's neo-Confederates often claim that Black soldiers fought for the Confederacy in great numbers. On the contrary, for most of the war, the Confederate Congress prohibited Black slaves or freedmen from taking up arms and participating in battle. Throughout the earlier part of the war, many slave owners brought their slaves with them to perform such tasks as cleaning clothes or carrying equipment.**

The first regiment of US Colored Troops was the Fifty-Fourth Regiment out of Massachusetts, an all-volunteer unit. The men's ability to learn tactical sequences and execute military drill was grossly underestimated, which not only led to many troops taking on noncombatant jobs but also resulted in a separate fight for equal pay. Black troops were eventually paid, though they received only a portion of what their white counterparts did, with white soldiers being paid thirteen dollars per month and Black soldiers being paid ten dollars per month. Unlike their white counterparts, Black troops were forced to pay for their uniforms.††

By the end of the war, 10 percent of the Union army was made of Black troops. Approximately 40,000 Black soldiers lost their lives in the war; eighteen Black soldiers and eight naval personnel received the Congressional Medal of Honor for serving "beyond the call of duty" in the Civil War.

Many historians today believe the Union would have lost without the contributions of Black soldiers. In an interview with the Wounded Warrior Project, historian Sam Collins explained that this was not just about numbers:

> The North could not have won if not for the Black troops—the United States Colored Troops—because in addition to additional manpower, many of them were former slaves who had important intel. What is often forgotten is that those runaway slaves knew the Southern territory and landscape. So not only did they take their physical bodies when they ran away, hurting the labor force of the Southern plantations, they also took intel with them. They knew where the creeks were; they knew where you could cross; they knew where [the Confederacy] was storing guns and supplies. So, they would have been able to share that information with Union officers.‡‡

---

* "War Department General Order 143: Creation of the U.S. Colored Troops (1863)," National Archives, accessed August 20, 2024, www.archives.gov/milestone-documents/war-department-general-order-143.

† P. Ferguson, *African American Service and Racial Integration in the U.S. Military*, February 23, 2021, Army.mil, www.army.mil/article/243604/african_american_service_and_racial_integration_in_the_u_s_military. (When we attempted to access this page on May 29, 2025, the "page not found" message read as follows: "We have deliberately taken some of our webpages offline in order to comply with Executive Orders and OSD Policy. The intent is to preserve our history, and we are working to re-publish content as soon as possible.")

‡ "Black Soldiers in the U.S. Military during the Civil War," National Archives, accessed August 20, 2024, www.archives.gov/education/lessons/blacks-civil-war.

** D. Peterson, "The Myth of Black Confederates," University of Illinois Urbana-Champaign College of Liberal Arts & Sciences, September 1, 2013, https://las.illinois.edu/news/2013-09-01/myth-black-confederates.

†† "African-American Soldiers during the Civil War," Library of Congress, accessed August 20, 2024, www.loc.gov/classroom-materials/united-states-history-primary-source-timeline/civil-war-and-reconstruction-1861-1877/african-american-soldiers-during-the-civil-war/.

‡‡ "Juneteenth Plays a Significant Part in the Nation's Past . . . and Future," Wounded Warrior Project, accessed May 29, 2025, https://newsroom.woundedwarriorproject.org/Juneteenth-Plays-a-Significant-Part-in-the-Nations-Past-and-Future.

Person, Rockingham, Brunswick, and Robeson Counties and other places. More than half of the state's 100 counties have documented some form of Reconstruction-era racial violence.[36]

These attacks and murders—"outrages," as they were called in trials and news reports—were certainly underreported. Many victims were threatened after attacks, as Caswell Holt had been, and were afraid to report crimes. For survivors, there wasn't often a reliable or trusted authority to make reports to, and many white-owned newspapers suppressed stories about white supremacist violence. Other victims were unable to identify their attackers or simply disappeared from history after their murders.

In some cases, the violence happened on the scale of mass murder: In Duplin County, in 1866, six Black men were lynched for demanding wages from a white landowner.[37] In Moore County, Daniel Blue, a Black man, testified against white men accused of racial violence. In retaliation, the Klan raided his home and murdered his pregnant wife and five children, then burned the house with their bodies inside it.[38]

What is the point of retelling these terrible stories? Of writing them here? One reason is to show that yes, white supremacist violence happened on a grotesque scale—some 2,000 documented murders of Black people between 1865 and 1877, the time period we know as Reconstruction. But our greater purpose is to show why the violence happened: not as a defense of white womanhood, as Klan violence is often remembered, or as another form of vigilante justice. It was perpetrated in almost every case because Black people were now living within the law, as citizens. They were testifying in court, working for their own living, and demanding fair payment for their labor. They served as law enforcement officials. They were voting and encouraging others to vote. In some cases, it was enough provocation for Black people to have their "own" anything—own corn, own wheat, own chickens, own schools, own churches, own homes.

In April 1869, North Carolina's General Assembly targeted the Klan with legislation that made it a misdemeanor to paint one's face or to mask the face in order to "terrify or frighten any citizen of the community." Section 2 of the law stated that "any person or persons, either singly or in association with each other, who, being disguised or masked, or otherwise concealed in the manner described in the preceding section, shall commit any trespass or act by force or violence . . . shall be deemed guilty of felony, and shall be imprisoned at hard labor in the penitentiary for a term of not less than one year, or more than ten years."[39]

This didn't quell Klan violence—in Caswell and Alamance, especially, the night raids, whippings, and atmosphere of terror only increased. The

Klan's targets were wide-ranging, including anyone who did not appear aligned with white supremacy and the Democratic Party, and the damage they did was indiscriminate. They attacked white men for patronizing Black men's businesses or for being "damned Radicals!" who voted the Republican ticket. They tore a white woman's home down to "the bottom log" because she had a biracial child and was considered "lewd."[40]

No one could tell when the Klan would visit, only that they might come at any time. In many parts of the South, the violence was so acute that Black men took to sleeping outside, abandoning the homes where they might be found, or sleeping separately from their wives and families in order to protect them.

In September 1869, white Alamance County resident John Allred was awakened past midnight by a "parcel" of disguised men on horseback. He hid under his bed and bade his wife tell the Klansmen he wasn't at home. The Klansman who spoke to her appeared to communicate in riddles, telling her that he "liked a woman that will tell the truth" because he was a woman himself. He warned Mrs. Allred that if her husband didn't change parties—from Republican to Democrat—and "be a white man" they would "make his throat red" the next Saturday night.[41]

In October, William Long, a Black shoemaker, was at the Alamance County home of the Tickle family, from whom he rented a house, making shoes by candlelight. Between eight and nine that night, several disguised Klansmen came to the house. They asked for "a negro," and though Louis Tickle asked the trespassers to "go back and behave themselves," they refused. Tickle sent Long to his fate, where the Klansmen tied him and carried him a quarter mile to a tree.[42] They threatened hanging and questioned him about a recent break-in and theft. Long denied it, they bucked him, and after considerable whipping—he later recalled that "there was no skin left"—Long broke. "I will acknowledge whatever you say," he pleaded, but the details he gave—entering a window instead of a door—were incorrect, and they decided, laughing behind the tree, that they had the wrong man. Still, they said, he had to leave the county. Long retrieved some shoes he'd contracted to make and had left at the Tickle house and then walked three miles to the home of Jim Sellers, a Black minister. From there he traveled to Graham, recovered for about two weeks, and fled to Raleigh.[43]

On a "powerful cold" Saturday night in late November, a Black man named Samuel Garrison was kidnapped from his home by five men wearing gowns and hoods with "great long ears like a mule's." He recognized two of them, John Rich Ireland and Asa Isely; Ireland was a deputy sheriff, and both men were Democrats. They struck and choked him and carried him a mile from his home. The Klansmen built a fire and tied him to a tree; when Garrison slipped the rope, they bucked him and whipped him with hickory sticks. The beating was so bad that he bore its scars years later. His wife and five children escaped to a neighbor's house, and after Garrison retrieved them they stayed with another neighbor, afraid to return home. No crime was alleged, but Garrison had been a Union League member and voted the "other side" from the Klansmen.[44]

Two Saturdays later, the Klan returned to Caswell Holt's home and banged on his door, demanding to be let in. He refused, unless they'd tell their names and what they wanted. This time, he had an ax and a knife ready to defend himself. He motioned to one of his sons, who reached for the ax.

"Open the door!" the Klansman shouted.[45]

"I shan't do it, sir," Holt answered from behind his locked door.

"Blow his brains out!" another Klansman shouted, and they shot through the door, striking Holt in the chest. As he clapped his hand over his breast, declaring, "I am shot," his son scrambled to help the rest of the family escape. The boy jerked open two loose planks in the floor, and Holt's four oldest children and Holt's wife hid beneath the house. The three smallest children remained in the house with him as Holt fell onto his back.[46]

The Klansmen burst through the broken door, angry with Holt for the audacity of being shot. "God damn you, if you had opened that door, you wouldn't have been shot!" one insisted. There was debate among the disguised intruders over whether Holt had indeed been shot, and one pulled away Holt's shirt to show the wound. They also saw the knife Holt clutched and took it from him, holding it to his injured body. "God damn you, I have a mind to run you through your damned heart," the attacker said. "God damn you, you said you was not afraid of any KuKlux in the county."[47]

Bleeding and prone, Holt denied it: "If you heard that you heard it from somebody else besides me. I didn't say it."

"Do you know me?"

"I don't, sir. I don't know anything about you."

The attackers then demanded to know where Holt's sons were and where his weapons could be found. He replied that he didn't have any more in the house, but they were welcome to anything they could find. They took his ax and knife and tossed them in the yard and found the two guns—a musket and a shotgun, procured since the last attack—and broke them both. They briefly considered burning the house, with everyone in it, but decided to "make quick time" and leave.

Holt was badly wounded, shot in his right lung and in both arms. The next morning, he sent for the doctor, who removed the bullets, and in the evening he borrowed a wagon from his landlord, Jerry Holt, and moved to Graham. The rest of his family and things came over the following day. Holt remained in critical condition through the new year. He contracted pneumonia and had to be seen by three different doctors. By the time he could work again, it would be spring.[48]

In *I Saw Death Coming: A History of Terror and Survival in the War against Reconstruction*, Kidada Williams warns against the "false impression," given by newspaper reports and some historians, that such attacks were preventable. Looking at history with arrogance, she observes, fools us into believing resistance was possible, and "driving off attackers, fleeing, or avoiding a raid altogether seems easy." Because survivors' testimony was long disrespected, she writes, "people who themselves have never considered the structure of violent coercion often mistakenly believe African Americans were either completely passive during strikes or possessed superhero strength to dispose of extremists."[49]

Caswell Holt's complex and painful story belies this myth. Here was a formerly enslaved man who was smart and successful. After surviving a first, unexpected attack, he went to his "old master" for advice, but he knew enough to take his words with a heaping spoon of salt. Holt protected his young family as best he could, securing weapons and refusing to open the door to men he knew wanted to harm him. He resisted falsehoods, refusing to confess to thefts he had no need to commit. He made quick, complex decisions that protected his family from physical harm and saved his life. He was resourceful, strong in body and mind, and incredibly brave—and still, he was almost killed.

We know about Holt's story, and so many others, because of a different kind of bravery than the one required in the moment of attack. This later valor was the courageous testimony given by Black men and women before lawmakers who were not positioned or inclined to hear the whole story. They spoke before state senators and US congressmen, traveling farther than they'd ever been to testify about what had happened. This is how scholars like Kidada Williams, descendants like Thomas Holt Russell III, and writers like us are able to know something about their characters and to piece together their stories—stories that are full of the worst heartbreak imaginable but also glimpses of ordinary life: the moments of rest and even celebration that freedom and citizenship promised and that Klan violence sought to destroy.

One week after Klansmen shot Caswell Holt inside his home, Jacob Murray and his wife hosted a party at their one-room house in Alamance. It was Saturday, a week before Christmas, when around twenty Black friends got together for a "frolic." We can imagine that there was food, storytelling, maybe music. The Murrays had a four-month-old child, and Mrs. Murray held the child in her lap in an easy chair among the "right smart" crowd of merrymakers.

Anyone who has cared for a four-month-old knows that a baby that age doesn't yet sleep on a regular schedule; he might be kept awake at a party or gathering and then fall soundly asleep at his mother's breast with noise all around. The Murrays' baby was healthy and had never been to the doctor for any illness.

Around eleven that night, eight Klansmen broke down the door, demanding Damon Holt. They wore white gowns and hoods with what Jacob later described as "quills in their mouths." They shot a gun inside the house, frightening the partygoers, and knocked the baby out of Mrs. Murray's lap.

One of the Klansmen stepped on the child, and Mrs. Murray cried, "You mustn't kill my child!" She picked the baby up, but the child had lost his breath.

"It was mashed inside and it never could be better anymore," Jacob Murray remembered.[50]

Amid this terror and mayhem, the Klansmen took Damon Holt, Greene Freeman, and Jerry Lynch out of the Murrays' home. With his shirt removed, Holt was made to "hug a tree" and was lashed some sixty times before being told to run away. The Klansmen shot at him but missed as he fled. Freeman and Lynch were whipped more than seventy times each, and Murray, who was tending his wife and baby, could hear them "hallooing" as they received the licks.

The three men lay suffering outside all night, and when Holt returned the next morning, to borrow a hat, the Murrays met him at the door but did not invite him inside. He saw that they were "uneasy" and went on his way.[51] The baby lived a week after the attack, dying on or near Christmas Day.

My child, Mrs. Murray called her baby. A beloved, tiny human she must have nursed, washed, made clothes for, played with, sung to. But also a *child*, a person she would have imagined living a whole and full life. A life different, maybe better and more prosperous and freer than the one she'd had.

The child's name isn't recorded anywhere that we can find, and his brutal killing—deliberate or accidental—is among the many uncounted deaths caused by the Ku Klux Klan.

CHAPTER TEN

ACCOUNTABILITY

Ordinary Notes by Christina Sharpe is a book of short essays about the experience of Blackness within, and filtered through, specific contexts—personal, political, historical, intellectual. We read the book together in the spring of 2023, shortly after it was published, and referred to it as we thought about Wyatt Outlaw. We argued with it, questioned it, admired it, were challenged by it.

It is a book literally wrapped in beauty. Sharpe does this in two ways. First, she offers as cover art one of her own photographs, a blurry violet image that fades to a peachy-golden sunset over what appears on the front to be a houseline and on the back to be a tree line. Sharpe has a practice she calls "beauty-everyday" in which she photographs "flowers, trees, the light, clouds, the sky, moss, water, many things, in order to try to insist beauty into my head and into the world."[1] This photograph, and some of the ones at the end of her book, appear to come from that project.

The second way she enfolds her book in beauty is through its dedication:

Ida Wright Sharpe
Once again. And always.

And its last note: "This is a love letter to my mother."[2]

Christina Sharpe's mother is the central image of beauty in the book, a woman who taught Sharpe "to build a life that was nourishing and Black."[3] Ida Wright Sharpe, writer of incisive letters to the editor, inscriber of books, held teas in which the family would dress in their Sunday best and recite poetry. She was a woman who made beautiful things, gardens and Christmas ornaments, with hands that Sharpe notes for their elegance. There are other images of beauty scattered within the book's pages—well-loved copies of Toni Morrison's *Beloved*, old family photographs, a checked cotton dress appliquéd with tulips for Sharpe by her mother, the text of an unexpected letter from a friend of her mother's, which brought Sharpe great, surprised joy.

There are also images and notes of painful ugliness and hate: a yelling white boy gripping a wrapped leather belt in a demonstration against integration; a racist Cream of Wheat poster; details about collections of lynching photographs, along with the context that "the collectors who lend these items stipulate that their names not be revealed." There are dates and details about modern-day lynchings and police killings, the racist murders of children like Tamir Rice and Trayvon Martin. There are personal memories: Sharpe's mother's remembrance of being served a greasy possum leg by her foster family. Sharpe's own memory of walking to the library in summer when "a car of whiteboys drives by and calls me ■■■■■," then pushes her into the hedges.[4]

By interspersing the beautiful and the ugly, the book produces a feeling of breathlessness in us as readers. We don't know which kind of note we will encounter next or how a beautiful moment—a woman gardening, a child walking to the library—will be interrupted by white supremacy in the form of an obtuse question: "Is this your house?" Or violence.

In Note 27, "I am still thinking on this," Sharpe considers the Legacy Museum in Montgomery, Alabama. Founded by Bryan Stevenson as part of his Equal Justice Initiative's work to reconcile America with our history of enslavement and mass incarceration, the museum does not allow photography inside its walls. Instead, tour groups and visitors often take photographs outside the building, "mark[ing] their visit with an 'I was here.'" Images outside of the museum include photos of Black children being sprayed with fire hoses, photos of Black teenagers wearing orange jumpsuits in a courtroom, and a "colorized triptych of the 1893 spectacle lynching of seventeen-year-old Henry Smith in Paris, Texas."[5]

Sharpe informs us that 10,000 white people participated in Smith's lynching, mostly as spectators, and asks, "How many more lookings? . . . What might it mean, or do, or make, for these particular and specific images to circulate now—with Black people in groups (maybe) smiling while a lynching plays out, in color triptych, over our heads?" Sharpe goes on to ask: "We leave with a memento of what experience? We look back on our collections of what experience? What work are we marking? What entanglement? What is the instruction here? And in what?"[6]

She ends the note with the same words as its title, "I am still thinking on this," addressing the complexity of even beginning to answer these questions. In a country that, before the 2018 opening of the Legacy Museum, did not have a single major museum dedicated to the history of enslavement or the aftermath of white supremacy, despite having sixteen Holocaust museums. In a country where forty-four states have banned or attempted to ban the accurate teaching of history in public schools.[7]

In an earlier note (20), she quotes an interview between Stevenson and Henry Louis Gates, in which Gates posits that the narrative around slavery has not changed substantially and asks, "What makes you optimistic that we can change the narrative about lynching?"

Stevenson responds, in part, "I want us to tell the truth about our history not because I want to punish America, I want to liberate us but we can't get to liberation if we don't acknowledge what we've done."

And Sharpe replies,

> To stand in Gates's and Stevenson's "I," "we," "us," and "our" requires a certain innocence and belief in, as well as a commitment to, reforming the nation. Entering this space, one is asked to assume a certain position; asked to embrace memorial narratives that offer Black suffering as a pathway to knowledge, national and "racial" healing, reparation, and reconciliation; asked to embrace a narrative that acknowledges violence only to frame it as anomalous and intermittent and not foundational and ever-present.
>
> "We" are not approaching healing; nor should "we" be reconciled.[8]

It brings to mind something we've heard activist Michael Harris say, more than once, at marches and rallies: "I don't believe in justice. I've been let down too many times. Instead, I believe in accountability."

Because how do you have accountability without reckoning?

But in that reckoning, and in the creation of spaces that promote it, how do you avoid retraumatizing people whose ancestors were the targets of the traumatizing violence and who continue to be targets of police and white supremacist violence? Is it possible to tell truthful stories for people who have been let down too many times? What about their stories and the way that they are entwined with this untold violence, which white people insist was "long ago"?

The NAACP defines lynching as "the public killing of an individual who has not received any due process." Lynching can and often has included police officer participation. The Equal Justice Initiative describes lynching as "terrorism—a widely supported phenomenon used to enforce racial subordination and segregation" and notes that these violent, public, traumatizing events "were largely tolerated by state and federal officials."[9]

Many of these atrocities, like the 1893 lynching depicted on the outside walls the Legacy Museum, were witnessed by large crowds of white people, including white women and children. Some were perpetrated by the Klan or the White Brotherhood, but often these murders were undertaken and observed by mobs of white people unconnected with those groups.

The message to white and Black people in the community was one of brutal white supremacy. Frequently, these "spectacle lynchings" were photographed and turned into souvenir postcards shared among white people, a practice that began in Reconstruction. It was not until 1908 that the US Postal Service banned the mailing of these postcards, which continued to be produced and circulated privately for decades.[10]

Many were held in private collections, in dusty attics and old bureau drawers and the back rooms of antique shops, and few were ever seen publicly and together until the 2000 exhibit *Without Sanctuary*. Comprising 100 historical photographic prints and postcards of lynchings collected by James Allen and John Littlefield, the exhibit opened in the Ruth Horowitz Gallery, a one-room space on the Upper East Side of New York City.[11] It has now been exhibited across the United States, opening in each case to record attendance as well as to questions that evoke Sharpe's inquiry: *What is the instruction here? And in what?*

In her 2020 review of *To Make Their Own Way in the World: The Enduring Legacy of the Zealy Daguerreotypes*, Parul Sehgal asks a connected set of questions about the oldest surviving photographs of enslaved people, daguerreotypes taken in 1850 at the behest of Harvard zoologist Louis Agassiz. These are racist images taken without consent, damning to Agassiz and to Harvard, which threatened a copyright lawsuit against artist Carrie Mae Weems over her reproduction of the photographs in a 1995 series called *From Here I Saw What Happened, and I Cried*. Weems and other artists, scholars, and essayists contributed to the book.

Sehgal asks, "Is there a correct way to regard these images? Should one view them, or any coerced image, at all? To whom do they belong? Do they quicken or numb the conscience? Does displaying them traumatize the living? Is it care or cowardice to keep them concealed? What do we owe the dead?"[12]

Reading Sehgal's questions, like reading Sharpe's, is to understand that there is not, and may not be, a correct or comfortable answer, though these sets of questions land in slightly different places.

Sharpe questions the possibility of healing or reconciliation, as well as the possibility of a first-person plural pronoun ("we"). She cites the Afropessimist scholar and poet Frank B. Wilderson III: "*Shared experiences in the realm of the social do not necessarily index shared positions in the realm of the structural.*"[13]

Sehgal quotes Frederick Douglass, the most photographed American in the nineteenth century and the source of the book's title: "Pictures, like songs, should be left to make their own way in the world. All they can reasonably ask of us is that we place them on the wall, in the best light, and for the rest allow them to speak for themselves."

But she also adds, "Daguerreotypes, as is often noted, are sensitive, mirrored surfaces. You need to find the precise angle that blocks out your own reflection. Everything you see depends on where you stand."[14]

• • • •

No photograph of Wyatt Outlaw survives, though two are frequently used to represent him. One is an image of a Black Union soldier, taken from an academic article about Outlaw, and the other is a photograph of Caswell Holt, a Black man and Union League member who lived in Alamance County when Wyatt Outlaw did and who was also a significant figure of bravery and tenacity (we write about Holt in chapter 9). Using Holt's image as a stand-in for Outlaw's demeans the lives of both men.

And while many Black men were falsely accused of rape and then lynched without due process, this was not an accusation ever levied against Outlaw during his lifetime. The lie that Audra Faucette heard as a child about the killing of Wyatt Outlaw and the actions of One Arm Bill was a second, violent demeaning of Outlaw's legacy. Somewhere along the line, someone in the Faucette family misremembered what happened to Outlaw through the lens of a later lie—the one that casts Black men as threats to white womanhood—when in fact it was white supremacist political power that he threatened.

It's impossible to know how many white families in Alamance heard or still believe this story. But examining the lie teaches something important about the history of lynching, which changed over time as the Klan, and overall white supremacist violence, changed targets and tactics. All acts of lynching were, of course, hideous injustices, and the Klan (which was behind many but not all lynchings) was a hideous institution. But documented Reconstruction-era lynchings were both more frequent and more tied to political power than the ones that happened during the Jim Crow era.

Like Wyatt Outlaw, many of the Black people killed during Reconstruction were not accused even of made-up crimes. Instead, they were killed for participating in public life as equals to white people: for demanding wages for a job. For voting and encouraging others to vote. For fighting for the Union side during the Civil War. For protecting, as Outlaw did, Black and white citizens against the violence of the Klan and other terrorist groups. Many of the cases documented by the Equal Justice Initiative also happened in mass killings. For example:

In New Orleans in 1866, white mobs killed thirty-three Black people marching in support of voting rights.

In October 1868, in St. Bernard Parish, Louisiana, 35 Black people were killed by white mobs attempting to suppress the Black vote. And in that same month, in Bossier Parish, white people killed at least 162 Black people leading up to Election Day.

In November 1870, in Eutaw, Alabama, white mobs attacked a political meeting of Black voters and their white allies, killing four Black people.

In Eufala, Alabama, on Election Day 1874, white men killed at least six Black voters at the polls.

In 1875, in Clinton, Mississippi, armed white mobs attacked and killed fifty Black people after a political meeting.

In Hamburg, South Carolina, in July 1876, a white mob attacked and killed six Black men stationed at the National Guard Armory.[15]

In all of these cases, and in Outlaw's, violence was targeted against Black participation in political life, because this was the highest priority of white supremacists during Reconstruction. White conservatives and terrorist groups like the KKK and the White Brotherhood needed to suppress the Black vote in order to maintain or regain power in their state legislatures.

Because the records are so scanty, these Reconstruction-era stories are harder to tell. Yet they're worth seeking out and considering. As we show, they closely match our present circumstances of voter and political suppression. They also have the potential not to retraumatize but to inspire.

The men and women who were killed in these attacks, like Outlaw, were incredibly brave. To be newly freed from chattel slavery, *then* to endure the kinds of terror visited on communities like Eutaw or Clinton or Hamburg or Graham, and *then* to organize a political meeting where people were threatened or killed, and *then* to go to the polls to vote took incredible faith in democracy—these brave acts require, as Sharpe says, "a certain innocence and belief in, as well as a commitment to, reforming the nation."[16]

These people were not *only* victims. They were heroes.

What do we owe the dead? is an important question.

But so is this one:

What do we owe the living?

CHAPTER ELEVEN

A PROTESTER'S STORY

"PRESSURE" BY MICHAEL HARRIS

Michael Harris is a US Army veteran, small-business owner, mentor, father, and activist who lives in Rockingham County, North Carolina.

All my life I've been a pushback, stand-up guy—not easily led or told what to do. If you want me to do something, you have to tell me why. Anything can be a form of slavery. School can be slavery, military can be slavery, prisons can be slavery. It's another way to control you. And if they can't control you, they get rid of you. And I found that out in the movement. Malcolm X, Huey P. Newton, Dr. King, Marcus Garvey, Wyatt Outlaw—they couldn't control them, so they got rid of them. They'll give you a little rope. "You can do this, but you can't do this."

A few days after Memorial Day in 2020, I originally thought I would take the kids to the Woolworth's Civil Rights Museum down Elm Street in Greensboro.[1] But when we got down there, I was told there was a protest for George Floyd. My lady at the time drove the kids back, and I stayed. I'd never protested before, never chanted, but I used to call cadence in the military. So I used that. My military training helped me understand strategy and the concept of squad and platoon formations. Another thing I learned from the army is debriefing. "What worked about what we did?" was asked after every action. When it came time, I used it all. From that point I traveled around putting out fires of injustice.

I came to Graham for the first time in 2020 because I saw an invitation on a flyer to gather at Wyatt Outlaw Park. I didn't know who Wyatt Outlaw was at the time, but that's when I met Sylvester, Spencer, Maurice, Avery and Quenclyn and Ann and Faith and Drumwright and the others. When I got there I immediately fell into the role of crowd organizer, trying to keep people safe and out of jail with the mentality of "live to fight another day." It was a role God apparently has been preparing me for my whole life.

I remember the time in Graham when we marched from Children's Chapel United Church of Christ after marchers had been pepper-sprayed a few weeks earlier, and all those Confederate people were standing out there and they thought we were going to back down, and we didn't back down. That moment sticks out more than any other. But Greensboro and Graham weren't my only stops.

I was also in Akron for a few nights protesting for Jayland Walker. We were tear-gassed that first night in Akron. But I remember that third night, when I was arrested and punched repeatedly in the face on camera by an Akron police officer. After taking me down to the jail, I told the officer that we were only there for accountability for Jayland Walker. He told me to my face, "Accountability was served that night when they shot him."

They told me I wasn't being cooperative but I was, so when they finally asked me my name I said, "Breonna Taylor," and when they asked me my address, I said, "Fred Cox." They asked me another question, and I answered, "George Floyd." So they threw me in the "bullpen" with a lot of lasers on me and said, "If you move we're going to tase you." I thought about trying 'em, but I wanted to see my family again so I decided to live to fight another day. I still chanted for hours. I was there in the bullpen for a day and a half, never receiving medical attention. Come to find out during court proceedings, they were following my social media live posts the whole time. I don't consider myself a Rodney King, but similar things were done to me.

I want justice for all stolen lives. Jayland was shot forty-six times and shot at ninety-some times. Why isn't the city on fire? I don't mean physically, I mean mentally. Let me stop traffic. Let me stop people from getting to work. Let us stop some things so we can start some things. Tobacco, gas, and alcohol are some of the biggest things. Money runs the country, so if we can stop those kinds of things, we can get some things done. If they're not listening, how do we get them to listen? How do we get some accountability? And some activist groups don't want that because they don't want their grant money to stop.

Michael Harris marching in Greensboro, North Carolina, on May 31, 2020. “Let us stop some things so we can start some things,” said Harris. (Photo by Kevin Greene.)

Now I coach Little League Football and run a business called Each One, Teach One Lawn Service, all while continuing the fight for justice and accountability. My grandparents taught me respect and leadership. My grandmother was an outspoken leader, attending city meetings and heading the community watch. She was always a voice in the community and set the example.

So it's been in me since birth and finally came to a rise.

Pressure busts pipes. I got that activist name from some comrades who know I like to apply pressure, so that's what they call me, *Pressure*. I always tell people, it's not a moment, it's a movement for transformative change. As the old people say, if they talk about you, you must be doing something right. What I would say is stand for something or fall for anything. This is about justice for the next generation. We may not see it, but our kids might see it.

My daughter has been to protests, and my son rides down the road in the back seat hearing me say "Black Power" and "Peace." My children were safest in the womb of their mother, but now that they're in the world it's up to me and the community to protect them in this Amerikkka world. So I'm going to stand for something. I may get looked at differently, but one thing's for sure and two things are for certain, I love everybody. And there is only one race: the human race. Appreciate our ancestors, because if it wasn't for their fight we wouldn't be where we are today. We are continuing the fight that our ancestors began. We're still chucking the wood in the fire the old folks started.

Justice for all stolen lives.

All praise to Allah.

All gas, no brakes.

CHAPTER TWELVE

BEWARE YOU GUILTY, BOTH WHITE AND BLACK

Much of what we know about the last hours of Wyatt Outlaw, Graham's first Black town constable and commissioner, comes from the testimony of his mother. Jemima Phillips was seventy-four years old in March 1871—"I shall be seventy-five if I live to see the 20th day of August," she said, perhaps in recognition of the precarity of her life as a Black woman in Alamance County, North Carolina.[1]

The trial was being held not on behalf of her son, a law enforcement officer who'd put his life on the line protecting the citizenry from the Ku Klux Klan, but to provide background and context for Governor William Holden's impeachment trial. After nearly three months of argument and testimony, Holden became the first American governor to be impeached and then removed from office.[2]

But more on that later. Let's now imagine Jemima Phillips, born some fifty-five miles from Raleigh, the state's capital, where she has traveled to testify before the senate. It is only the second time she has been inside a courthouse, and it must be a fearful place for her, seated in that dim, cavernous legislative chamber, the only woman present. Richmond Pearson, chief justice of North Carolina's supreme court, presides. Jemima listens as the clerk of court calls the roll of some forty-two senators. Forty of these senators are white men, and only two are African American.[3] All are looking at her.

She has been sworn in, and now she must give testimony about the last time she saw her son alive. She remembers this momentous, terrifying night in vivid and precise detail. She tells how twenty men broke into the house, smashing the door's latch in half. These men, some of them holding "great torches" and armed with swords and pistols, strode into her room first, threw the covers off of her, and demanded to know, "Where is Wyatt? Where is Henry Holt?" They argued about what to do to her—"Cut her head off!" "Blow her brains out!" "Let us set the house afire!"—before moving to the middle room, where Wyatt Outlaw slept.[4]

She heard "the baby," her five-year-old grandson, Oscar, crying "Oh, Daddy! Oh, Daddy!" She flung open the door to her son's room and saw him struggling to get dressed. Thinking quickly, she ran back to her own room to grab a stick, which she used to try to defend her son from the intruders. She struck them, an enraged and determined mother, but she could not overcome them. They dragged Wyatt out of the house: shoeless, shirtless, coatless. That was the last time she saw her son alive.

The questioning attorney circles back to her description of striking the white men—all of them disguised, carrying weapons, and who have already threatened to cut her head off and burn down her family's house. Did she really hit them? Had he heard that correctly?

Jemima backtracks, establishing precisely when she'd hit them—not when they were leaving her room but when she saw them surrounding her son: *Then* she struck. "You said that when they got around him, then you commenced striking?"

She repeats that part of the story, which makes perfect sense to her: the part about her wailing grandson, her son half-dressed in a room of torch-bearing men. Provocation and mortal threat to all she holds dear. "They were surrounding him, and I say, who would not fight for their child?"[5]

The attorney is on her side—at least he is on the side of Republican governor Holden, who had declared all of Alamance County in a state of insurrection after Outlaw's murder. Maybe it's better to say that the attorney *needs* her testimony. But he is getting flummoxed by it, perhaps by her matter-of-fact description of her own remarkable courage. Is her testimony credible? We can imagine that a seventy-four-year-old woman does not seem like much of a match for twenty armed men. It must seem hard to believe, too, that she would admit to such behavior in a court of law and before the highest judge in the state.

"You don't answer my question; I ask what you did to them, when you raised that stick?"

Jemima is unflinching. "I said I struck at them as hard as I could."

She recalls what the men did to her: They "stamped" her, three times, on her breast and head and arms, and each time she rose again. She followed them as they left—they had her son, her *child*, which is how she refers to the fifty-year-old Wyatt throughout the excruciating testimony. She took a back route, not the direct path along North Main Street, and heard the men "hollowing like geese" and thundering down the street on their horses. She did not follow them, but she cried out. *Murder!*[6] Jemima's cry of murder establishes that she knew what was to come, if not precisely how it would happen. Maybe she tended to the children inside or to her own wounds. No one in court asks her that or offers any sympathy for her terror.

We can imagine her neighbors, hearing her screams along with the stampede of horses, looking outside their windows at the disguised men, a familiar and frightening sight in their long robes and white hoods, some of them adorned with painted, blood-red devil horns. Many of these men and women were called to testify at the Holden trial, and it is only through their brave, frankly shared memories that we can piece together what happened that February night.

One of these witnesses was Henry Holt, a Black fellow constable and Loyal League member who lived close enough to hear the first "lick" struck at Wyatt's door. The Klansmen also sought Henry Holt in retribution for his night patrols of the town, and—presumably—his participation in the Loyal League. Holt had gone home early in the evening, had taken a nap, and was sitting by the fire around eleven that night, talking with his sister, when he heard the commotion. He went to the doorway and watched—he lived close enough to see a light struck outside Wyatt's home. He watched as a group of robed men headed toward the courthouse.

"Don't you go too far," his wife implored, but Henry told her not to worry. He left the house and got close enough to some of the Klansmen that he could hear them talking. "Come on, come on; pshaw! Let us go." He saw some of the hooded men going toward his own house; they didn't see him, but he feared they might. "I heard a fuss like they broke down the door and I got scared and stayed right still and listened," he remembers at the Holden trial. "They made a terrible fuss like they were stamping all over the house."[7]

Mary Holt, Henry's wife, was in bed with their baby when the Klan broke in. We know about her experience the night of Wyatt's murder because she also testified at the Holden trial, traveling to Raleigh to sit before the same group of mostly white men.

Like Jemima's, Mary's testimony is exacting and precise, but there is also a polished, clipped quality to her responses. She says what she knows with confidence but also admits to what she could not know or remember. "I was so frightened that I didn't know how many were in the house," she answers, when asked to number the intruders.

When the Klansmen demanded to know where Henry was, Mary told them he wasn't home. One Klansman didn't believe her and threatened to shoot her if she didn't tell. "I told them they would have to shoot," she said, "for I didn't know where he was." When a Klansman asked Mary whether he stayed there "all night," she told him, "Not often, sometimes he did and sometimes he didn't." They had the idea that she could lead them to her husband, but when she asked whether she could take her baby with her, they relented and left.[8]

Holt could not see or hear what was happening to his family but watched and listened to their progress, up and down Main Street, from Peter Hardin's home, where he'd taken refuge. Hardin was a white man, a magistrate, and a Republican who employed Henry Holt to "wait on" him. Hardin, his wife, his grown children, and Henry Holt all watched helplessly as the men made a racket—"hallooing and making a noise and singing," Holt remembers. Mrs. Hardin counted eighteen men. They returned, dressed all in white "except one who was dressed in black," riding single file and "hallooing" at houses where they knew they might find enemies: They hollered at William Albright's home and circled back to Henry and Mary Holt's.[9]

They reentered the door they'd broken, demanding "a piece of rope" from Mary, but the only rope she had was in the bed, latticed beneath the mattress.

Mary climbed out of bed, perhaps holding her sleeping or drowsy child. The hooded, robed intruders turned over her mattress and cut a length of cord from the headboard to the foot—long enough to make a noose. When they left, disappearing into the late-winter night, she had no idea if they'd use the rope on her husband. Unlike Henry and Jemima, she didn't follow them, didn't cry out. Perhaps she prayed or wept or comforted the baby, but she told the senate that she didn't leave the house for the rest of the night or all the next day.

Henry returned near daybreak to find his door broken, the cord cut from his bed. In the dawn light, he went first to Wyatt's house "to see what was to pay up there."

Here is some of Henry Holt's testimony from the trial:

Q: What did you see?

A: I found the door broken. They had broken two doors. The one where his children were lying they broke first.

Q: Describe the house with reference to the front doors?

A: Both front doors were broken. There is no door on the backside except one room where his mother slept. They broke her door open next. He had opened his door, I suppose, for it was not broken.

Q: You did not see what took place?

A: It was all broken. The first one they broke was where the children were that was mighty near knocked to pieces.

Q: The front door?

A: The front door. Both front doors were broken open.[10]

No witnesses in this trial are invited or permitted to give voice to their outrage, their sense of violation, or their helpless anger at what was done to them, to their families, and to the community—"I don't care about that," witnesses are told when they go off-script by sharing emotion. But with some of the witnesses, especially those closest to Wyatt, we can see deliberate references to the most outrageous acts of terror. Notice how Henry Holt repeats the words "broke" or "broken" nine times over the short exchange and reiterates that there were children there—children sleeping in their beds. Notice his references to Wyatt's mother and the room where she slept. It's hard not to read the references to sleeping and family relationships as a reminder of the Klan's diabolical violence, the breaking of the peace and sanctity of the home.

The next day, a Sunday, Wyatt's body was found hanging from an elm tree directly across from the courthouse. In all, some 100 white men had watched as Outlaw was murdered, his body mutilated. They had blocked every exit leading away from the courthouse, perhaps a sign of their own fear of Outlaw and of the white and Black citizenry who might defend him. And they left him there so that people would see him as they made their way to church the next morning. Henry Holt saw his body from a distance, but he "did not go to him."[11] His testimony is clipped and vague about who committed the murder or what, specifically, he saw—he still lived in Graham when he testified. When called to testify a second time in the trial, he refused to respond.

Wyatt's mother, Jemima Phillips, had moved away and had little to lose. She had already seen the worst that a mother can imagine, the mutilated, lifeless body of her child. She saw him not where he hung but laid out inside the courthouse the next day. Though her son, as constable, must have entered and left that building frequently, it was her first time inside. She identified his body and noted his bare feet and chest. Perhaps she touched him—her child, who had done so much in his life, establishing a prosperous business, a school, a church. Her child, who'd died for defending his community against night raids by men who would not show their faces. He was wearing only underwear, some purplish breeches, and suspenders.

But Mr. Merriman, the cross-examining attorney, doesn't ask her about any of that. Instead, he asks six times whether she told the coroner, after swearing on the Bible, that the man who held the torch inside her home was a Black man. Six times she answers that she did not. "I said it once and I say it again, I never told anybody so."

It rained that day, she tells him. Mightily.[12]

• • • •

So much is contained within this moment of testimony, and so much is left unsaid. It was nearly six years after the end of the Civil War, and America was rebuilding itself—not physically, in the way some of us are taught to think about Reconstruction, but politically and socially and economically. Millions of formerly enslaved men had gained, at least on paper, full voting rights and citizenship. Some, like Wyatt Outlaw, had also become political leaders, representing the Union League at Republican conventions and encouraging their neighbors to vote.[13]

Jemima Phillips would not live to see her own right to vote realized, but in seventy-four years her life had changed dramatically, and its contours tell a story that is triumphant as well as tragic. She may have been born into slavery as the property of Chesley Faucett, a wealthy merchant and planter as well as a member of the North Carolina legislature. Though he denied it in the press, Faucett was a member of the secretive Red Strings, an antisecessionist group that promoted Republican ideals. It was not unusual for Red Stringers to be slaveholders or to deny their membership publicly.[14]

Faucett was also reputedly the father of her child, Wyatt. No one today knows whether her biracial son was the product of a consensual relationship or a coercive one or was the result of rape. Wyatt Outlaw's birth itself was undocumented, so his birthdate is something of an estimate—between 1816 and 1820.

It is also unclear whether Faucett freed Jemima and her son. A letter by a white visitor to the county referred to Wyatt as the "free nigro son of ches faset."[15] Other documentation suggests that Wyatt was sold to the nearby Outlaw family, tobacco planters who gave an enslaved man named Wyatt small amounts of freedom (which they did not extend to other enslaved people)—allowing him to learn to read and write, to learn the trade of carpentry and sell his services, and perhaps to buy his own freedom and his mother's.[16]

Jemima's 1871 testimony reveals something significant about the way that her life changed after the end of the Civil War. The fact of her testimony itself is significant; before the ratification of the Fourteenth Amendment in 1868, Black people could not testify in cases that implicated white people. Before that year, which coincided with the early gains of Reconstruction and the rise in political power of men like Outlaw, the right to give testimony—to say what happened, defend oneself against accusations, and seek justice—was denied to many Black, Indigenous, and other people of color. This was true not only in the South but across the country, a complicated patchwork of rules that varied from state to state. In New York, free Black people could serve as witnesses, but not enslaved people. In Virginia, a white plaintiff could not use the testimony of a Black person against another Black defendant—but a mixed-race person could testify against a white person, as long as that mixed-race person was less than one-quarter Black. In North Carolina, the declarations of an enslaved person could not be made in court or under oath but were admissible, as told to a white person, in the same way that the noises of an animal were admissible. Even after North Carolina's 1866 Civil Rights Act, which allowed Black people some rights, such as the right to sue or give evidence in court, Black people could give evidence implicating white people only if all white people who were at party to the case agreed.[17]

This is part of what makes Jemima Phillips's testimony so powerful—it was a right that she had held for less than three years, yet she exercised it with little inhibition. She said that she had lived with her son, in his four-room house and workshop, for five years, or since "the surrender," a sly reminder that, no matter the sympathies of her interrogators or witnesses, the Confederacy had indeed lost.[18] Perhaps it had taken until the end of the war, and emancipation, to gain her own freedom. Or perhaps she had been free, but it was only upon her son's return to Alamance and the founding of his business that she moved to that four-room house on Graham's North Main Street.

Both Wyatt Outlaw and his mother were also examples of the emerging economic power of free Black people, Wyatt because of his work as a mechanic and carpenter and Jemima because she was removed from the workforce—no longer enslaved and, because of her son's relative prosperity, no longer available for cheap domestic labor.

This was true for a significant number of Black families in Alamance County, where railroad work had replaced field labor for many. Working for the railroad paid in cash and, unlike sharecropping, was not subject to a white man's "benevolence," which often meant families did not get paid at all. Thanks to the railroad, many Black mothers and grandmothers were able to stay home to raise their children and grandchildren, to cook and tend house and care for their community.[19] This did not sit well with many whites.

The emerging political leadership of Black men like Wyatt Outlaw was seen, by some, as an even greater threat to white supremacy.

Aside from military service and the inhuman records of enslavement, men like Wyatt Outlaw left few official traces in the antebellum South. Births, which took place at home, were not recorded—this is why we don't have an official date of Wyatt Outlaw's birth. Black people, even free Black people, could not legally marry, and so although Outlaw is believed to have been married, we don't know his wife's name or what happened to her. Black men could own property and land, but few did, and many whites refused to sell land to African Americans. Though in some places they could vote, own a gun for hunting, and preach and found churches, operate stores, and open bank accounts, these freedoms were short-lived. After the 1831 Virginia rebellion led by Nat Turner, North Carolina joined other Southern states in passing new, harshly restrictive laws that prevented voting, court testimony, and other forms of civic participation of free Black people.

North Carolina's "Act concerning Slaves and Free Persons of Color" was a ninety-one-part Black Code. Among other restrictions, it made it illegal to teach an enslaved person to read, write, and do math; illegal for enslaved people to hunt; illegal for enslaved people to raise livestock; illegal for enslaved or free Black people to preach in public.[20] Black Codes were again written into North Carolina law in 1866, a year after the Thirteenth Amendment, outlawing slavery, was ratified in the state. These new Black Codes continued many of the conditions of enslavement, making it illegal for Black men to vote or for Black people to testify against whites in court.

It also made it possible for white men to have Black "apprentices," forced to work for free—slavery by another name.

Yet in this same year, Black men like Wyatt kept the faith that their trajectory moved toward full citizenship.

In April 1866, Wyatt Outlaw was recorded as a bondsman for a marriage license, his first civilian appearance in the public record. Newly freed African Americans could now marry legally, and several of the marriage licenses recorded by Outlaw were for Black veterans of the Union army (bondsmen "secured" the statement of a marriage bond, or intent to marry, before the clerk of court).[21] He opened his carpentry shop on North Main Street. He made coffins, repaired wagons, and sold liquor at his shop, which became a gathering place for white and Black workingmen. His political influence must have started here, in the web of multiracial networks he'd built through work and family connections.

Later that year, Wyatt Outlaw attended the convention of the North Carolina Equal Rights League of Freedmen, in Raleigh, as one of two representatives of Alamance County. It is there that historians believe he met William Holden, a former governor, appointed in 1865 and defeated by special election in 1866. Holden was one of the few invited white dignitaries to attend, and he addressed the meeting, remarking that "knowledge is power." He told the assembled freedmen that education for their children should be their priority, along with buying land. North Carolina was "the home of the black man as well as the white," he told them.[22]

Outlaw got to work on both. He organized a Loyal League chapter in Alamance County, which accepted both white and Black members. The goals were multifaceted, but all connected to the ideals of constitutional republicanism—that is, that all people have unalienable rights, that the government exists to protect those rights, and that one of the most important ways people participate in a republic is by voting.

Outlaw knew that for people to fully participate in republican democracy, they needed a basic education. This was one of the reasons he started the league chapter—to provide a structure for founding a school and a church for Black people, who had no such structures in place for them at the end of the war. The chapter's meetings were formal and dignified, with recitations that helped instill courage and enthusiasm for voting among its members, who were known as Pioneers. Like Red Stringers, Pioneers wore strips of fabric in their lapels and discreetly but knowingly tapped them as they passed fellow Loyal Leaguers. They stood guard near polling places to be sure their members were not molested and also to make sure that people voted. Voting, and the rule of law, was paramount in the Loyal League.[23]

In 1867, as president of North Carolina's Union League, William Holden commissioned Outlaw as a member of the league's Grand State Council, giving Wyatt Outlaw the authority to instruct other Union League founders, install officers, and supervise their proceedings. In 1868, Wyatt and four other men bought a tract of land on North Main Street, where they intended to build a church and likely a school.[24] Later that year, newly elected governor William Holden appointed Outlaw as a town constable and commissioner of Graham.

The story of Wyatt Outlaw's life, as told by the records we do have, was one of discipline, service, courage, and exposure to the wider world. As a community member, he'd worked to educate people with fewer opportunities. As a businessman, he interacted with people from the government and the emerging working and middle classes of Graham and Company Shops, the small railroad community nearby. And as a Union League officer and Loyal League leader, he would have had to speak publicly, influencing people who were moving through an exciting, dangerous, world-changing time.

But the Loyal League was not the only group holding meetings. The year 1868 was also the one in which the Ku Klux Klan, known locally as the White Brotherhood, established itself in Alamance County. Early local Klan leaders, called chiefs, were former Confederates who had spent time in a Union prison, where they developed a secret language of whistles and signs. Other members were shopkeepers, tradesmen, and farmers. These first Klansmen wore fake beards and papier-mâché hats and horns, masquerading as the souls of dead Confederates. Even their horses wore robes. They swore blood oaths to the group and were initiated in elaborate, sexualized woodland rituals that were the opposite of Loyal Leaguers' dignified gatherings.[25]

The choice of Alamance, and the Piedmont in general, was deliberate. The Klan was searching for a foothold to help right-wing Democrats win elections. The large number of newly free African Americans in the eastern part of the state made that area unlikely as a source of victory. But Alamance, Person, Orange, Caswell, and Guilford Counties made up an area where suppressing the Black vote, and the white Republican vote, would be consequential and where white supremacists could exploit white resentment over Black competition for lucrative railroad jobs. Though some parts of the Piedmont leaned Unionist, there were also large swaths populated by former Confederates and wealthy, embittered former slaveholders.

Klan raids in Alamance County began in 1868. Hooded white men, some in elaborate and fearsome horned costumes, rode through town with guns, clubs, swords, and torches. They burned homes and barns. They threatened and whipped people for everything from allegedly stealing chickens or exposing themselves to white women to teaching school to Black citizens and voting Republican. Their attacks often involved ritual, sexualized humiliation and were debilitating, even fatal.[26]

Some Black citizens, understandably fearful as well as mistrustful of the legal system, thought that they should arm themselves against these masked terrorists. Caswell Holt, who had been repeatedly attacked, whipped, and tortured by the Klan, sought help from multiple sources: his white employers, his former master, the legal system. This only brought more attacks from Klan members, including on his children.[27]

But Outlaw, whose life story and Loyal League leadership expressed a belief in the rule of law, counseled them to wait. "Leave it quiet" and "be as industrious as possible," he told them. "Allow law enforcement to do its job."[28] In early 1869, newly elected Graham mayor William Albright established a night patrol of five armed constables. This small group dispatched at least one raiding group of Klansmen, but they did so within their legal rights as officers of the law. And they were led by Wyatt Outlaw, a Black man and a Republican.[29]

A year later, an armed group of twenty Klansmen kidnapped Wyatt Outlaw, refusing him clothes and shoes. They threatened to kill his mother, they beat her, and they terrified his children. They drove him down the street to the town square, horse hooves thundering. Nearly 100 Klansmen blocked every exit, and then they hung him in front of the courthouse, the very symbol of law and order. Included in this crowd were not only law enforcement officials but likely some of Outlaw's own half-brothers and half-cousins who had joined the White Brotherhood.[30] No one knows what Wyatt's last words were or whether he recognized the men surrounding him. One of the Klansmen slashed his mouth with a knife, punishment for his "mouthiness," and others pinned a note to his scanty nightclothes: "Beware you guilty, both white and black."[31]

• • • •

How must the community of Graham, particularly the Black community, have mourned Wyatt Outlaw? How did they seek justice? Here was a man with a family and a community who depended on him. A man who was instrumental to many at different points in their lives: as a bondsman for their marriages, a repairer of carriages, a carpenter and builder of coffins for the final rests of family members who must have grown up with no guarantee or even likelihood of a proper burial. His shop was a gathering place; at the end of the workday, he poured drinks for tired railroad workers. He brought them, Black and white, into Union League membership, providing a society of dignity and purpose. With other Black men, he bought land for a church and made plans for a school.

A multiskilled, energetic, and brave man like Wyatt Outlaw must have been called on at all hours of the day to help his community. We can imagine his advice sought when disputes arose, and we know that he counseled those who depended on officers of the law to protect them against the growing violence and terror of the Klan. He died, as it turned out, because he dared to protect his neighbors and because he believed that the law was on their side. Though he certainly had enemies, he must have had many friends.

One of these, we can imagine, was William Puryear. There are no records documenting the relationship between Puryear and Outlaw. But Puryear died because he sought justice for Outlaw, claiming that he knew and could identify two of the men who killed him and reporting them to authorities some two weeks after Outlaw's lynching.[32] This too must have taken extraordinary bravery. Puryear's widow, Matilda Puryear, testified about the terrifying abduction of her husband, which happened shortly after he spoke to the authorities. Many details of her testimony echoed the experience reported by Jemima Phillips. Disguised men wearing hoods and horns broke into the Puryear home in the middle of the night, threatened to cut Matilda Puryear's head off, abducted her husband, hatless and wearing only one shoe, and locked Matilda and her three young children "bound up" inside the house. To free them, Matilda's son had to climb out through the chimney.

Matilda testified that Puryear had been "distracted," a reference to mental distress. She said that he was convinced that his life was in danger, ever since he "went to Graham and reported those people" who killed Wyatt Outlaw. Similar to the cross-examination of Phillips, attorneys tried to discredit Puryear, suggesting that his wife had taken out a "peace warrant" against him and repeatedly asking her whether he was having problems with his Black neighbors. Like Jemima Phillips, she denied their assertions with plainspoken eloquence: No, she did not take out such a warrant, and no, he was not in dispute with his neighbors. He was not "raving and swearing," Matilda told them. "He said no one should touch him—he was a free man."[33]

The Klan's brutality was not limited to Alamance. On May 21, Klan members stabbed and garroted John W. Stephens, a white state senator from Caswell County who was closely aligned with the Black community, "radical" Reconstruction, and Governor Holden. They did not attack on horseback under cover of night but inside the county courthouse, claiming afterward that the assassination was carrying out a verdict in a Klan trial in which Stephens was defended "in absentia."[34] Such brazen tactics—assassination inside a courthouse, at a meeting of Democratic politicians—was just one sign of the increasing terrorism of the Klan, as well as its connection to the Democratic Party.

Klan violence, and the disappearance of Puryear, may have been why Jemima Phillips moved away from Graham, "across the river," as she said she did on April 5.[35] It's very likely she was fearful for her life, as an eyewitness whose life had already been threatened. Not long afterward, Puryear's body was discovered, weighted and bound, in an Alamance County mill pond. Matilda Puryear testified that, although his body was badly decomposed, she knew it was him by the brass buttons on his shirt and the single shoe on his foot. The date of his lynching is not known—there is no death certificate—but his death was reported on June 1, 1870.[36]

On March 7, Governor Holden declared Alamance County in a state of insurrection, followed by Caswell County on July 8. He suspended the writ of habeas corpus and imposed martial law in both counties in an effort to round up Klansmen and hold them accountable for their actions.[37] Colonel George Kirk, an unpopular Union cavalry officer who was known for his harsh tactics, was placed in charge. Kirk, along with more than 300 state militiamen, arrested and jailed some 100 suspected Klansmen in both counties. This became known as the Kirk-Holden War, characterized by Democrats as a battle of Old South valor against brutal Republican force.

Right-wing newspapers like Josiah Turner's *Sentinel* were primed to take advantage of what seemed to some citizens like a dangerous overstep of government authority. Turner fabricated stories about hangings and whippings of Klansmen, and one even proclaimed that "all the murders, whippings and barn-burnings had been done by the Loyal Leaguers under the barb of Ku Klux!"[38] This would be echoed in the Holden trial, when attorney Merriman repeatedly questioned Jemima Phillips about the "Black man" who held the torch.

The conservative ploy worked. People bought what Josiah Turner was selling: that Black political power meant corruption, that complaints against the Klan were overblown, that Black political power would also mean white political and economic disenfranchisement. In November, the Black vote was sufficiently suppressed and white anger sufficiently stoked to ensure huge Republican losses.

On December 14, 1870, Holden was impeached by the new Democratic majority. On December 19, seventeen African American state representatives wrote an open "Address to the Colored People of North Carolina" in support of Holden and denouncing the Democrats' partisan "wrath." They did not mince words: "After impeachment, his enemies will not be satisfied until he is hanged, unless happily their own gallows should overtake them. When Gov. Holden is disposed of those whom he protected will be the next victims. For the blood of one man will not satiate their thirst. They are mad because their slave property is lost. They are mad because the Reconstruction measures have triumphed, and we are permitted to represent you in this body. They are mad because we refuse to bow the knee to them."[39]

This address is a significant document because of its very existence and because of its seventeen signatories, each representing constituents in counties across the state, which they attributed to Reconstruction success. Their address to "the Colored People" identifies African Americans as having their own power, as voters and citizens, and neatly dissects the rationale for Holden's impeachment. The incantatory repetition of "they are mad" efficiently strips the Democrats of any claim to reason and justice. Taking up "arms of flesh" will not be effective, the representatives say, suggesting instead that people turn to God for power and justice, the "source that never fails." The letter goes on to ask that African American ministers make January 13, a Friday, a day of fasting and prayer on behalf of the governor and "suffering people" of North Carolina.[40] This was not a turning away from government and its earthly powers but a deliberate connection between the faith community and social justice that had persisted from Reconstruction to the civil rights struggle and continues into the present era.

The trial began in January, and it lasted nearly three months. On March 22, 1871, after testimony from 174 witnesses, including 113 defense witnesses who detailed the atrocities and lawlessness of the Klan, Holden was convicted of six charges, including unlawfully raising troops, illegally declaring insurrection, and illegally searching and arresting citizens.[41] He was the first American governor to be removed from office. Because the Democrat-controlled legislature extended pardons to any members of secret societies, including the Klan, no one was held accountable for Wyatt Outlaw's death, William Puryear's death, or any other lynchings or political assassinations in Alamance County, Caswell County, or other places around the state.

Republicans would struggle again, in Black and white alliances, to regain control and influence, achieving remarkable success in a fusion: a Republican and Populist coalition that swept the legislature in the 1890s.[42] Fusionists won both Senate seats and took back the governorship, and passed some progressive educational and labor laws, focusing on workers' rights and providing for a "general and uniform system of public schools."[43] But this success was met with a state-level, right-wing backlash of "Redeemers," which is what white supremacist Democrats across the South called themselves. They sought to "redeem" the South from Black political leadership and progress through Black Codes, Jim Crow segregation, and poll taxes, literary tests, and Klan intimidation that led to the near-total suppression of Black voters in North Carolina. Their voter suppression efforts were upheld by a conservative-majority US Supreme Court.[44]

TODAY'S "REDEEMERS"

In *The Third Reconstruction: America's Struggle for Racial Justice in the Twenty-First Century*, historian Peniel E. Joseph characterizes three Reconstruction periods—the first, in the years after the Civil War; the second, during the civil rights era; and the third, starting with the historic election of Barack Obama and continuing through Black Lives Matter and the Biden administration. He writes about the backlash of so-called redeemers working against reconstructionist goals in each time period—white supremacists fighting against voting rights, economic and educational equality, and a full participatory democracy for all. Joseph suggests that the duality that made it hard for Black Americans to "forge a coherent identity in a nation scarred by racial slavery" is reflected in a dual identity, a clash of "warring ideas," for the entire nation. He writes, "There is the America that we might call reconstructionist, home to champions of racial democracy, and there is the America that we might call redemptionist, a country that papers over racial, class, and gender hierarchies through an allegiance to white supremacy. Since the nation's birth, its racial politics have been shaped by an ongoing battle between reconstructionist America and redemptionist America."*

Joseph sees the Third Reconstruction as "the most volatile yet," a bold statement when you consider the brutal attacks on Black Americans and the proponents of a multiracial democracy during the first two periods.† But consider the election of Donald Trump, post-Obama, and his blatantly (and increasingly, as the years went on) racist and antidemocratic rhetoric and policies; the Biden years of somewhat surprising reconstructionist progress; and the reelection of Donald Trump even after he incited a violent and deadly insurrection on the US Capitol, and you will recognize that the backlash against progress in the Third Reconstruction now seems supercharged. We have a right-wing media devoted to spreading dangerous misinformation; state and national legislators committed to making it harder, not easier, to vote; and a president who reportedly suggested, repeatedly, that police and military "just shoot" Americans protesting police violence.‡

"History," writes Joseph, "is a balm capable of healing America's deep-seated racial wounds."** Certainly the true history of this country is harrowing. But even, perhaps especially, within our most violent and antidemocratic periods, there is inspiration to be found in the bravery and fortitude of historic reconstructionists.

---

* Peniel E. Joseph, *The Third Reconstruction: America's Struggle for Racial Justice in the Twenty-First Century* (New York: Basic Books, 2022), 10.

† Joseph, *Third Reconstruction*, 13.

‡ Michel Martin and Tinbete Ermyas, "Former Pentagon Chief Esper Says Trump Asked about Shooting Protesters," *All Things Considered*, NPR, May 9, 2022, www.npr.org/2022/05/09/1097517470/trump-esper-book-defense-secretary.

** Joseph, *Third Reconstruction*, 35.

In 1914, the United Daughters of the Confederacy erected a marble statue of a Confederate soldier standing with a gun, atop a tall granite column, directly in front of the Alamance County Courthouse and across from the site where Wyatt Outlaw died. Inside the monument's concrete base is a copper box containing the names of 1,100 soldiers from Alamance County who fought for the Confederacy in the Civil War.[45] Jacob Long, who was the leader of the Alamance Klan when Wyatt Outlaw was murdered and who had been arrested by Governor Holden, spoke at the monument's dedication.[46]

Monuments like Alamance's are common throughout the South and are often found in front of courthouses and in other public spaces. People pass them all day long as they go about their business: working at law enforcement or clerical jobs, recording deeds and marriage licenses, petitioning the court or the county board of commissioners. According to the Southern Poverty Law Center, North Carolina still has seventy-one statues and monuments like the one in Alamance, though twenty-four were removed in 2020 after the murder of George Floyd.[47]

Defenders of the statue will often say, "You can't erase history." Or, perhaps, "You can't erase *my* history." What many don't realize is that most of these statues were erected decades after the end of the Civil War, and they had a deliberate and nefarious double purpose: to promote white supremacy and to tell Black people that they had no place in the political and legal business of Southern towns like Graham. Made of marble or tin, often mass-produced in Northern factories, these statues were a cheap, ugly seal on Black economic, political, and legal disenfranchisement.

They also leave out, whitewash, and misinform. North Carolina's Civil War history is far more complex than the image a "stalwart" white soldier, gazing northward, represents. North Carolina was the last state to secede, with a smaller and less-powerful class of slaveholding elites than in South Carolina or Georgia, for example. Contrary to Southern mythology, these elites often did not send their own sons to the battlefield but conscripted boys from poor families to do their fighting. North Carolina had many yeoman farmers, an economy that was less dependent on enslavement than Deep South states, and strong Unionist support, particularly in the mountains. North Carolina's politicians and people knew that the war would mean tremendous casualties and economic losses, and many resisted. North Carolina had some 10,000 white soldiers who fought for the Union side. And although neo-Confederates like to trot out examples of Black volunteers for the Confederacy, North Carolina had many more Black soldiers who volunteered to fight for the Union. More than 5,000 Black soldiers from North Carolina fought to end slavery.[48]

Alamance County's political history was particularly complex and poorly represented by that marble soldier. Alamance was home not only to many Unionists and Red Stringers but also to a significant population of Quakers, who had settled in sizable numbers in Randolph and Guilford Counties. These pacifist abolitionists formed manumission societies, which bought people out of slavery or transferred their ownership to the Society of Friends. Technically still enslaved, these people were allowed to live freely on Quaker land. Alamance County's small, pre–Revolutionary War town of Snow Camp was also a stop on the Underground Railroad.[49]

There is no statue or monument in Alamance County to represent *this* freedom-loving history or the dark history of the Klan. There are some thirty roadside markers recognizing historical people and events in Alamance County but none telling anyone about Wyatt Outlaw, one of the most historically significant citizens ever born in Alamance.[50]

• • • •

When Jemima Phillips and Matilda Puryear testified about the abduction and murder of their loved ones, it was the first time either woman had appeared before a court. Only three years earlier, their testimony would not have been admissible in North Carolina or in many other states because of the color of their skin and because their testimony concerned the affairs of white people. Neither Phillips nor Puryear had the right to vote. But voting, particularly the Black man's right to vote, was why their loved ones were killed. Again and again, white and Black witnesses to Klan violence named voting as the primary motivator. "Since the war, I think as a general thing, the democratic or the conservative party in my county have had a prejudice against the colored people," Graham magistrate Peter Hardin said at the Holden trial. He clarified that the prejudice arose not from general freedom but "since they have been permitted to vote."[51]

Phillips and Puryear both appeared as witnesses for the defense—they were there to help Holden's side prove that Alamance County was indeed in a state of insurrection, overrun with Klan violence. They were not there to seek justice for their loved ones—at least, not directly—but to establish that they had been terrorized by the Klan. The goal of the impeaching, conservative Democrat state senators was to remove Holden from office and to establish that protecting the citizens of North Carolina from the Ku Klux Klan or other white supremacists was outside his authority. The point was that murder, torture, and intimidation done in the name of white supremacy and voter suppression were not crimes. This is not far from the same argument that Donald Trump and his supporters have made, implicitly, when defending the insurrectionists who stormed the Capitol on January 6, 2021. Some of those Confederate-flag-waving marauders came from Alamance County; they returned home without ever being questioned or apprehended, and they faced no consequences for their criminal behavior.

Phillips and Puryear were interrogated by attorneys on both sides who seemed not to understand them at times and who offered not a single word of comfort or sympathy for their losses. Phillips and the defense attorney had a confused, frustrated exchange over the meaning of "arms," and a cross-examining attorney snapped, "I don't care about that" when Puryear described seeking help from her neighbor, whom she identified as "a Black woman," after her husband's kidnapping.[52] Reading their attempts to understand and be understood in a room full of mostly white men is painful, and it's important to remember that even today, the courtroom remains a racially imbalanced space, with a disproportionate number of white judges and attorneys (77 percent of sitting judges are white, as are 85 percent of lawyers).[53] Even court reporters often err in transcribing testimony; 85 percent of court reporters, nationally, are white, while only 4 percent are African American. A recent study of more than 2,000 transcriptions found that court reporters transcribed testimony in African American English with only 82 percent accuracy. Often, these errors have a substantial impact on how testimony is understood—the same study showed more than 30 percent of the errors made in transcribing dialect changed the content of the testimony.[54]

Another echo: Cross-examining attorneys attempted to discredit the women, asking irrelevant questions, like whether Puryear had children from a previous relationship. They also insisted, to both women, that they had told others that the intruders were Black men. "Didn't you swear that the man who held the torch, before the coroner, was a black man?" The prosecuting attorney asked Phillips some form of this question six times. Each time, she answered with a definitive no. Matilda Puryear was asked seven times whether she appealed for a peace warrant against her "distracted" husband, and seven times she said that she did not.[55]

Their testimonies end abruptly, when the prosecutors couldn't get more from them. Both women disappear from the historical record after that. We don't know how afraid they may have been when they returned home, what threats or harassment they faced, or how they took care of the children left behind by Wyatt and William. We do know that no one was ever tried or convicted for the lynchings of Wyatt Outlaw and William Puryear.

To read the testimony of Jemima Phillips and Matilda Puryear, and of so many of the Black witnesses for Holden's defense, is to be immersed in a time period that is almost unimaginably brutal. Witness after witness describes being whipped and beaten until they were scarred or permanently disabled, or threatened with hanging, or made to kneel and pray while Klan members beat them or argued about what to do with them. They describe their children and wives hiding under porch floorboards, their homes invaded, their livelihoods destroyed. Matilda Puryear tells how, to escape her home and look for her husband, one of her sons had to climb through the chimney, scramble down the side of the house, and unlatch the door.

Before testifying, each witness placed a hand upon the Bible and swore to tell "the truth, the whole truth, and nothing but the truth." That swearing-in process is the same today as it was in 1871, and it's not the only thing that has remained the same.

Race, racism, and even the outcome of the Civil War still bitterly divide Graham and Alamance County as a whole. After the 2020 marches, neo-Confederates frequently clashed with Black Lives Matter protesters at rallies around the still-standing Confederate monument, which is protected by a tall, $32,000 new fence.[56] At protests, Black Lives Matter activists have been disproportionately arrested and charged with everything from disturbing

Installed in 2021, the eight-foot-tall iron fencing surrounding the Confederate monument in Graham, North Carolina, cost taxpayers $32,000. (Photo by Anthony Crider.)

the peace to inciting a riot. Policing these protests and protecting the statue cost taxpayers more than $750,000 in 2020; this is not inclusive of the legal costs of prosecution, of defending the city and county against multiple civil rights lawsuits, or of settling with the plaintiffs.[57] Despite growing public demands, the 100 percent white, 100 percent Republican city and county governments have refused to consider removing the monument or setting funds or space aside for a park, memorial, or even a marker honoring Wyatt Outlaw.

"I am not a racist. I don't like to be called a racist. And most of the people in this town and county aren't racist. But don't step on our feet. Don't step on our feet," the county commissioner Bill Lashley Sr. said in response to community activists in August 2020.[58] They were requesting, again, that the board remove the Confederate statue that still stood outside the Historical Courthouse, even after dozens of similar statues had been removed across the state.

Lashley, who was succeeded by his son Bill Lashley Jr. after the 2020 elections, was used to having the floor—he'd served as commissioner for twenty-two years before he died, just after Thanksgiving. He was closely aligned with the long-serving sheriff, Terry Johnson, who survived a US Department of Justice investigation that found patterns of discriminatory policing within his department and who has also made frequent statements about his own lack of racism.[59] It's hard to imagine either man uncomfortable or silenced in a courtroom.

"There hasn't been an attempt to truly connect with the community," said Dreama Caldwell, who campaigned for a seat on the Alamance County Board of Commissioners. Forty-five years old, a mother of two and former preschool teacher, she came to politics after learning about her county's hidden history: Wyatt Outlaw and Reconstruction-era Black excellence, the lynchings that happened in that era and during Jim Crow, the Burlington protests where police killed a fifteen-year-old, Leon Mebane, who'd been a student at her own high school. "I was educated here and I never heard any of these stories in school."[60]

That's what everyone in the movement says. *I never heard; I didn't know.* Now that they do, they're making sure no one else has their history concealed from them or loses the chance to share it.

CHAPTER THIRTEEN

NOTHING BUT A POLITICAL FEELING

Why did the Alamance County White Brotherhood, or Klan, regularly terrorize Black citizens starting in 1868?

Why was Caswell Holt repeatedly attacked in his home, beaten until he couldn't work?

Why was Henry Holt's home broken into, his wife threatened?

Why was a teacher of Black schoolchildren whipped, his schoolhouse burned? Witnesses intimidated and killed?

Why was Wyatt Outlaw kidnapped and assassinated, his body left in the town square for all to see?

It was about the vote.

It was always about the vote and the full expression of equal rights and citizenship.

Let's look at the history of voting rights and voter suppression in North Carolina until the white supremacist violence prompted by Reconstruction. It won't take long, because before Reconstruction, voting rights were meted out to a very select few.

In 1776, North Carolina ratified its first state constitution, which allowed any white man who paid taxes to vote for his state representatives, and any free man who paid taxes and owned more than fifty acres of land to vote for state senators. This included free Black and Native men who paid taxes and owned at least fifty acres—less than 1 percent of the total population.[1]

In 1835, four years after Nat Turner's rebellion in Virginia, North Carolina's legislature amended the state constitution, giving landless white men the vote but stripping suffrage entirely from free Black, Native, and mixed-race men. The new constitution allowed all white men to vote for governor and for state representatives. It still took white men considerable wealth—ownership of fifty acres—to vote for state senators, and these men had to own even more land (a minimum of 100 acres) to serve in the general assembly. Until the Civil War, most legislators in North Carolina were slave owners, and legislation followed their priorities: Reward the wealthy, protect enslavers, restrict rights for poor people, and disenfranchise people of color.[2]

After the Civil War and emancipation, Black freedmen began to join societies devoted to voting rights, like the Loyal League, the Union League, and the Equal Rights League. But enabled by the Confederate sympathizing and leniency of President Andrew Johnson, the white-led legislature passed what came to be known as the Black Codes, which restricted the rights of newly freed or already free Black citizens. These laws determined that any persons descended from Black parentage should be considered "persons of color," established an apprentice system that was nearly identical to slavery, allowed for the forced labor of convicted criminals (also akin to slavery), and denied Black people the right to vote, serve on a jury, or give testimony against a white person.[3]

The leagues fought back, continuing to meet, educate, and spread the word about Reconstruction and demanding fair representation, including their right to vote. After the federal Reconstruction Act of 1867 was passed, extending suffrage to all Black men, the freedmen registered in droves. More than 70,000 Black voters in North Carolina delivered the Republican Party control of the general assembly in 1868, which now included more than a dozen influential Black members.[4] At the local level, Black men were being appointed and elected as constables and commissioners. They bought land and built schools and churches, which white supremacists knew to be sources of power and voting education for Black people.

The year 1868 is also the same one in which the Klan became active in Alamance, Caswell, and other Piedmont counties. After swearing an oath of secrecy and loyalty, its members disguised themselves in white robes and fearsome masks to terrorize their communities, assault Black families, burn churches and schools, and threaten white Republicans who made common cause with Black people or tried to bring Klansmen to justice.

It wasn't only Black people and their white political allies who testified about Klan motives; in the three-month Holden trial, a number of white former Klansmen also spoke plainly about why and how they committed their acts of terror. John W. Long testified at length on the trial's thirty-fourth day, admitting that he joined the White Brotherhood in 1868 in Company Shops, under camp chief John Trollinger and county chief Jacob Long. At that time, according to Long, there were 700 to 800 Klansmen in Alamance. At the beginning of his testimony, at the request of the senate, Long donned a white gown and headdress with red tasseled horns. He admitted that this was the type of disguise he wore at night, as his camp "never done business in the day."[5]

He couldn't recollect the full oath he took, but he clearly remembered the purpose of the group: "to keep the colored man from elevating himself with the white man and to overthrow the Republican party; to go around before elections and to scare the Republicans or the colored men, to keep them from voting." Further, Klansmen were meant to defy legal accountability—Long testified that "if anybody should get arrested or put in jail we were to release them and stand around and get on a jury, if possible, and bring out a verdict in favor of the prisoner."[6] One camp could order the actions of another camp—say, to burn a schoolhouse or whip a targeted person—and that camp would comply. This was one of the Klan's many ways of avoiding accountability.

Long saw all of this as a member. He watched the burning of a schoolhouse that taught Black children. He whipped people. He participated in a unanimous vote to drown Caswell Holt because "dead men told no tales," though he claimed to have abstained from voting on it. By the time Long testified, he had moved to Alabama, afraid he would be killed for disloyalty to the Klan. "I was in it and could not get out of it," he said.[7]

Throughout his extended testimony, he was asked about the purpose of the Klan. Was it to deprive Black men of citizenship? Was it to return the state to the time "before the Fourteenth Amendment and the rights of the Negroes was put in?"

Long did not understand or pretended not to understand: "How is that?" he asked. "I don't know whether I said about citizens or not." This part of his testimony, including the grammatically confusing "whether I said about citizens," reads as if he's missed something essential. Could he conceive of Black people as citizens at all, or did he not understand what "citizen" means?

What he did affirm is very similar to what he said at the start of his testimony. He understood that the Klan's objective was "to keep [Black men] from going to the polls and voting and keeping them from elevating themselves to white people."[8]

Going to the polls

Voting

Elevating themselves to white people

Stephen White, a Company Shops postmaster, railroad agent, and magistrate who was elected to the general assembly, was asked about the "state of feeling between the two races in Alamance County." White appeared before the court in the Holden trial because he was a witness to the whipping of a Northern-born schoolteacher who worked with Black children. He characterized the feeling as "very bitter" and when asked, "On account of politics?" responded, "I know nothing else."

"The feeling between the two races is a political feeling?" he was asked.

"Nothing but a political feeling," he responded.

"The colored people generally and almost unanimously vote the Republican ticket?"

"They do."[9]

Merriam-Webster defines "citizenship" as "membership in a community."[10] But we also like the more specific definition used by the Center for the Study of Citizenship, a global institution based at Wayne State University: "a *participatory* member of a *political* community" (emphasis ours).[11]

This is the community that the Equal Rights League, Loyal League, and Union League encouraged and inducted people into. Their politics were about protecting workers' rights, expanding educational access, and growing opportunities for working people of all races. They advocated for progressive and inclusive rights, including access to the ballot and to the basic rights of shelter, food, and health care.

Reconstruction, with its vastly expanded opportunities for Black political participation and Black political leadership, did not help only Black men and other men of color. After the degradation and violence of enslavement, Radical Republicans generally held progressive views that were about freedom and peace for all. They opposed the death penalty, supported women's suffrage and pacifism, and advocated for land reform and an end to political corruption. They worked in mutual aid societies and helped create our current system of free public education—for Black and white children. According to a 2020 study, each Black politician working in a Southern county increased per capita earning and per capita tax revenue by a significant amount.[12] Black political engagement was the rising tide that lifted all ships.

But equality on any terms looked threatening to conservatives, who abhorred the idea of sharing the wealth and power they'd built with stolen labor. In *Iron Confederacies*, Scott Reynolds Nelson documents Josiah Turner's speeches made in Alamance County: "In Alamance he told the story of his faithful servant named Dick, whom Turner had always treated like a son. But, Turner reportedly said, 'If Dick should ever vote the radical ticket, Dick should never eat my meat and bread; damned if Dick could ever eat my meat and bread.'"[13]

Putting aside the dubious claim that any slave owner ever treated an enslaved person "like a son" or that any such person as the faithful "Dick" existed (Nelson suggests that Turner was prone to yarn-spinning), it's useful to unpack Turner's speech. Josiah Turner saw "meat and bread" as solely belonging to him and as resources he could remove as a penalty for voting against his interests—voting "the Radical ticket." The vote was what Turner most opposed; he had argued in speeches and in print for a "white man's government."[14]

Men like Josiah Turner could not abide Black men like Caswell Holt saying, "I have got plenty of wheat and corn of my own."

They could not abide Black men and their families defending themselves, physically or legally.

And they especially could not abide Black men holding leadership positions, voting and encouraging other Black men to vote.

• • • •

Wyatt Outlaw was publicly killed in an act of terrorism, but was he *lynched?* He did not receive due process, but despite later misinformation, he was also not accused of any crime. He was a well-known, well-respected person of "good character" who did government work, ran a tavern, patrolled his community, and led the Union League. His town square killing was so public and so orchestrated, with nearly 100 Klansmen in attendance and guards blocking every exit, not because of what he'd done but because of *who he was.*

One morning at the coffee shop in Saxapahaw, we had Christina Sharpe's book between us and were thinking about Wyatt's inspiring life and tragic death, along with Sharpe's question: *What is the instruction here?*

How does it affect a Black child to hear that "once, there was a Black leader, and he was lynched right there next to the courthouse"?

We began to wonder, Would it be more respectful, more empowering, and more *truthful* to say that Wyatt Outlaw was *assassinated?*

We looked up definitions of "assassination" and read them aloud to each other.

From *Merriam-Webster*: "Murder by sudden or secret attack often for political reasons: the act or an instance of assassinating someone (such as a prominent political leader)."

From the *Cambridge Dictionary*: "The murder of someone famous or important."

From *Britannica*: "The murder of a public figure. The term typically refers to the killing of government leaders and other prominent persons for political purposes—such as to seize power, to start a revolution, to draw attention to a cause, to exact revenge, or to undermine a regime or its critics. Such politically motivated murders have taken place in all parts of the world and in every period of history."

From the *Oxford English Dictionary*: "The murder of a person (esp. a prominent public figure) in a planned attack, typically with a political or ideological motive, sometimes carried out by a hired or professional killer; a murderous attack of this kind."[15]

Wyatt was an important person. He was famous in the community where he lived—everyone knew him and what he stood for.

The motive for his murder—for all the outrages committed in Alamance and the surrounding counties—was political. He was killed by men who kept their identities secret, who killed at least one witness and intimidated many more.

We wonder whether claiming his killing as an assassination would return to him some of his power, some of his legacy. Whether it would dispel lies like the one that Audra Faucette heard.

Because his body was not hung and forgotten but marked with a message for everyone in the community to see: "Beware you guilty, both white and black." His life was mourned not only by those closest to him but by neighbors, league members, judges, writers, politicians, and more.

Word spread.

And spread.

And what happened next in the state of North Carolina could surely be counted as a revolution.

CHAPTER FOURTEEN

THE WAR AGAINST THE KLAN

We are conditioned from early school days to think of revolution as a positive, or ultimately necessary, act. The American Revolution threw off the tyranny of British colonial rule; the French Revolution abolished France's monarchy; the Haitian Revolution was a multi-ethnic revolt against French colonial rule. We don't always use the word in a political sense—the Industrial Revolution made the economies in America and Europe efficient and productive. When companies tell us a new product is "revolutionary," they mean it will change our lives for the better.

But "revolution" simply means an attempt—usually violent—to end the rule of one government or social order in favor of another. And to revolve is to turn in a circle, or curved path, around an axis.

The social and political order being challenged by Klan violence throughout the South, including the assassination of Wyatt Outlaw, was one of ascendant Black power and progress. These emerging Black gains were accomplished within the legal system, through the Reconstruction amendments and the resulting freedom to participate in civic life. Black men were voting and holding office in record numbers. Seventy percent of 1 million eligible Black men cast ballots in elections across the South in

1870, and in that same year Black politicians and community leaders held 15 percent of elected public positions.[1] Black families also made huge gains, buying land, building homes and churches, and sending their children to school. By 1880, the Black literacy rate was 30 percent—up from only 10 percent in 1860.[2]

Wyatt Outlaw provides an opportunity to see, in a single man's life and death, the revolutionary but peaceable and legal Black gains and the counterrevolutionary, violent backlash happening simultaneously in a small North Carolina town. Wyatt was financially successful and politically powerful, running a carpentry and mechanic's shop by day and leading Union League meetings by night and, through all of it, working side by side with a Republican mayor, Republican judge, and fellow constables to protect Graham's townspeople from Klan raids.

His assassination happened after more than a year of escalating violence and terror by Klansmen who desired a return to antebellum days of slavery and subjugation. Their targets were primarily Republican voters and organizers of Republican voters because, like the people they terrorized, they understood that the ballot was the ultimate source of power and progress for Black people. The vote was the axis around which both sets of revolutionaries—Black people seeking equality and white supremacists attempting to destroy it—revolved.

Officially, the Klan's violence was called by another name after Wyatt's assassination. Using the powers granted earlier that year by the Shoffner Act, Governor William Holden declared Alamance County in a state of insurrection on March 7, 1870, citing Wyatt Outlaw's hanging just days earlier and decrying the acts of "disguised assassins and murderers." In the proclamation, he voices his frustration with the lack of response by the public and local officials in "repressing these outrages" and in "preserving peace and order." He concludes that the people who have complained have had their lives endangered and that "many of the citizens of the county are so terrified that they dare not complain, or attempt the arrest of criminals in their midst. The civil officers of the county are silent and powerless."[3]

Though many white law enforcement officials were in league with the Klan, the Republicans weren't entirely friendless. John Stephens, a thirty-five-year-old white Republican elected to the state senate by Black voters whose rights he championed, bravely continued his work in the face of Klan threats; he was garroted and stabbed to death on May 21, 1870, in the Caswell County courthouse at a daytime meeting of Democrats. Union veteran, writer, lawyer, and judge Albion Tourgée sounded the alarm about Klan activities and the murders of Wyatt and Stephens, writing to senators and newspapers about the way national Republicans had abandoned brave loyalists to be killed by "the very dregs of the rebellion, the scum of the earth."[4]

An insurrection is, by definition, a violent uprising against an authority or government, and the legal use of that word—declaring an insurrection—gives governors and presidents the power to call in the National Guard or other troops to stop it. Though the words can describe similar acts, insurrection almost never has the same positive association with change and justice as revolution. Insurrection implies out-of-control, rampaging violence and destruction. An insurrection is by its nature difficult to quell and requires an extraordinary response.

Perhaps this is why, after the planned, organized, and violent attack on the US Capitol on January 6, 2021—an attempted coup orchestrated by outgoing president Donald Trump and his allies—right-wing politicians and their lawyers resisted the label "insurrection" and downplayed the seriousness of the crimes committed. In February 2024 arguments before the Supreme Court over Trump's eligibility for public office (Colorado had banned him from its presidential primary, citing the Insurrection Act), Trump's lawyers claimed that the attack was "a riot; it was not an insurrection. The events were shameful, criminal, violent—all of those things—but it did not qualify as insurrection."[5] Perhaps they'd read the column by conservative *New York Times* opinion writer Ross Douthat, who argued in January 2024 that "since the paradigmatic example [of insurrection] is the Civil War, in which hundreds of thousands of people were killed, a five-hour riot probably doesn't clear the bar."[6]

THE INSURRECTION ACT, THEN AND NOW

First enacted in 1792 as the Calling Forth Act, the Insurrection Act allows the president to deploy the nation's armed forces against civilians in cases of rebellion or lawlessness. Often criticized by legal experts as dangerously broad, as it does not define "insurrection," the law has been invoked thirty times in US history, from the Whiskey Rebellion of 1794 (a Pennsylvania revolt against liquor production taxes) to the 1992 use of federal troops in Los Angeles, California, to quell civil unrest after four white officers were acquitted in the taped beating of Black motorist Rodney King. Notably, the president who invoked the

(continued)

Insurrection Act the greatest number of times was Ulysses S. Grant, who sent federal troops into Southern states six times between 1871 and 1876, primarily to address Klan violence. During the civil rights era, Presidents Dwight D. Eisenhower, John F. Kennedy, and Lyndon Johnson all used the Insurrection Act to enforce court-ordered desegregation.*

Though reports by the Department of Justice suggest that President Donald Trump and his attorney general, Bill Barr, came close to invoking the Insurrection Act to dispel Black Lives Matter protests in Washington, DC, on June 1, 2020, it was Trump's own actions that reminded Americans of the word "insurrection" and its history.† On January 6, 2021, Trump addressed 53,000 followers at the White House Ellipse, a park south of the White House, telling them to proceed to the Capitol and "fight like hell" to prevent the certification of elected President Joseph R. Biden. Thousands swarmed the Capitol after Trump's speech, with between 2,000 and 2,500 rioters illegally entering the Capitol Building, where they vandalized, looted, and attacked police officers.‡

Also reflective of Reconstruction era politics, Trump has repeatedly lied about the events of January 6. In his third campaign for president, Trump falsely claimed that "nobody was killed," that the insurrection was "caused by [Democratic House Speaker] Nancy Pelosi," and that the rioters were unarmed. In addition, Trump has suggested in campaign events that he would invoke the Insurrection Act on his first day in office—among the reasons nonpartisan policy organizations like the Brennan Center for Justice advocate for its reform.**

---

* Joseph Nunn, "The Insurrection Act Explained," Brennan Center for Justice, April 21, 2022, www.brennancenter.org/our-work/research-reports/insurrection-act-explained.

† Josh Kovensky, "DOJ IG Details How Close Trump Came to Invoking Insurrection Act in 2022," Talking Points Memo, July 31, 2024, https://talkingpointsmemo.com/news/doj-ig-details-how-close-trump-came-to-invoking-insurrection-act-in-2020.

‡ Ryan Lucas, "Where the Jan. 6 Insurrection Investigation Stands, One Year Later," NPR, January 7, 2022, www.npr.org/2022/01/06/1070736018/jan-6-anniversary-investigation-cases-defendants-justice.

** Michael Waldman, "Trump's Insurrection Act Threat," Brennan Center for Justice, November 28, 2023, www.brennancenter.org/our-work/analysis-opinion/trumps-insurrection-act-threat.

The January 6 insurrection caused seven deaths and more than $2.7 million in damage to the Capitol.[7] Some 140 US Capitol and Metropolitan Police officers were assaulted and injured.[8] Insurrectionists erected a wooden gallows on the lawn and threatened to hang Vice President Mike Pence. That day reminded many Americans of the Civil War's insurrection not because of the body count or destruction caused but because many of the insurrectionists carried Confederate battle flags, wore Confederate flag bandannas, and displayed other emblems of white supremacy and hatred. They yelled racist epithets at Black police officers as they assaulted them. The specter of the noose and gallows clearly evokes the violence of the time just after the Civil War, when Black votes were so feared by white supremacists that they created the Ku Klux Klan.

The Insurrection Act, giving executive authority to suspend laws and call on troops to fight against citizens, dates back to the late eighteenth century. North Carolina's Shoffner Act, sponsored in December 1869 by Republican state senator T. M. Shoffner of Alamance, and the federal Enforcement Act of 1870 were each created with the specific purpose of protecting citizens from the terror, violence, and voter intimidation of the Ku Klux Klan.[9]

When we think about insurrection, we think of lawlessness and never feeling safe, not even in one's own home or workplace. This is what life was like in Alamance County, Caswell County, and some of the surrounding Piedmont when Wyatt Outlaw and other Reconstruction leaders attempted to protect their community from violent white supremacists.

In declaring an insurrection, Governor Holden suspended the writ of habeas corpus, meaning that accused Klan members could be apprehended and imprisoned without trial. Using a spy network that included detectives who infiltrated Klan meetings, Holden prepared indictments on hundreds of Klansmen. He appointed two officers, William Clarke, a Confederate colonel, and George Kirk, a Union officer, to a militia that moved secretly from the western part of the state into Alamance using the railroad.

In command of 400 troops made up of white Union veterans recruited from western North Carolina and eastern Tennessee, Kirk plowed through Alamance and into Caswell's county seat of Yanceyville, arresting dozens of men. Some of these arrests, including of Caswell County's ex-sheriff suspected of witnessing John Stephens's assassination, were harsh and threatening. Josiah Turner was interrogated and imprisoned in the same room in the Caswell County courthouse where Stephens was killed. The ex-sheriff claimed to have been whipped, and Turner, soon released, trumpeted his time in "Holden's Bastille."[10]

These short-lived rough tactics came nowhere near the murders, rapes, castrations, and skin-flaying beatings perpetuated by Klan members for many months. But with a member of the opposition in charge of a right-wing newspaper and many Klansmen in positions of power and authority in their communities, it was easy to exaggerate the violence and overstep of Kirk and his men. Though Holden had urged the militias to treat prisoners "humanely," Turner invented stories about violent interrogations, whippings, and hangings. He even promoted a false flag theory that acknowledged violence and unrest but blamed it on Klan victims: "All the murders, whippings and barn-burnings had been done by the Loyal Leaguers under the barb of Ku Klux!"[11]

In July, Holden asked for backup from President Grant, who sent in 700 troops to keep the peace. By the time violence had been quelled, some 200 Klansmen had been jailed, mostly from Alamance and Caswell Counties. Holden had enshrined habeas corpus as a basic right of North Carolinians in the state's new constitution, but he refused to honor writs issued on behalf of prisoners. Judge Parson, a Republican ally, ruled that he had this right. Attorneys representing the Klansmen appealed to federal district judge George Brooks, who ruled that the Fourteenth Amendment protected the Klansmen's rights. As Fergus Bordewich notes in *Klan War*, the constitutional amendment written "to protect freedmen from arbitrary arrest . . . was now being exploited on behalf of accused terrorists."[12]

At Holden's direction, Kirk released his prisoners after Grant's attorney general, Amos T. Akerman, ruled against the North Carolina governor. Two judges, Brooks and Pearson, received the prisoners. George Brooks released all of his immediately, and Richmond Pearson held fifty-nine of the hundred he had. But with no one willing to testify against them, all of the Klansmen, including anyone connected to Wyatt Outlaw's and John Stephens's murders, went free.

Conservative Democrats began calling this four-month period the "Kirk-Holden War," leaving the Klan out entirely, as if every violent act was the responsibility of the governor and his colonel. Unlike the nearly two years of Klan terrorism, no one died or was grievously injured. No one slept in the woods, had his house or property burned down, or saw his family terrorized. The Klan quieted its night raids; its work, for now, was done. Black and pro-Black leaders had been murdered, witnesses killed and maimed. By election time, Republicans had been thoroughly intimidated from the polls even as Democrats, full of righteous anger over Holden's use of state and federal power, flooded them. With Republican votes suppressed, conservative Democrats gained a majority of seats in the state House and senate.

Kirk-Holden War marker in Graham. (Photo by Belle Boggs.)

On December 14, 1870, William Holden was impeached on eight counts, and after a trial lasting seven weeks, he became the first US governor to be impeached, convicted, and removed from office.

He was pardoned by the North Carolina Senate in 2011. Unanimously, the state senators declared that Holden "dispatched the State militia to Alamance and Caswell counties to stop the violence being caused by the Ku Klux Klan . . . and [his] steadfast resistance to the Klan led to his being impeached and removed from office."[13]

The significantly more conservative House, led by then-Speaker Thom Tillis, did not take up the bill (though Tillis, as US senator, would in 2024 cosponsor the "No More Political Prosecutions Act" shortly after Donald Trump was convicted by a jury of thirty-four felony counts).[14] The pardon remained incomplete.

Today, the "Kirk-Holden War" is memorialized in Graham with a historical marker on Main Street, less than a mile from where Wyatt Outlaw was assassinated.

There is no marker for Wyatt.

CHAPTER FIFTEEN
GOVERNMENT

Dreama Caldwell belongs to a Facebook group called "Dreama-Drema-Dreema," a place for women who share her first name, if not its spelling. Many of the group's more than 400 members, mostly white women over forty, trace their names to relations in West Virginia, but that's not where her mother got the name. Dreama, who is forty-seven and Black, traces her family through North Carolina's Piedmont, in Alamance and Caswell and Person Counties. Her mother named her that because, when she was born, her eyes looked dreamy.

In 2020, Dreama ran for the Alamance County Board of Commissioners, a group that consisted of four white men and one white woman, all Republican, which remained all-white and all-Republican after the election. "It's not the end for Dreama," her campaign manager, Rion Thompson, told a crowd of masked organizers inside a Burlington church on a cold night, two weeks after the election she lost. Dreama, who was working, couldn't be there, but the crowd clapped and cheered for her.

The photo on her candidate page showed her standing next to a large mural across the street from the Alamance County Courthouse in Graham. LOVE ALWAYS WINS reads the mural, in tall black letters on a mottled pastel background. Painted in 2018, presumably in response to Donald Trump's racism and xenophobia or to the controversy surrounding the Confederate statue, the mural often shows up in local Instagram shots. Dreama stands just below the words, arms crossed and smiling warmly, next to a cut-out image of a girl holding a paintbrush. Her blue floral dress matches the blue in the girl's old-fashioned frock. The girl, who is white, stands on a stack of books whose titles are painted onto the spines: *Lord of the Flies*, *War and Peace*, *Charlotte's Web*, *Oliver Twist*. Two books stand out—*Gone with the Wind*, that famously racist romance, and *The Count of Monte Cristo*, the only book in the stack by a nonwhite author.

Had Dreama been elected, she would have been the first Black woman commissioner in county history and the first Democrat in six years. Though she is aware that Blackness is often perceived by white people as a threat, she has learned to approach spaces of community power in a methodical and patient way, aware that, at least in her community, it can take a long time for things to change, and she is determined to approach that change using the best options in front of her. She wanted to "get into the system, change things from the inside," she said, even though she knew it would mean sitting next to commissioners who expressed open hostility to causes she championed, like better funding for Title I schools or ending police brutality and harassment of people of color.[1]

County commissioners set the budget for the sheriff's department, appropriate funding for county public schools, and hear requests and commentary from the public at bimonthly meetings. Dreama was first introduced to this insular local process through Down Home North Carolina, a grassroots organizing group founded in Alamance and Cabarrus Counties in 2017 by Todd Zimmer.

Down Home started with the core belief that a multiracial, working-class coalition of rural folks could make change at the local level, and through this work they could grow leaders that didn't look, talk, or act like the politicians people were used to. Down Home members and leaders are substitute teachers, mechanics, bus drivers, and shift workers. Many have kids or grandkids and are used to choosing between fixing a car and paying rent, putting gas in the car or buying groceries. Some have criminal records or are in recovery; most are part of a huge constituency long ignored by the Democratic and Republican Parties.

The group starts in discussion, education, and community-building, offering everything from childcare to full meals for families at the early evening meetings. Dreama would take her two kids before her third-shift hotel manager job because, she said, "I always knew they'd be fed, and I always knew they'd have some fun."

Not that it was all barbecue and coloring pages—Down Home's slogan is both welcoming and serious: "Come on in y'all, we've got work to do." Unlike other local Democratic and progressive groups, it's not made up of retired people or folks with a lot of leisure time. Most Down Home members identify as working poor and pay a one-dollar-a-month membership fee.

Early on, the group was small, and members took turns drawing political engagement assignments from a hat. Dreama drew county commissioners and was at first disappointed by her "boring" assignment. She went, and it *was* dull in parts, but she also learned a lot about local governance and got to see and hear things that surprised her. She noted how little the commissioners seemed to care about funding the schools, in particular, and how unguarded, offensive, and out-of-touch the meetings felt. One commissioner, admitting that his family had been slaveholders, said that his family never called enslaved people "slaves"; they were just "workers."

"I couldn't believe the things people were saying," Dreama said. She reported everything she heard to her fellow members, and they began attending too, attracting notice from commissioners and community members. "How we got here," she likes to say now, "is because we weren't here."

Dreama volunteered in a Down Home campaign to end 287(g), a Department of Homeland Security program that allowed the Alamance sheriff's department to hold suspected immigrants for US Immigration and Customs Enforcement, or ICE, indefinitely in the Alamance County Jail.[2] The program had been halted after the Department of Justice, in 2012, found it led to discriminatory policing of both Latinx and Black people, but Sheriff Terry Johnson managed to rejoin the program in 2017, under the new Trump administration. Dreama and her Down Home colleagues attracted the attention of the ACLU, which filed suit against Alamance.

The next year, Dreama took a Down Home–organized bus tour of Alamance County. "I learned things I never knew," she said. She passed by the Confederate statue she'd always objected to and heard about Wyatt Outlaw's murder. She rode through downtown Burlington and found out about racial unrest that led to the police killing of Leon Mebane, a fifteen-year-old student of the same school Dreama had attended. "How did they cover it up so well?" she wondered. "I went home and I just cried."

In 2020, with the backing of Down Home, she made the decision to run for county commissioner. She attended Black Campaign School in DC, studying alongside the Reverend Gregory Drumwright and other Black community organizers. She came home and started knocking on doors again, talking to Black people and poor people who never voted because they'd never believed their vote counted.

LEON MEBANE

Ask someone from Alamance County who has now reached a certain age—say, early sixties on up—if they know the name Leon Mebane, and they'll probably nod grimly before telling you what stuck with them about that awful week in May 1969: schools closed by a walkout, a citywide curfew, a young man shot by police or National Guardsmen—some say seven times, others say seventeen. But if you weren't there to experience what became known as the Burlington race riots, you might have never heard the name Leon Mebane, whose unsolved death remains a deep wound for many in the community.

"This town won't talk about those riots unless its back is up against the wall," Lisa Mebane, Leon's sister, told the *Greensboro News and Record* in May 2001.* In 2020, she returned to Alamance County, where she marched in Burlington and Graham with other Black Lives Matter protesters, carrying a handmade sign that read, "Ask me about Leon Mebane."

The riots happened after unrest at Williams High School, a formerly all-white high school in Burlington that had added 66 Black students to its roster of 1,700 pupils. Many felt that white students were given preferential treatment by the faculty and that Black students had little say in the workings of the school. After spring cheerleading tryouts ended with zero Black students chosen for the squad, Black students walked out of Williams. They were joined in a sit-in protest by Black students from nearby Jordan Sellars High along with local college students and attempted to negotiate demands with the school administration. The next day, many white students stayed home from school; some who came got into fights with Black students. The town's long history of segregation, police violence, and economic injustice began to boil over.

Late on Friday, May 16, crowds of people thronged Rauhut Street, part of Burlington's historic Black Bottom neighborhood. Black residents faced off against police and National Guardsmen, who fired shotguns into the air. Rioters threw bottles and rocks, looted stores, and burned buildings. Leon Mebane, a fifteen-year-old eighth grader at Turrentine Middle School, went to the streets along with everyone else in his neighborhood. He was unarmed, and no one saw him destroying property or fighting.

(continued)

At about 3:30 the next morning, he was shot and killed in front of Countryside Grocery, which had burned earlier in the evening. Some witnesses said he was just looking around and put his hands up in surrender, while others said he was looting the building. His family never received any official answers or details about what happened, and no one from the city or state apologized. The family never fully recovered from their loss, the lack of closure, the absence of answers.

"What it boils down to is this: An unarmed black boy was killed," said Lisa Mebane. "For what?"

---

* Charlie Frago, "Violence of 1969 Still Haunts Victim's Family," *Greensboro News and Record*, May 19, 2001, https://greensboro.com.

"I don't vote, but I'll vote for you," they told her. Some sent her their "I voted" stickers as proof. Still, Dreama acknowledged, she knew there was a good chance she'd lose.

"Alamance is a long-game county," Dreama acknowledged. "It's about putting one leader in place at a time."

Dreama fought a hard race while working full-time as a night auditor at a hotel in Durham. She would often go directly from community events or candidate panels in Graham to Durham, where she'd work all night reconciling the day's receipts and making sure the hotel was stocked with soap, towels, shampoo, and coffee. Back home again, she'd stay up, responding to campaign emails and deleting or blocking abusive comments on her Facebook page. "Take care of your own community," commenters posted, though Dreama had never lived anywhere but Alamance. "Take care of the Black babies being aborted."

"I started off thinking all this was because of my past," Dreama said. "But then the realities came out. I was a Black female."

The week before the election, Sheriff Johnson ran a full-page ad in the *Alamance News*, the conservative local paper, depicting each of the three Democratic candidates at protests and marches. "Celebrating lawlessness," reads the caption below Dreama's picture. It shows her standing before the Graham courthouse's Confederate statue protesting the harsh penalties—a felony record and fines—levied against local citizens who voted illegally in 2018 while serving probation for minor crimes. Dreama knew how a record and court costs could follow a person—it was why she worked third shift at a hotel instead of in the profession she trained for, and why she rented a small house from a friend who would not put her through the hassle of a background check.

On the last day of early voting, October 31, 2020, Dreama waited near the polling place across the street from the sheriff's office. She was there to meet the marchers and early voters who planned to make their way to the polls with Reverend Drumwright, who had organized the I Am Change Legacy March to the Polls. This march, the second large march held in the county after George Floyd's murder, was focused on building electoral power through issues important to the Black Lives Matter movement—the removal of Confederate monuments from public lands and ending police brutality and disproportionate charges for Black and Latinx citizens.

Drumwright's vision for the Halloween march was dramatic. He had asked attendees of all ages and races to dress up, but not in the usual Marvel Comics or Disney princess costumes. "We're gonna march down these streets with Skittles in our hands in honor of Trayvon Martin's legacy," Drumwright said at an October 14 press conference on the courthouse steps. "We're gonna march down these streets with hoodies on our heads, with George Floyd's name on our backs."[3]

On Halloween, the polls closed at three, the last chance for unregistered voters to register and cast their ballots. Dreama waited, looking at her phone as the minutes ticked by. Refreshing her Facebook feed, she saw photos of bright-faced children and Black Lives Matter signs giving way to reports of tear gas, pepper spray, and arrests. Dismayed and fearful, she walked one block to the jail. She saw K-9 units, an armored vehicle, officers in tactical gear—nothing like what Dreama, or march organizers, had envisioned.

"Everybody always asks me about things wearing and tearing on me, but I don't expect anything else." She said this matter-of-factly, in a considered tone that communicated not defeat but awareness of a long battle behind her—and more fighting ahead.

• • • •

Dreama grew up in the Beaumont Apartments, a public housing complex of two-story brick buildings on the east side of Burlington. Her mother studied nursing at Alamance Community College, where Dreama would later study early childhood education. As a baby, she was cared for in the college's childcare center, and later she went to Eastlawn Elementary and Broadview Middle School, two schools serving primarily Black and Hispanic students.

At Eastlawn, her kindergarten teacher was Black, and there were other Black teachers and staff. It was a welcoming place, and she loved school. As Dreama got older, she was often in trouble, especially with white teachers, for talking. "My conduct scores were terrible," she remembered, "but I got A's in everything else."

Her third-grade teacher, a Black woman named Mrs. Isley, finally realized that Dreama was finishing her work before anyone else—she was bored. "This child needs to be tested for the gifted program," she told Dreama's mother. She explained how to request testing and how qualifying Dreama for the extra classes would challenge her and use up some of her restless energy. It took a while to arrange the tests—school administrators told her mother that they didn't have gifted kids "coming out of Beaumont"—but as Mrs. Isley suspected, she qualified. Dreama soon learned they didn't have many kids in their program at all. The gifted teacher was shared with another school and didn't have her own classroom. But they sometimes took special field trips, like one to the aquarium in Greensboro, where the children dissected a squid. They learned rudimentary computer programming, solved puzzles, and played word games. Dreama's behavior improved, though she still loved to talk.

Dreama remembered other children who probably should have been tested, like her, but whose parents or teachers were less persistent. Still, the kids in gifted and honors classes looked like her, and she excelled.

When Dreama was in seventh grade, her mother graduated with her degree in nursing, and they moved out of public housing. Dreama transferred into West Burlington's more affluent middle school, and "everything changed." Her new school had photography classes, a horseback riding club, and kids who went to country clubs and cotillions. On the first day of seventh grade, the students in Dreama's honors English class told her she was probably in the wrong classroom. She remembered stepping outside, her face burning, to check her schedule and then steeling herself to go back into the all-white space. No one apologized. Dreama later realized that for many of her new peers, it was the first time they'd really interacted with a Black person. She decided she would have to educate them, and she became known for speaking her mind.

Her favorite class was band, where she played the flute and no one argued about race. Sometimes before class they'd sit around, playing "I Never," and Dreama surprised her classmates with some of the things she'd never done. "What do you mean, you've never been to the state fair?" they asked her. She didn't tell them that there were places in their own county, even in their own town, where she wouldn't dare go. Dreama laughed, remembering their shock. "There are places I still wouldn't go."

She went to the same high school, Williams, that her mother attended in the 1970s. In the 1990s, when Dreama was in high school, it often seemed like nothing had changed. When Black students wore Malcolm X T-shirts after the Denzel Washington film premiered, white students responded with Confederate flag T-shirts that read "You wear your X, I'll wear mine." Once, Dreama came home upset that the sculpture of the school mascot, a squat bulldog, had been painted in blackface, and her mother told her about the time someone spray-painted "Colored" and "Whites only" on the outside of the school. The administrators and teachers let the graffiti stay up an entire day.

"All those people grew up," Dreama mused. They became teachers, principals, business owners, county commissioners. Her mother, who had put herself through nursing school, wanted Dreama to focus on her own success, and she worried about Dreama's tendency to challenge authority, to ask questions, to push. "She's about bettering yourself," Dreama explained. "I have a mindset to better my community."

Dreama and some of her friends in high school started an African American culture club, as well as a gospel choir, and they petitioned for an African American history class. The principal told them that if they could find a textbook and curriculum and a teacher, they could have the class. At the time, Dreama and her friends were so excited to have a chance to learn more about their history than slavery that they didn't mind doing the legwork. They found a white female history teacher who was willing to take on the class. She shared that some of the other teachers stopped speaking with her, but the students were grateful. "It was exactly what we needed," she said. "We were yearning to know our history."

Around that time, racial tensions at Williams escalated, and the administrators banned Confederate flag T-shirts. One white student brought a Confederate flag to school. He ran through the school hallways, yelling the N-word directly at his peers. Outraged Black students beat him so severely he had to be hospitalized, and administrators began policing the students' every move—especially, in Dreama's recollection, the Black students. They positioned police officers in the hallways, and when some of Dreama's friends had matching T-shirts made up—burgundy, with their nicknames in iron-on letters—they called them a gang and made a rule that no one could wear matching T-shirts or even dress up for Twin Day.

"It was the beginning of criminalizing our behavior," Dreama said, remembering how her Spanish honors teacher pulled her aside to ask whether she'd really joined a gang. How could she do something like that?, the teacher wanted to know. Dreama's response was simple: "If anyone else had worn the shirts, you would have called them a social club."

Throughout high school, Dreama made good grades—A's and B's, all in honors classes—while continuing with extracurriculars and working part-time at the library. She was often selected to represent the school in community outreach programs and joined the "Bulldog Buddy" program, a kind of Big Brothers/Big Sisters geared to at-risk local kids. Despite her leadership and good grades, no one talked to her about college. There was no meeting with a guidance counselor to talk about college applications or the SAT, and her parents didn't know how to navigate those gateways any better than Dreama did.

In the end she followed a path not dissimilar to her mother's: She got pregnant young, went to the local community college, and didn't leave the county. What would she study? Her passion for justice had once inspired her to imagine becoming a police officer or a lawyer. But a bad experience getting lost and being pulled over by officers who drew guns on Dreama and her friends soured her on policing. And it was too late, she felt, to be a lawyer. So, she began taking nursing classes, and while assigned for work study to the school's early childhood education, where she'd gone to day care, she had her aha moment. "Those little kids," she said, "they were like sponges." She realized that there was a path to change right in front of her.

• • • •

Daniel Ayers, born Daniel Osborne, grew up in Graham not far from the courthouse. He was homeschooled along with his older sister and younger brother by parents who enjoyed the freedom to take as many field trips as they wanted. His dad, an engineer at Duke Energy, earned enough to allow his mom, a nurse, to stay home with Daniel and his sister. The family did a lot together, participating in the nearby Snow Camp outdoor theater, which performed an annual show about Alamance County's history as a stop on the Underground Railroad. They took many trips to Gettysburg. Daniel and his dad both got into Civil War reenacting, though their Quaker family, which they trace back to the 1750s in what is now Alamance County, were all pacifists and abolitionists.

"My parents wanted me to see things about the world," Daniel said. "Other kids went to Disneyland. I've never been. I joke that we always went to places where large numbers of people died."[4]

Unlike Dreama, who didn't think of her high school activities as political, Daniel assumed he'd get into politics one day. In tenth grade, he entered the Hawbridge School, where Belle was his tenth and eleventh grade English teacher. He was an exceptionally polished student in the way that certain homeschooled students can be—worldly, well-spoken, tolerant of less-than-mature peers. The school didn't have student government then, but if it had,

Daniel surely would have been president. His peers naturally looked up to him, and he was popular, but he just as often spent his lunchtime playing music or joking with friends as he did talking with Ocasha Musah, who taught history. That was Daniel's favorite class, his natural home.

In 2013 Daniel left for Roanoke College, which gave him a scholarship, to study political science and came home in the summers to work. The summer he interned for Kay Hagan, a Democratic senator in Greensboro, he realized that maybe politics wasn't for him. He'd pictured himself talking policy and learning about the ins and outs of Democratic organizing, but instead he spent the summer answering phone calls from angry constituents. There was a panic room in the office, and he had to wear gloves and a mask to open the mail in case it was poisoned.

After graduating in 2017, he came back to Graham. Though he felt adrift and slightly abashed to be back where he started, his sleepy hometown had new signs of life—a coffee shop, a creperie, a record store. "I was so optimistic that Graham was turning a corner," he said. Though the town had always had a Mayberry-like feel to him, he knew from his studies about its racist past and agreed that the Confederate statue needed to come down. Surely, he thought, that would happen now.

Unlike Dreama, whose two children were born by the time she was his age, at twenty-two Daniel had few responsibilities, other than supporting himself and making use of his education. He was into Hunter S. Thompson and playing music—his sister had her own successful bluegrass band—and he thought about "going rogue," traveling the country as a vagabond. But he also found himself thinking about history class with Mr. Musah and transmitting that same love of learning to the next generation.

This was how Daniel wound up teaching history and social studies to middle school kids, in the basement of the same small charter school he had once attended. Like Ocasha Musah, he'd never studied education, so he was limited to schools that would hire him; regular public schools require a teaching certificate, but Hawbridge could allow up to 40 percent of its teachers to be uncertified, "lateral entry" educators. Also like Ocasha, he was drawn to the opportunity to create his own units and by a project-driven approach to North Carolina and American history.

Though Daniel learned about American history through field trips, deep reading, and experiences like the performances in Snow Camp, he taught it at Hawbridge through discussion. Part of Daniel's task was to teach American history through the history of North Carolina. Because there is no way to talk about North Carolina history without talking about race and racism, he'd begin with that. "It's in the DNA of the state," Daniel said. "Most kids have not been exposed to complex discussions about race. They don't realize it was invented."

In the Civil War unit Daniel taught, he emphasized three things: The war was America's bloodiest, the South came close to winning, and the war was fought over slavery. Almost all of his students are surprised by the first two facts. Many white students are surprised by the third.

"I always get a kid," Daniel began, then stopped himself and started again: "I always get a *white kid* who says, 'I thought the war was about states' rights.' I ask them, 'A state's right to what?' If they try some argument about freedom of trade, I say, 'Freedom to trade what? Who do you think was harvesting that tobacco, that cotton? What was the entire economy based on?' It's not controversial."

Daniel's classroom sounds like the opposite of the rural Virginia classrooms Belle attended as a middle school student, where the curriculum venerated Robert E. Lee and the idea her teachers corrected was that the war was about slavery. It was different from Sylvester's middle school in Graham, where he and his peers learned that slavery happened, and the Civil War happened, but no one made the connection between slavery and the war. In different ways, we each remember feeling that we weren't allowed to challenge their correction, that the teachers had access to some protected historical distinction that was at odds with what we instinctively knew.

Though they quieted us, our teachers never convinced us, and we're both sure they didn't convince many of our Black peers, either. In his predominantly white classes, Daniel also had stubborn outliers. These tend to be students from southern Alamance County, kids who grew up hearing about states' rights, heritage, and the valor of their ancestors from grandparents and parents.

Once, early in the school year, Daniel asked his seventh graders to design their own album cover, using images that represent them. One student brought a cover decorated with the Confederate flag and guns. Privately, Daniel asked this student why he'd chosen those particular images. The guns, the student explained, were about the importance of the Second Amendment. The flag was chosen because he wanted a Christian symbol—he claimed that he'd searched for an image on Google.

"What did you type on Google?" Daniel asked. "I typed in 'Confederate flag,'" the boy told him. After explaining the difference between the St. Andrew's cross and the Christian cross, he talked to the student about the symbolism of the flag, its history, and what it meant to some people—the student's own peers. Could he try again? The student did some more

Googling of Christian flags and then brought Daniel a new cover with an image of the Gay Pride flag, which he'd carefully labeled: "hot pink to represent sex, red for healing, yellow for sun, green for serenity with nature . . . I like to picture him seeing a Pride parade and thinking to himself, those people are really excited about Jesus!" Daniel said. "I told him that it was better, but let's not take that one home."

Seventh and eighth graders are so young, Daniel reflected. They don't always know what they're saying or why they're saying it. They're searching for identity in ways that don't always make sense, especially if you know little about the seventeen hours they spend outside of school. Another time, a student changed his laptop's background to a Confederate flag, and when Daniel noticed and asked him to change it, he refused.

"I asked him, in the hallway, if there was a reason he wouldn't change his background, and he said, 'I'm afraid that the Blacks are going to enslave us white people. They're going to take our guns,'" Daniel said, before explaining that the strangest part about the exchange was that the student himself was not, by a nineteenth- or even twenty-first-century understanding of that word, white. Exasperated, Daniel pointed through the window at the other students—an unusually diverse class for Hawbridge. "Do you think he's going to take your guns?" he asked, indicating a Black kid. "Not *him*," the student said. He couldn't answer who would or how such a thing would happen.

Eventually the student was suspended, and his parents pulled him from the school. Daniel, who'd convinced his peers not to harden against him—they'd only lose him that way—was sorry to see him go. "I want a class of Trump kids," Daniel admitted. "I want to teach them."

• • • •

"Hate in this county is generational," Dreama said. She saw it in some of the things the children she worked with in Head Start would say to her: "This is an N-word-mess. I don't have to listen to colored people."

"What color people is that?" she'd ask the children, and then she'd make them repeat what they'd said to their parents, who always exclaimed, "I have no idea where my child heard that!" Other parents were less veiled in their racism, even asking Dreama, at the start of February, not to teach their children about Martin Luther King or Rosa Parks.

She knew that all her students—Black, white, Latinx—were growing up in poverty and that the services she was providing were essential: nutrition and socialization and culture and helping families access dental care.

"I'm about changing the child's behavior," she said. "I know the garbage they're getting at home. I was an adult before I learned about local history, that we'd had a race riot in Burlington or about Wyatt Outlaw's murder. I didn't even realize that the riot had a direct correlation to my high school. All of those things were not taught."

Dreama might not have found her way into politics and organizing, might have stayed a teacher all her life, had a terrible accident not happened at the preschool where she worked in Chapel Hill. After years of schooling and countless exams, she had become a licensed teacher and administrator with a good job and a school of kids she loved. A bus monitor left a child on the bus on a hot July day, where she sat for six hours. Dreama, who had driven the bus, was the executive director.

"It was a hard, hard time," Dreama said. The school was closed down immediately, and she never got to say goodbye to the child, who survived but was taken to the hospital for dehydration. Dreama turned herself in and was held on a $40,000 bond. That meant that she needed $4,000. No one she knew had that much cash, and it took her sister three days to work things out with a bail bondsman. Dreama spent those days in jail. "If my sister didn't have access to a 401K, I would have spent a very long time [there], probably a year."

The next expense was a lawyer. She was facing so much potential jail time that she was afraid to get a court-appointed attorney, but the lawyers she consulted quoted fees of $13,000, $15,000, $20,000 to take the case. Finally she found one of her cousin's sorority sisters who agreed to represent her for $5,000. The attorney didn't have experience with felony cases, and she urged Dreama to take a plea deal. In exchange for her freedom and a waiving of court costs, Dreama accepted a felony record and the end of her twenty-year career in education.

She looks back on the decision with sadness but no regrets. "I accepted the responsibility, and I still have a raw spot for that child," she said. She apologized to the child's mother in court and asked the judge whether part of her sentencing could include talking to other day care workers about how to avoid a tragedy like this one.

The judge didn't take her up on the offer, and Dreama knew she had to turn the experience into something positive. She began learning about the movement to end cash bail and how being held in jail while waiting for a trial wasn't about guilt or innocence or even danger to society but about what kind of resources you have at your disposal. "That's how I found Down Home," she said. She joined a working group called Stop Criminalizing the Poor and learned about Kalief Browder, a Black man from the Bronx held for three years, much of that in solitary confinement, on charges of theft. Though Browder was released, his charges dismissed, those years in solitary damaged him, and he eventually committed suicide.[5] Dreama knew she had to try to end cash bail in Alamance County, and she began telling her story. This was how she became a candidate for county commissioner.

Though she never hid her past, there were people who acted like she did. They'd post her mug shot—Alamance County releases those, which get published in local papers—to her Facebook page or Twitter, calling her a piece of shit, a Black b——. A well-known local pastor made comments to Facebook so harsh the Graham police chief asked him to take them down.

Like the rest of Dreama's career, her new political life is bigger than her own story. It's about reckoning with the inequalities that surround her family and friends and telling people in power that they must do better. Why are there the same temporary learning trailers at Eastlawn as there were when she attended that school? Why do Black people represent a third of Alamance County's population but more than half of the prison population?

Why did it take her so long to learn about Wyatt Outlaw or Leon Mebane? What did it cost for sheriff's deputies to guard a Confederate monument twenty-four hours a day, and what else could the town do with those resources?

"The Confederate sympathizers, they're as much a victim as we are," Dreama said. "They only know what they've been taught."

• • • •

When Daniel Ayers looks at downtown Graham—the circle around the courthouse and the small businesses that line Main Street—he is used to seeing a familiar, welcoming space. *There's the barber where I had my first haircut, and where I still had my hair cut at eighteen,* he thinks. *There's the soda shop where I went with my friends. There's the theater where I had my first date.*

That sense of comfort in the familiar began to change after George Floyd's murder. In the summer of 2020, he went to a Black Lives Matter march and stood, masked, before the statue. He chanted Leon Mebane's name and Wyatt Outlaw's name—histories that he too learned only recently.

Across the street, counterprotesters stood jeering and unmasked. They held Confederate flags and chanted, "Four more years of making liberals cry like bitches." They chanted, "My black turd matters." Daniel looked into the crowd and was startled to see someone carrying a German flag and sporting a swastika tattoo.

He shook his head, remembering the scene. "I was in this place where I spent all my formative years. And I was standing right next to a Nazi. Where do we go from here?"

As a student and teacher of history, of course Daniel knew the reference to Dr. King, but his words had the feeling not of quotation but of a real question—one without easy answers. Trump was voted out in 2020, but not by North Carolina. Statues were coming down and buildings were getting renamed, but not in Graham. Not in Alamance.

What's next? How do we fix this?

• • • •

On a Monday night in June 2024, the Alamance County Commissioners held their monthly meeting in the administrative courthouse. Before the meeting, some twenty Down Home members stood in front of the Historical Courthouse, just a block away, with signs reading "Our Kids Are in Need! Fund Schools to Succeed" and "Pam Thompson Said: No More Band-Aids for ABSS Budget." Commissioner Thompson had been targeted as a potential ally by Down Home in its spring 2024 campaign to secure full funding for the Alamance Burlington Public School system. Though Thompson was a Republican, she'd made statements sympathetic to public schools and the repair of a system so neglected and underfunded that in August 2023, the entire school system was closed for two weeks after toxic mold was discovered in sixteen schools.[6]

Ebony Pinnix, a Down Home organizer and Alamance native, was one of the parents whose work and family life was disrupted by the last-minute school closure. She'd gotten involved with Down Home back in 2020, when she served as a medic at the July 11 Black Lives Matter protest.

"I was seeing those blue [Down Home] T-shirts everywhere that summer," she said, including at protests. With Down Home, she picked up important skills and leaned into existing capacities. She also met new mentors. "One day, I was on the side of the street, and the police were looking right at us and laughing. But standing beside me was this lady who was so nice. 'Don't worry about those folks,' she told me. 'They're ashamed that we're building this much power.' That was Dreama Caldwell."[7]

Though Ebony had to take a yearlong break from organizing after the traumatic experience at the October 31 I Am Change Legacy March to the Polls, where she was pepper-fogged along with more than 200 other protesters, she returned to Down Home in late 2021 and now works for the organization full-time. Ebony's Alamance County chapter has focused especially on issues in public schools, and her experience as a parent and a former Alamance–Burlington student motivated her leadership of Down Home's "Fund Our Schools to Succeed" campaign, which started in 2024 with school board listening sessions. After strategizing with school board members, including Seneca Rogers, the county's only Black school board member, she and her fellow organizers attended dozens of meetings, read through hundreds of pages of budget documents, and organized parents, students, and community members to send emails and make public comments.

At this final commissioner meeting, Ebony wore a bright yellow "Elect Working People for Everything" T-shirt, one of Down Home's core slogans. Her long braids were tucked into a kente cloth head wrap, and she smiled warmly at supporters, new arrivals, and media.

Ebony passed out stickers to the small sign-holding crowd, took video, and spoke to local television reporters, who positioned their cameras awkwardly on the west side of the Confederate monument. Close to six o'clock, the crowd made its way to the courthouse, where supporters filled the seats in the courtroom. In the adjacent spillover room, twenty-five Down Home members and school budget supporters, including Ebony, leaned forward to watch the proceedings on a video feed from the courtroom. They were hoping for full approval of the school board's $59 million budget request—an increase that would help fix the decaying buildings, prevent teacher and staff layoffs, and restore summer school classes cut during the budget crisis. In heated talks, the commissioners would commit to only a third of the board's increased ask.

Daniel Ayers, who had this year started a popular North Carolina politics-based podcast, *The Hometown Holler* ("like every white guy with an opinion," he sheepishly joked), settled into a bench on the side. He was one of more than a dozen speakers to make comments in favor of public school funding. He'd quit teaching at Hawbridge in 2022 but now worked as a consultant and tutor, helping local kids earn scholarships to college. Other speakers included students, parents, former teachers, and retirees.

Finally, Republican commissioner Craig Turner proposed a compromise that would get the school system within $4 million of its targeted budget—not the whole pie, but much closer to whole than many expected. Commissioner chair John Paisley opposed the increase in taxes, but Turner's proposed budget passed, three to two.

During and after the vote, Ebony Pinnix showed no sign of celebration or defeat. She took notes and approached the screen to take photos of projected budget numbers with her smartphone. Dreama, the mentor and friend who'd coached her through strategies of co-governance, wasn't there and had in fact moved away from Alamance County to a modest house on a quiet street in Greensboro. But she hadn't left the fight. In 2020, after losing the county commissioner election, she began working full-time as an organizer for Down Home. In August 2021, she was appointed the organization's co-executive director, alongside founder Todd Zimmer.

Since then, wins for Down Home include the passage of Medicaid expansion in North Carolina, which brought health care coverage to some 600,000 residents; numerous state and local election wins, including electing the first Black woman to Burlington City Council; preventing a Republican supermajority in 2022 (later undone by the defection of former Democrat Tricia Cotham); and many local issue-driven wins, including successfully funded anti-eviction, public park, and school supply programs in rural counties around the state.

In many ways, Down Home looks different from the Union League meetings held more than 150 years ago. There's no script to follow, and meetings aren't held in secret. Union Leagues sometimes included women and white people, but they were predominantly male and Black, while Down Home boasts racial, gender, ethnic, and generational diversity. Radical Republicans, including Union League members, were often part of mutual aid societies that assisted poor and working-class people, but Down Home is able to fundraise and organize to include resources for an expanded group of members and recruits. At most Down Home events, there's a wide range of things to keep people feeling comfortable and welcomed: quiet rooms for folks who need to take a moment, Narcan for anyone who may be in an opioid emergency, and frequent check-ins to make sure that members are being heard.

Down Home trainings offer childcare, food, and transportation assistance. Instead of adopting an elevated formality (it's hard to imagine one of today's organizers intoning, "All present are true and worthy" after calling roll), Down Homies, as they call themselves, lean into their accents and vernacular. They lead raucous trainings, with chants from different county groups and short skits illustrating the disappearance of the social safety net. "That ain't right," members will call out when fellow members talk about a recent injustice they've been fighting: unfair evictions, environmental racism, bus service that stops at 6:00 p.m.

"We're all swimming in the same stuff," Dreama said.

But like Union Leaguers, they understand that they're fighting to be heard in a political climate that would prefer to ignore poor and working-class people. Ebony's bright yellow "Elect Working People for Everything" T-shirt—which Dreama and others wore too—represents a core value that Wyatt Outlaw and his fellow Union Leaguers would have shared.

Working people in Alamance County during Reconstruction were Black and white and Native, poor and middle-class, male and female. Today's coalition is even more diverse, and as it was in the 1860s and 1870s, that's entirely by design. As Fergus Bordewich writes in *Klan War*, "The league

Down Home members wearing campaign T-shirts.
(Photo by Chris Ashley, courtesy of Down Home North Carolina.)

represented precisely what conservatives most feared: a dynamic Black political movement allied with Radical whites and determined to revolutionize government in the South."[8]

Down Home members also focus on education, access to the polls, and growing leadership from within.

"Campaigns, for us, are about training and development of community leaders," Dreama said. This is why, though she was not in attendance for the commissioner vote to increase education funding, she called Ebony right away to congratulate her and reinforce the scale of the accomplishment achieved by her group, which required convincing three Republicans to vote to increase taxes in support of public education. "Alamance wins always look different," Dreama allowed.

That's part of growing leadership too—teaching idealistic progressives that meaningful change can be incremental, as long as people keep fighting.

Like Dreama and Daniel, Ebony acknowledged the challenges but has no plans to quit.

"We're not ending the campaign there," she said. "We still need a full building study. It'll go through the fall, and maybe into next year."

There's one more thing that connects Union Leaguers like Wyatt Outlaw, Henry Holt, and Jim Williams to today's locally focused social justice workers, like Dreama Caldwell and Ebony Pinnix: the danger, and the burnout, of fighting a status quo established by white supremacists. As much as the experiences hurt her, Ebony was matter-of-fact about the threats and harassment she's faced. "Anytime you do anything for good, you're in danger," she said.

Dreama sought somatic therapy after the trauma of 2020's protests and politics, and she believes that the intense pushback, while harmful, needs to be remembered and reflected on by the community.

"People always ask why I share memories, every year, of Halloween 2020," Dreama said. "I do it because it put an indentation in my life."

An indentation in my life—a divot, a hole, a crevice—but also a furrow. Somewhere for water to flow.

CHAPTER SIXTEEN
OF ANGELS AND DEMONS

SYLVESTER

Somewhere along the line, maybe I was sixteen or seventeen years old, I was told by a Graham townsperson about a man being hung in Court Square. I don't remember who told me, and I don't remember the feeling I got from that information. What I do remember is thinking that that must have been a long time ago, *because of course things like that don't happen nowadays*. It seemed like some distant happening of the past, completely separate from my life. It would take a move away from Alamance, several years, and a return to Alamance before I heard the story again, and with any names attached to it. You see, unless you're talking to the right person in Graham—and those folks are hard to find if you don't know where to look—local history is cherry-picked, the good always ready to be spread like wildfire, and the bad and ugly sent to the graves with the ol' folks.

By my senior year at Graham High, my brother, Timothy, had been diagnosed with lupus; my mother had long since been laid off from Kayser-Roth, a sock and hosiery weaving plant in west Graham; and in all of life's traffic, I had determined that I was supposed to be some kind of family savior.

I had been lugging a gold-lacquer junker Yamaha tuba with no case back and forth to school throughout my freshman, sophomore, and junior years.

The tuba is great for learning music, not great for making friends. But for a quiet kid who found conversation awkward, the "practice room" became a place of refuge. I became a better musician every year, winning the John Philip Sousa band award and participating in All-State orchestras. I remember the thrill of blasting OutKast from my sousaphone bell as we marched in step across grassy football fields in our red and black "devil" uniforms during halftime shows.

We played "I Like the Way You Move" and "Hey Ya!" ad nauseam at games that almost always drew in shoulder-to-shoulder, ball cap–wearing, potbellied country crowds. In the offseason, concert band and jazz band were the classes that kept my attention, more so than any other subjects in school. Stravinsky's *Firebird* and excerpts of Berlioz's *Symphonie fantastique* were all but glued to my music stand. I'd pull my instrument out a few minutes before the start of class to play fast scales and flashy presto passages just to see the look on other kids' faces as my fingers manipulated the valves of the tuba at rapid speeds like a typewriter. Those kinds of moments were the only times I felt validated and useful in school. And the band hall is where we, at least on occasion and even outside the month of February, would study the works written by people who looked like me.

So, I decided that this would be my magic carpet. From then on, I started to grab every piece of wisdom I could, bugging well-seasoned musicians with questions and using my grocery store paycheck to pay for lessons.

I took piano from a gospel musician named Joe Jeffries, a warmhearted Black man in his seventies who wore collar shirts neatly pressed everywhere he'd go. I would pick him up on Saturdays in my new-to-me 1992 navy blue Chevy Lumina and take him to Children's Chapel United Church of Christ in Graham, where a deacon would meet us to unlock the doors. It was the one we attended after transferring from St. Luke Christian Church during one of my family's many moves. The three arched stained-glass windows look down on Highway 54 in "Trinity" fashion. There's a cemetery behind the church, dug on land where enslaved people use to meet for worship on Sunday mornings. The first Children's Chapel building was constructed in 1876, but the enslaved had been meeting on the land to listen to Reverend James Willis Wellons, a white man who helped build up Black church communities and went on to cofound Elon College—now Elon University. One of his assistants, Daniel A. Long, brother of Reconstruction-era Graham KKK leader Jacob A. Long, called the worshippers "children," a term often used by whites to describe even adult slaves. This is where the church gets its name.

As we sat at the sanctuary piano, Joe would take a leftover Sunday service program, roll it up, and slap my hand with it every time I tried to look down to see what I was playing.

"Now, have those keys moved the last time you looked down, sir?" he'd ask with lips pursed, brows raised, and one fist on his hip.

"Not this time, Mr. Joe," I'd laugh.

Those piano lessons had a profound impact on me as a high school senior. Not only were they lessons about passing diminished chords or sharp eleventh extensions or how to pick up a key by ear, but they were lessons in the sharing of stories. There's so much value in sitting and playing with the older generations. Joe was a storyteller. He lived a modest life with a modest home and no car, but the music, he was eager to pass that along. Gospel is loaded with the sounds and messages of the enslaved and their descendants. Playing melodies written so long ago was like having a direct landline to their composers, the music growing in style and richness with each generation.

Later, after receiving a tuba scholarship, I stored away my basketball and packed some boxes, loaded my Chevy Lumina, and headed west (though only thirty minutes away) for Greensboro College. Just making it to college felt like a major accomplishment, since my mother had to drop out in eighth grade and my stepfather in second grade. I wanted to make them proud. Naively, I stepped onto campus with every ambition to become Harry Connick, Quincy Jones, Mozart, and Luther Vandross rolled into one.

• • • •

After hiking a few wide granite steps to the entrance of Odell Memorial, the music and theater building, and swinging open the glass doors, I'd enter a spacious lobby with a marble-topped wrought-iron table, a sparkling chandelier, and eggshell-white-and-gray marble floors. Offices of professors and department heads lined the lobby walls. On the other floors were dance studios and costume shops, music classrooms and digital music studios. If you had told me this was heaven, I would have believed you.

But my time in college proved to be very arduous. There were the late-night stocking shifts at Lowes Foods, at times walking home when my car wouldn't start, and the early-morning music theory classes. There was the jarring transition from small town to "city life" to contend with and the workload that came with rehearsals and general education classes. And then there was the undiagnosed dyslexia, which gave me headaches when I read anything long and maintained a tight grip on my organizational skills and ability to get through assignments in a timely manner. Nonetheless, I took full advantage of my time there. I transcribed modal jazz improvisations from Miles Davis's *Kind of Blue*. I learned to scat Charlie Parker solos. I performed harmonic analysis on complicated works like Pyotr Tchaikovsky's Violin Concerto in D Major, op. 35, and William Grant Still's "Afro-American Symphony No.1 in A-flat Major."

One of the great differences between high school and college was that all of a sudden I was studying artistic geniuses of all races with an endless catalog of work. I remember sitting and reading about the great African French composer Joseph Bologne, Chevalier de Saint-Georges, born of a wealthy white French father and a Senegalese enslaved mother. He was a true Renaissance man, stretching his brilliance to many fields, crafts, and disciplines. His classical music was made of beauty and sophistication, and he was a contemporary and friend of Mozart's. I recall the story of Saint-Georges being suggested as maestro of the Paris Opera but ultimately denied because three sopranos in the company wrote to the queen about their discomfort with a man of mixed race. I learned that Saint-Georges was attacked and assaulted by police in Paris in 1779. It reminded me of the story of Miles Davis, who was beaten up by police during a set break of a show at a nightclub and went back to finish the second set with blood on his forehead. I thought about how racism and police brutality had reared its ugly head across the African diaspora . . . and across time. I thought about what knowing this history meant to me, the good and the bad, and how the gaps in knowledge of history have often resulted in a skewed perception of the African American reality—an unawareness of or apathy toward the struggle, even by your own friends.

While in class or passing time in the lobby of Odell, I would occasionally get comments from other students like "You sound white" or "I know you're not from the hood" or, from some of the white kids, "I probably have more soul than you," as if there were some expectation or litmus test to what Blackness should feel and sound like. I found those comments painful. I don't know why. Maybe because I wanted to be more accepted for who I was. Did I truly *know* who I was? Maybe it was because somewhere deep down and in the back of my mind, I felt a sense of betrayal. Not betrayal toward me but *from* me.

Were they right? Whatever "Black" was, was I enough of it? Was there some style or phraseology or code of conduct that I had missed the memo on and needed to study and become? After all, I was used to, and even fatigued from, hearing those kinds of judgments from not only white but Black people from varied generations. These are the kinds of questions that could easily plague a young Black kid—as they did me.

I remember stepping into Benjy Springs's jazz band class for the first time after being asked to join in on bass trombone. Benjy, himself obsessed with Basie and just as well known for his catch phrases as for his master trumpet playing, was always happy to give the butt-kicking that young musicians needed. If we came in late or made it obvious that we had not practiced the music, with a Southern drawl suitable for any North Carolina band hall he would tell us we were "FIRED, FIRED, FIRED." And, yes, we would hear it often. It was how he used to let us in on what the professional world would be like. It wasn't enough just to play the music; it had to be done authentically. Swing where it's supposed to be swung. Pay tribute to the ones who created the music every time you play.

The proscenium stage in the 787-seat Huggins Auditorium at Greensboro College has red show curtains just large enough to swallow a nervous young actor. Robert Overman, director of vocal studies, a big and tall baritone who won over the auditioners at the Metropolitan Opera in the late 1970s, told me I should audition for a character named Roger from *Grease* after hearing me sing.

As green as I was, I agreed to show up.

With my teeth chattering, my knees knocking, and sweat dripping down the back of my neck, I felt myself almost walking backward onto the Huggins stage to do a cold read. When told to *go*, I flung myself around, turning my back "upstage," away from the audience, and remained that way as I whispered the entirety of the scene. They couldn't see me; they couldn't hear me. I was sure I wouldn't get the part until it came time to sing a song called "Mooning." I closed my eyes, stood center stage, and crooned and overproduced my vibrato, but I got through the thirty-two bars. I somehow got the part.

I attended the first several rehearsals of *Grease*. I would think about Mama, Timothy, Carla, and my aging stepfather, Willie, who had broken his leg while I was away. That sense of responsibility alone kept me in the midnight grocery aisles stocking canned pork and beans and oversize jugs of laundry detergent instead of in the dance studio. I initially struggled with even the idea that education came before work. It's not what I was taught. It was immediate survival first. Much like Willie, who was pulled out of school to work in the fields in rural South Carolina and never again stepped foot in a classroom from second grade on, that same lesson had unintentionally been passed on to me, a first-generation college student.

I never finished *Grease*. Professor Schram asked me to step aside after I had missed too many rehearsals. I felt ashamed for having squandered an opportunity. And I knew it was time to start breaking generational curses. I started to take theater seriously, eventually being cast in shows like *Man of La Mancha*, *The Secret Garden*, *Fiddler on the Roof* (yes, I played a Black Lazar Wolf), and numerous other theater productions in my undergrad.

And in my time away at school, things had changed. After all that education, doors that were once slammed shut were being held wide open. I felt an odd sense of freedom. I was no longer sure that I ever wanted to go back.

Aaron, a slinky guitar student from Maryland who often chuckled after his own jokes, had just won a guitar position in the Air Force Band.

He said, "You know, all the military bands are good. You should give this a shot."

His suggestion lingered with me. I was still looking for something that I left home to find, though I wasn't sure I knew what that was anymore.

• • • •

Camp Red Cloud was stationed between Seoul and the demilitarized zone in South Korea. It's a small base with a golf course right in the middle. To get to the army band hall, which is where we rehearsed and trained every day, we would walk a fifteen-minute path from the barracks to the company area. In the winter, that meant trudging in wet socks, with frozen toes, through several feet of snow for months at a time. The Second Infantry Division was constantly in training mode. With no peace treaty signed with North Korea, we rehearsed attack scenarios on a regular basis, early in the morning and late at night. Band member or no band member, you trained like the others. I now had a rifle in one hand and a tuba in the other.

African Americans had been fighting in American wars throughout the country's history, though much of it came by way of segregated units until 1948 when Harry Truman, whose reputation was anything but that of a progressive antiracist, ordered the desegregation of forces. This gave way for Black people to be promoted more often—eventually.

In the first years of Obama's presidency, the active-duty army received a spike in Black enlistment. In 2010, 22 percent of active-duty members were Black, a leap from 16.1 percent in 2008. So by the time I arrived at the Special Troops Battalion at Red Cloud in 2009, there was plenty of representation to go around. There were Black sergeants and warrant officers, Black sergeants major. But that somehow didn't stop even those in high positions from maintaining a worldview that often degraded their own kind.

The band's first sergeant, a tall pale bald man who loved to have "theater chat" and always looked like he was chewing on gum even when he wasn't, sent me to the promotion board seven months after I arrived at the unit. However, the promotion board was being held in three days—not a lot of time to prepare. I dug into my study guide, shaped up on every regulation I could memorize, and meticulously polished every piece of brass on my Class A uniform. I thought, *I'm definitely as ready as I can be.*

I was laughed out of that promotion board room. Literally. I mean, as soon as I started to speak. I couldn't tell whether they were laughing because something was funny or whether it was all a part of some intentional tactic to apply pressure. I walked back to my barracks in my shiny shoes and neatly formed beret. I closed the door, sat on my neatly made bed, and stared at the wall with watery eyes. I knew I hadn't been recommended for promotion.

Later in the evening, I ran into one of the first sergeants who sat on the board. "Can I tell you something?" he whispered closely in a room full of off-duty soldiers. "You sound like a white man."

"What does that mean?" I asked.

"Intellect. You sound intellectual. No offense. It's just funny."

He wasn't the only one. I got other comments in the coming days, similar in kind, from other Black army leaders. I realized that it wasn't the individual comments that bugged me. Those were easy to brush off. It was the mentality. Where does it come from? Why does it persist? Much like the kids back at school, others' perception of Blackness seemed narrow. It wasn't just about how much *soul* you have or a certain way of walking; it was about a lack of knowledge as to what Black people had contributed to our society even pre-emancipation. Even serving under the first Black commander-in-chief couldn't sway them.

Over time I began to obsess about the matter—what people knew and didn't know about the history of Blackness in America. I went on from Korea to serve at Fort Lee in Virginia and even did some temporary duty at Fort Sam Houston in Texas. But I became more and more restless, eager to get home. Once my contract was up, that's what I did.

Driving past Children's Chapel UCC, the church my family had transferred to after moving from Mebane to Graham, I was reminded of the after-service conversations I'd have with church musicians, bugging them with questions like "How did you do that?" and "Can you teach me?" Seeing the windowpanes of the church evoked images of that sharp-dressed kid sitting in the pews with a Bible in his hands pretending to hang onto every word the preacher said while daydreaming about being a superhero.

The street signs were familiar. The storefronts, recognizable. The food, nostalgic. Yet it wasn't till I set my duffel bag down on the living room floor and pulled off my boots and stuffed them in the corner of the closet that it hit me. I was home again.

Army life changed the lens through which I viewed the world. I was older and more attentive to detail. I started to notice more often what I'd taken for granted before. White churches and Black churches, white bars and Black bars, white parts of town and Black parts of town, white events and Black events. The separation and division, with few exceptions, was more obvious after being away.

There was something different about Alamance County, I realized. All the beautiful landscapes and friendly Southern hospitality could be quickly juxtaposed with memories of being followed a little too long by a police officer after leaving a night shift, or being called the N-word repeatedly by a drunken cowboy on a crazy late-night bar rant, or being stopped in broad daylight while coming home from college in my fully packed sedan, just so the officer could make sure the stuff in the back seat wasn't stolen.

"That's 'cause Alamance racist as hell," one of my Black Greensboro friends told me.

This was something the older generation in town already knew.

"You got your passport?" an older Black man said to me once.

"No, I don't," I replied.

"Well, get it. 'Cause you're a king everywhere else you go."

He went on about the weight he feels when he's here in the United States and particularly in his own hometown. He was from the area, but he was gone all the time. And it was true. I did feel a weight at home that I didn't feel in other places. And that's maybe why when I got back into the theater, I was drawn to plays that had a message, playing characters like *Ragtime*'s Coalhouse, a well-educated musician during the Harlem Renaissance whose future is ripped from him when his fiancée is killed by police.

My activism remained mainly onstage, as I performed pieces written by others about injustices and sparked conversation that way. I was content with theater being my voice for years. I was content until May 2020, when I saw a video of a Black man being murdered by Minneapolis police in front of my eyes. It was on Facebook. It was public. A public lynching.

• • • •

By early 2020, I knew that the United States was already in for a historically divisive election, with Trump's last three years having been some of the most racially tense in recent history. But we didn't have to wait for the summer for the climate to heat up the political aisles. After the video of George Floyd's murder was released and spread like wildfire to the public, protests, riots, and collective actions began happening everywhere, including outside the country.

Maybe the most unlikely place for that civil unrest was right here in Graham, North Carolina. Unlikely because the tactics that racists used to induce fear had been passed down through the generations. There were many places in the country where you could exercise your First Amendment right and never fear you wouldn't make it home safely. Not here. Any action, big or small, was sure to be met with violent opposition. Even silent demonstrations garnered attention from law enforcement, neo-Confederates, and Trump supporters.

Through a complicated history, Alamance County had an undoubted reputation for treasonous rebellion and sympathy for the rebellious. The strongest evidence of that was the Confederate monument that stood thirty feet high in the middle of town on the north side of the courthouse. And in light of the protests that had broken out all over the country, the sheriff's department, the Graham Police Department, and Confederate sympathizers began preparations to protect not only private property but public heritage. Whether your intention was to harm the statue or not, they would assume that was your intention. And leading up to the George Floyd murder, tensions between police forces and their citizens in town were already on edge.

Bobby Harvey, a forty-one-year-old Black man, had been assaulted by Burlington police in October of the previous year. After a call to the residential area about a potential assault and after a small conversation with Harvey, police body camera footage showed a quick escalation by the police and Harvey responding aggressively, and in fear, to the attack. This all happened as onlookers shouted, becoming visibly upset over what they were seeing.[1]

And in January 2020, twenty-year-old Jaquyn Light was killed by Graham police as they attempted to serve a warrant for larceny. Light was unarmed. Marcus Pollock, a Black officer posted behind the house under the cover of night, reportedly pulled the trigger reactionarily as Jaquyn exited his front porch. No charges were filed.[2]

On May 18, 2020, then–County Commissioner Bill Lashley commented on his former days as a police officer at a commissioners meeting. "You can't do now what we could do when I was on. I used to beat the hell out of them, but you can't do that now," he said, eliciting a laugh from Sheriff Terry Johnson and others in the meeting room at Alamance County Offices. Though he later apologized, the damage was done. We'd seen, briefly, a public window into the mentality of policing.[3]

County and city officials made numerous unconstitutional attempts to diminish protest rights. Though no damage had been done in any protest,

JAQUYN LIGHT

The May 25, 2020, Minneapolis police murder of George Floyd, an unarmed forty-six-year-old Black man and father of five, sparked protests and demonstrations in cities and towns around the country, including Graham. These protests communicated immediate outrage over Floyd's murder—recorded on a smartphone and shared with the public by quick-thinking seventeen-year-old bystander Darnella Frazier—but were also primed by years of policing that targeted and harmed people of color, especially Black men.

That spring, Graham was still recovering from the police killing of Jaquyn Light, a twenty-year-old Black man and father-to-be. Just before midnight on January 28, 2020, Light was killed while exiting his front porch by Graham police officer Marcus Pollock, who was attempting to serve a warrant for a probation violation and two misdemeanors. Pollock, a Black twenty-year police veteran, did not turn his body camera on as required before serving the warrant. In a statement on January 31, Police Chief Kristy Cole said, "As the officers spoke with occupants of the residence, Mr. Light was attempting to avoid detection and crawled out from under the plastic. As he turned, presumably to flee, he ran into and contacted Officer Pollock. At this time, Officer Pollock's weapon discharged striking Mr. Light in his abdomen."*

Pollock was put on probation, according to protocol, but not charged with the killing. On July 17, 2020, District Attorney Sean Boone held a press conference and released findings concluding that Light's death was caused by an "accidental discharge caused by an unintentional collision between Pollock and Light." According to the report, Light was handcuffed before being taken to the hospital, where he died from significant blood loss about forty-two minutes after the shooting. "There is no evidence whatsoever that Light was shot in the back by the officer," Boone said.†

Light's death, and the months it took for the community to receive information—including whether or not Light was armed, the number of times he was shot, or where the bullet struck him—contributed to the community's fear, anger, and suspicion of the Graham police force. Despite community calls for reform, in March 2021 Graham's police department hired Doug Strader, an officer fired by the Greensboro Police Department for using "unnecessary, deadly force," including shooting at a fleeing vehicle. Strader was also one of eight officers involved in the hog-tying killing of Marcus Deon Smith, an unarmed man in Greensboro. Like Derek Chauvin, the officer who choked George Floyd, Strader had an extensive history of abuse and violence against unarmed citizens.

Jaquyn Light and Doug Strader did not receive the national attention of George Floyd and Derek Chauvin, but locals see them as part of the same, all-too-common story.

Derek Chauvin's conviction of second-degree murder, in April 2021, was the first time in Minnesota history that a white police officer was convicted for the murder of a Black person. Darnella Frazier, then just eighteen years old, testified in the Chauvin trial, and her video was crucial evidence. "If it weren't for my video, the world wouldn't have known the truth," Frazier posted later on Instagram. "My video didn't save George Floyd, but it put his murderer away and off the streets."‡

Darnella Frazier received the Pulitzer Prize in 2021 "for courageously recording the murder of George Floyd, a video that spurred protests against police brutality around the world, highlighting the crucial role of citizens in journalists' quest for truth and justice."**

Chauvin was sentenced to twenty-one years in prison in July 2022.

In September 2024, a federal judge ordered the City of Graham to pay Jaquyn Light's family $725,000 in a wrongful death lawsuit. The money will help support his only child as she grows up.††

---

* "GPD News Release—Officer Involved Shooting," Graham Police Department, January 31, 2020, www.cityofgraham.com/gpd-new-release-officer-involved-shooting/.

† Isaac Groves, "No Prosecution in Light Killing," *Topeka Capital-Journal*, July 17, 2020, www.cjonline.com/story/special/2020/07/17/no-prosecution-in-light-killing/41725029/.

‡ Joe Hernandez, "Read This Powerful Statement from Darnella Frazier, Who Filmed George Floyd's Murder," May 26, 2021, NPR, www.npr.org/2021/05/26/1000475344/read-this-powerful-statement-from-darnella-frazier-who-filmed-george-floyds-murd.

** "Darnella Frazier," The 2021 Pulitzer Prize Winner in Special Citations and Awards, Pulitzer.org, accessed May 29, 2025, www.pulitzer.org/winners/darnella-frazier.

†† "City of Graham Ordered to Pay $725K to Settle Wrongful Death Lawsuit," *Alamance News*, September 12, 2024. https://alamancenews.com/city-of-graham-ordered-to-pay-725k-to-settle-wrongful-death-suit/.

they called states of emergencies on several nights in May and June, allowing for curfews to be imposed and therefore permits for protest to be denied. Orange cones, designating "free speech zones," marked the small spaces where protesters could stand without moving along the sidewalks. Barricades blocked the Confederate statue and demonstrators were prevented from getting close to it, even to hold up signs and silently protest. On one occasion in July 2020, members of the NAACP were arrested for holding signs near the statue.

Silent Sam, the Confederate statue on the campus of the University of North Carolina at Chapel Hill, had been toppled. Governor Roy Cooper's orders had allowed for all Confederate monuments on state capitol grounds in Raleigh to be removed. Neo-Confederate groups like ACTBAC (Alamance County Taking Back Alamance County) were formed to protect the one at the courthouse in Graham. All indications pointed to an imminent head-to-head standoff between two sides: one with members who had the collective mentality of exposing an unjust system, and the other with those who had orders in hand from their commander in chief to do their part to "Make America Great Again." To rewind the clock on a post–Barack Obama America. To get back to the America they used to love. But unlike the chaos going on in every direction around us, Graham started out quiet and small.

On May 31, 2020, a Black man named Von decided to act. He dressed in all black and headed out to Court Square, sat on the northeast bench across from the statue, and read a book for several days in a row. It was unintrusive, uninviting of contention and hostility, yet it immediately made local law enforcement nervous.

Separately, Dionne Liles, Court Square's only Black business owner, and her employees Madeline and Sophie made "Black Lives Matter" and "Justice for George Floyd" signs. Dionne and Madeline made their way to the courthouse steps while Sophie stood on the corner near Dionne's store. Graham PD's Lieutenant Flood and Sergeant Payne quickly approached them and forced them to disperse, claiming a breach of city ordinance. Email had been sent by downtown development coordinator Mary Faucette to the businesses surrounding the county courthouse, warning of a possible protest on that Sunday. For this town, the warning was enough to induce threats of violent vigilantism.

From inside Farm Services, a shop close by the statue on Court Square and owned by city councilwoman Jennifer Talley, a video was posted on social media declaring "No looting in Graham." In the video, men displayed their rifles, shotguns, and revolvers, giggling at the thought of the chance to quell any protests they encountered. "No protesting in Graham. Stop them before they even get to the courthouse," one man said in another part of the video. As if he didn't understand or care about the difference between looting and protesting.

As the world engaged in demonstrations all around us, would-be protesters in Graham were met with faulty explanations about why they couldn't gather, nonsense city ordinance recitations, and aggressive enforcement. The fear tactics, threats, and runarounds had already begun. Though small in number, these activists refused to give up, even at their own risk.

On June 27, a twenty-seven-year-old Black man named Greg Cates came down to Court Square alone to perform a peaceful protest. He wore an NC ball cap and a black hoodie that read "Why Y'all Scared? I'm Beautiful." Matthew, a young white man in a peach-colored Hawaiian shirt, who'd come alone as well, stood side by side with Greg. Not long after their arrival, multiple police vehicles assembled around the square. Matthew, carrying a white sign that read "Destroy Hateful Heritage," was immediately thrown to the ground and placed in handcuffs. Greg was threatened with the same treatment. Videos of the interaction between Greg, Matthew, and law enforcement were posted on social media. It reminded me of the note the KKK pinned on Wyatt Outlaw's body after he was hung. *Beware you guilty, both white and black.*

But Greg Cates never got a chance to protest in downtown Graham again. One day later, Greg Cates was gone, having drowned in Lake Norman two hours south in Mecklenburg County.[4]

Alamance County cops collected numerous unjust arrests in a very short time, attracting local media outlets to what started to look like ground zero for injustice. Hearing of the unlawfulness on the part of the city and county, activists from the surrounding areas began to file into the small town, and numbers continued to grow over the next several weeks. Sure, it started with 1- and 2-person protests, but that number grew to 3, then 8, then 60, then 200. Graham wanted to stop protests here before they even got started. But the town miscalculated the outlaw mindset of those who cared about fairness and equality. And unjust laws weren't going to stand. More and more people began to see that this was the code that needed to be cracked. *If we could change Alamance County, we can change any place.*

The same summer, Dejuana Bigelow, an activist who spoke out against the Confederate monument at a commissioners meeting, was visited by a man in what looked to be a long white hood and white gown. The man pounded on the garage door of her residence in the middle of the night and ran off to a getaway car. His threatening behavior was caught on her security cameras and was posted on social media the next day.

And Faith Cook, a mother, health care worker, and resident of Graham, received a distressing call one day after coming home from work. At a store close to her home, her twelve-year-old daughter and a friend of her daughter were nearly hit by a car being driven by a white woman who called them "Black hoes" and tried to run them over. Faith reported the woman to the police but also posted her own tearful and angry response to Facebook, where within two days it was viewed more than 20,000 times.[5]

As the weeks went by, demonstrations became more frequent. Silent protests, rogue sign holders, living library walks. Each time, the public and law enforcement seemed to know ahead of time before protests began. Neo-Confederates would infiltrate social media groups and try to hack message threads. They routinely showed up in counterprotest, sometimes openly carrying their pistols on their hips despite a state law forbidding open or concealed carry at any gathering deemed a protest, parade, or demonstration. Activists were doxed, their homes were visited, and pictures of license plates were taken. Still, the number of activists grew.

The Reverend Gregory Drumwright and his activist group, Justice 4 the Next Generation, led a march and rally of several hundred people on a humid Saturday in July 2020. It was the first event of that nature and magnitude I'd ever seen in all my years of being raised in the town. The march was entirely peaceful. The rally at the end, however, was crashed by a small contingent of counterprotesters who'd had a spot carved out for them on the northwest corner of the square, just off to the side of where the rally was scheduled to take place. The augmented police force had to form the line using their bicycles and their bodies to keep the protesters and counterprotesters separate, as Confederate flag-wavers littered their corner near Sesquicentennial Park where the large bell commemorating the 150th anniversary of the town sat perched on a brick stoop. One sign read "The South Shall Rise Again." "No Free Color TVs Today" read another.

Confederate sympathizers and Trump supporters worked hard to drown out any positivity throughout the post-march rally in the square. One of the counterprotesters, even though the police were close enough to stop them, rang the bell continually, covering any guest speakers who came to the podium. But Sheriff Terry Johnson and his deputies instead arrested Maurice Wells, an activist who'd come with Drumwright to the march, for ringing that bell.

What was clear about the place I called home was this: Trump's rhetoric of racism and xenophobia emboldened other racists and xenophobes in the country. I remembered some racially charged encounters as a child, but this was more blatant; it was a hero complex. They thought they were on the

AN ACTIVIST'S ARREST

Maurice Wells was one of the activists arrested on misdemeanor charges that kept him in and out of court in the fall of 2020 and spring of 2021. A thirty-five-year-old father of two, he grew up a military brat, traveling around the world with his family before his parents settled in Greensboro. Maurice was a straight-A student from a stable, middle-class home, but as a teenager, after his parents' divorce and a head injury suffered during a four-wheeler accident, he fell into drugs and trouble with the law. After a tumultuous young adulthood, including drug convictions, he went back to school, got his life together, and found a job he liked working in Winston-Salem at an IT company. In January 2020, he moved with his family to Mebane, a small town in Alamance, because it was affordable, quiet, and a reasonable commute to work.

On a cool evening in September 2021, we met up with Maurice at Sesquicentennial Park, which he and others in the antiracist movement call Wyatt Outlaw Park. He was still waiting on a court date for the appeal of a conviction—inciting violence—from an arrest that happened fourteen months ago, in July 2020.

Maurice was wearing work clothes—gray slacks, black dress shoes, and a polo shirt. He took out a cigarette, lit it, and leaned back on one of the park's polished stone benches as he thought about how to characterize his participation in the movement and his motivation for returning to this spot, or somewhere near it, almost every day after work for a year. "I've always been a strong believer in fighting for what's right," he said, noting that he'd been involved in antiracist protests in Durham and Raleigh.* And as a Black man, he was no stranger to racism or unjust policing. But the overt racism that he found in Alamance, especially in Graham, was shocking.

"That was my first time seeing a Confederate in person," he said, referring to the crowd of Confederate flag–waving counterprotesters who gathered at the park across from the Confederate monument in Graham on July 11, 2020. That day, he said, "I saw Confederates. I saw a 'No Free Color TVs Today.' sign. Somebody had their *child* holding that sign." He shook his head. "That's what got me."

Not far from where he sat was the brick pedestal that, until May of this year, displayed a brass bell taken from the original Alamance

(continued)

County Courthouse. It was removed in May before a celebration, by neo-Confederates, of North Carolina's secession from the Union 150 years ago. The bell was also at the center of Maurice's first arrest in over a decade.

The July 11, 2020, march was about a number of things: police brutality, removal of the Confederate monument, and acknowledging the suppressed history of Alamance County. The march's organizer, Reverend Gregory Drumwright, had planned a procession that would take people from the town of Burlington, with its higher minority population, into downtown Graham and right up to the Confederate monument. Along the way marchers would pass, and learn about, sites important to the life of Wyatt Outlaw: the land he bought, along with four other Black men, for building a church; the site of his workshop and home; the spot near the courthouse where he was lynched by members of the White Brotherhood. Drumwright, who grew up in Burlington, gave a mini history lesson at each of these spots and saw how much Outlaw's story affected the marchers. "I saw young men with tears running down their faces," he said.†

Maurice was so affected by the story that by the time the 700-person march made it to the town square, where a cluster of neo-Confederates stood ringing the bell in an attempt to drown out Drumwright's words, he'd had enough. He stepped up to the brick pedestal and took his turn, clanging the bell in response: not to drown out, but to say that it was as much his as theirs.

The neo-Confederates didn't care for that. "Hey! He's ringing our bell!" they complained to Sheriff Terry Johnson.

Johnson had been Alamance County sheriff for nineteen years, making him one of the longest-serving sheriffs in the state, and Black Lives Matter activists believed he often sided with neo-Confederates. Sheriff Johnson heard Maurice scoff at one of the complainers: "You mad 'cause I rang your fuckin' bell?"

And Maurice was promptly arrested.

His first appearance in court was at the Historic Courthouse, where he experienced firsthand the hostility and incongruity of walking past a Confederate statue to appear before a judge in the year 2020. After that, he began going back to Court Square, at first with a cardboard Black Lives Matter sign and then with a flag. He was there every night after work, sometimes on weekends with his kids. He took his mama to the Halloween march, where they both got pepper-fogged.

He wasn't convicted of two other misdemeanor charges, thanks in part to bystander cell phone footage. The video clearly showed that a car he was accused of hitting with his Black Lives Matter flagpole had actually run the yield sign while Maurice was in the crosswalk (the driver was not stopped or apprehended). Before finding him not guilty, District Court judge Lunsford Long told him, "You might be innocent of these crimes, but you're not completely innocent."

Maurice was convicted by the same judge on the July 11 charge of inciting violence. He could have taken what's called a "prayer for judgment continued"—a kind of criminal case disposition specific to North Carolina, where as long as you stay out of trouble, the judgment isn't entered into the record. Maurice didn't like the idea of messing up his record after more than a decade without so much as a moving violation, but he liked admitting guilt even less. He wasn't trying to incite violence that day—certainly no more than the neo-Confederates were, endlessly clanging that bell near the very spot where Wyatt Outlaw died. Why was he the only one arrested?

"I don't see why I was singled out," Maurice said. "If 'You mad 'cause I rang your fuckin' bell?' makes you mad, then you mad."

He rejected the plea bargain. More than a year later, he was still waiting for a superior court trial on appeal. Maurice stood, threw away his cigarette butt, and paced around Sesquicentennial Park, which he and dozens of others asked the city council to rename Wyatt Outlaw Park in 2021. The city council refused, citing the people who'd paid to lay bricks with their names around the bell, back when the park was built, along with the impossibility of knowing "exactly" where Wyatt Outlaw died.

"It will always be Wyatt Outlaw Park to me," Maurice told the city council.

---

* Maurice Wells, interview by the authors, Graham, NC, September 20, 2021.

† Reverend Gregory Drumwright, interview by Belle Boggs, Greensboro, NC, October 1, 2020.

front lines making sacrifices for good reasons and for good causes. They thought they were the heroes in this story.

Even after the July march, the barrage of racial slurs and threats of violence didn't reduce the number of activists pouring into Court Square. Protests continued, often met with aggressive arrests and instigation from police. Lies and misrepresentations from some local news outlets splattered the front pages. The cops would spark agitation from the otherwise peaceful protesters, and the news would print a title that implied that we were the aggressors. It was infuriating to know that no matter the story, no matter what really happened, as long as the town controlled the media, they controlled what the townspeople thought. I knew this. We all did. We knew how emphatically they believed what they believed and how desperate they were to protect it. Even so, I never thought I'd see with my own eyes what I saw at a get-out-the-vote march on October 31, 2020.

• • • •

When I parked my brown '98 Chevy Blazer in the Wayman Chapel parking lot that morning, cars had filled the spaces in ways few present-day Sunday services can. Vehicles were decorated with pointed messages. One white truck sported wooden signs along the bed of the truck that read "Trump ignored Putin's bounty on US troops" and "Embarrassed by Trump? Restore dignity. Biden–Harris." Another woman held a sign that said "Jaquyn Light's life matters." Yet another wore a red hoodie that read "Paper Gods." Pan-African flags flew. I didn't know her yet, but Belle was there with her daughter Beatrice, a six-year-old girl in a green hoodie and face mask.

Many marchers wore hoodies in honor of Trayvon Martin, but I took what I could from my closet and matched what I thought might be Wyatt Outlaw's Reconstruction-era look the best I could. It was a beautiful day, in the mid-sixties, and so along with my suspenders and khaki pants, I threw on my long khaki trench coat and took a wide-brimmed black hat and folded it down over my eyes.

Activist Kani Adon X had the most standout costume. Dressed in all-white with a feather halo hovering over his head, he came portraying a guardian angel, one who had "come to heal the world," as he wrote on a later Facebook post. He burned sage in the parking lot, allowing for other participants to engage in the ceremony of smudging, the practice used to ward off negativity and evil spirits.

We were preparing to march along a portion of Highway 87, known as Main Street as it bisects the town. State troopers lined the road in preparation to escort the marchers, as city ordinance required protesters to request police presence for any form of protest.

Kani Adon X wore an angel costume to the I Am Change Legacy March to the Polls in Graham, October 2020. (Photo by Anthony Crider.)

Led by Reverend Drumwright, the action was called the I Am Change Legacy March to the Polls. It would begin at the church and end near the polling place, with a rally en route to honor Wyatt Outlaw, George Floyd, and others lost to unjust policing and racism. It was also the last day to register to vote, and many of the marchers were excited to register in concert with the others. It was a day to fully engage in the democratic process, putting to full use our right to speak freely, to assemble, and to choose our representation in public office. It was a learning day for the children. Present in solidarity were the family of Christian Griggs, who had been shot to death by his preacher father-in-law in 2013, and the niece and nephew of George Floyd.

With Drumwright, civil rights leaders, and Ian Baltutis, the mayor of Burlington, heading the front row, we began to march in columns, one behind the other with the police escort, down Main Street, sometimes in silence, sometimes chanting. The entire quarter of a mile was peaceful, reflective, and harmonious. I thought, *This is the moment that Graham needed.*

And the police escort was an important part. They were marching for change as well, weren't they? They were working with us on this day because they'd finally realized the changes that needed to be made within the system—within their system and the country itself. They were sympathetic to the cause, weren't they? They were with us this time.

As we came upon the Harden Street and Main Street intersection passing the First Baptist Church where Wyatt Outlaw's house once stood, we began to chant the lyrics to the Archie Eversole hip-hop song with a slight twist: "We ready, we ready, we ready for CHANGE." Then, Haikoo X, a slender man with a styled 'fro and black headband, was handed the megaphone and started to ad lib over the rest of us singing, his bright coloratura tenor voice ringing over the block. It was church. It was powerful. It was musical. It was peaceful. Young and old, Black and white. Singing together. This was the Graham I wanted to see.

When we arrived at the north side of the county courthouse, we knelt in silence for eight minutes and forty-six seconds, the time then believed to be the span that Derek Chauvin knelt on George Floyd's neck.[6] We then observed another powerful moment with fists raised and mouths closed for reflection. At the conclusion of that time of silence, Drumwright notified the marchers that the stage had to be set up. The space had been reserved for the rally until 2:00 p.m. "If you have to just party, the streets belong to us," he said over a mobile system microphone.

Seconds later, the pepper spray began.

The streets went from silent and pensive to confused and angry. Folks began pulling their COVID masks from their faces to find breath. Children cried. We didn't know why, after escorting us to the spot where we knelt, we were then perceived as "traffic blockers" in a space we thought had been reserved and where past neo-Confederate rallies had taken place numerous times with no interruption from police.

Eyes and throats burned as protesters exclaimed, "Why are they pepper-spraying?" "There are children," I heard people saying. Police would later say they told the crowd to move out of the streets after the moment of silence. Some didn't hear it. Others were confused by it. Others tried to move but got sprayed anyway. Either way, we weren't given much time. Police body cam footage later revealed one police officer saying playfully to another, "I knew you'd spray first. I knew it. I love it. I love it" and laughing about the incident. Reverend Drumwright grabbed the microphone. "Chief Kristy Cole, you maced children. This is how your administration is starting."

As protesters were being moved to the sidewalks, the discharged chemical still clogging the air, I couldn't help but think how strange the pepper-spray attack was. The July 11 march had also been in the street, and the rally that followed had remained in the street. And there were no major outbreaks of violence during the July march, and no effort was put into an attack on the statue. Yet for this rally, there were droves of officers in full battle dress uniforms posted on the roofs. Their gas masks were mounted on their uniforms as if they expected a major riot. What reason would they have to believe that this day would be any different from July 11?

With the irritant still burning our eyes and throats, the speeches from the stage began. Although most of the next several moments were a blur, I heard Wyatt Outlaw's name in the speakers' words and thought of how Wyatt had motivated so many others to carry on his legacy. I took stock of how many times we'd said that name in this very square. Now the spirit of Wyatt Outlaw was being uplifted in the place where he died and in front of a statue erected by those who killed him. Coalition groups like Forward Motion Alamance, Alamance Agents for Justice, and Justice 4 the Next Generation stood in solidarity to take the place of hate in a courthouse square built on it.

During Kani Adon X's speech, I looked to the northwest corner of the square where we'd usually see the MAGA counterprotesters clumped in groups. There was no one there. They were standing on the northeast side of the square this time, completely out of the way. At first, I thought that was a good thing. The police had moved them on purpose, but for what reason?

• • • •

"Medic. Medic. Medic. Medic. God damn y'all."

"I need water!" a woman screamed as she fell to her knees, surrounded by panicking demonstrators. "I can't open my eyes," a man said, wiping one clean hand over his tearful, reddened face. Blinded people bumped into each other as sound equipment crashed to the ground. Someone yelled, "Get a medic down here!" The nightmarish screams coming from the northeast and northwest sides of Court Square were hellish, maybe fitting for a march on Halloween.

Janet, a disabled woman once seated comfortably on her motor scooter, was now convulsing. As she collapsed to the asphalt, fellow marchers tried desperately to calm her and keep her from going into shock. But the spray was everywhere. And there was more coming.

Medics sprinted toward those who desperately needed saline in their eyes. But the screams for help were coming from everywhere. Choosing who got saline, who got medical attention at all, would be the medics' most daunting task. They were hurting, too. And they were scared.

It would later come to light that the commotion started when a sheriff's deputy, after orders to remove the generator used to power the sound system for the rally, grabbed the handle of that generator to disconnect it. Over the confusion about what was happening, there was a tug-of-war over the generator and a quick escalation of tension between the two sides. Bodies began to gather around the generator, and others came in to help the first officer. The dispute was over whether the generator was allowed, based on the protest permit. Confusion between parties escalated, and so the chaos continued.

One sheriff's deputy, his lower face wrapped in a "Thin Blue Line" face mask, raised his right arm over a tussling crowd by the pop-up stage and discharged a large cloud of spray into my eyes. I covered my face for protection and scrambled to find a spot around Court Square where I could find any trace of uncontaminated air to breathe.

To the children, the oblong plastic cutouts on police gas masks must have looked like demons' eyes. Long rifles and spray guns draped over their bodies for swift and immediate use. Some seemed to be laughing. I know the neo-Confederate onlookers were laughing. This was the show they'd come to see.

"Kendall, get over here with me." Parents tried desperately to keep up with their young ones. "Don't lose me again."

"You're pepper-spraying children!" one man screamed in teary frustration. Others cried, "Why are they doing this?" "What did we do?" "They don't want us here."

"You're fucking spraying children," I screamed, in an uncharacteristic loss of control.

How did this happen? How did we go from kneeling in silence to screaming in pain in a matter of seconds? How did we go from listening to speakers onstage to calling for medical attention? *This was peaceful. This was peaceful. What happened?* This was the land of Southern hospitality. This was Graham, North Carolina, where "love always wins."

In the chaos, I stopped and looked at one of the Graham PD lieutenants and said, "This was peaceful. You know this is y'all's fault, right? Why would you do this?"

"Not even close," he said as he waved folks on to clear the area, and his officers continued to spray around us.

The march never made it to the polls. There were numerous arrests, including Reverend Drumwright, Haikoo X, Faith Cook, Avery Harvey, Kani X, and more than a dozen others. The incident would lead to the sheriff's department and Graham PD being sued multiple times and was covered by the *Washington Post*, CNN, TMZ, and a long list of national outlets. I spoke to NPR; Belle spoke to the FBI, which investigated the police violence. Burlington mayor Ian Baltutis, who was also pepper-sprayed, said it was the worst display of policing he'd ever seen. My partner, Karla, who watched from a seated position on a low brick wall, said she had never seen anything like it and didn't understand why the police got so aggressive so fast.

Counterprotesters, who were told by police to move from the northwest to the northeast side of the square before the rally started, later posted a video to social media explaining what they thought was the reasoning behind the move. "Most of the time we're on the other side of the street. The cops literally moved us. . . . Now we know why. So when they went off and when they used the tear gas it wouldn't get none of us. So I guess it worked out the best."

The worst part is that no policing was necessary until the police created the necessity. Some called it an infringement of free speech; some called it voter suppression. It's hard to believe that something like this would happen on a neo-Confederate stage or at a MAGA rally—and it's hard not to connect the violence to the many instances of police and white supremacist violence faced by Reconstruction-era voting rights leaders.

I've heard some people say that Alamance County is the most prejudiced place they've lived in. And whether one sees it as a quaint and delightful town, a repressive and divisive one, or in some weird way a mixture of both, no reasonable person could argue against the certainty that what happened during the march to the polls on Halloween 2020 was undemocratic, unjust, and uncalled for. It was in part the motivation behind writing *The Spirit of Wyatt Outlaw*, because the evil Wyatt experienced in 1870, just across from the courthouse, somehow still had a strong hold on downtown Graham.

In the end, the *Alamance News* told the story as if we were hoodlums coming in to wreck an otherwise civil town. Though Graham is a conservative town, and that side of the aisle is known to tout their religious moral superiority, all the eyewitness accounts, video evidence, and personal experience confirm that we were the angels that day, and they were the demons.

What I saw was a police force that showed up to a peaceful protest with gas masks, similar to what we wore in the army. So this must have been a war zone. Because this couldn't have been home.

BELLE

The march started peacefully and with prayers.

"Did any of you bring a gun?" the Reverend Gregory Drumwright asked the 200 people assembled for the I Am Change Legacy March to the Polls on Saturday, October 31—the last day of early voting in North Carolina. "Did you bring a weapon of any kind? Do you have any intent to harm businesses? Do you plan to pull down this monument?"

"No!" the people answered, again and again.

"Did you come in peace?"

"Yes!"

I kept my hand on my small daughter's shoulder. Beatrice (we call her Bea) was six and in first grade, which so far had been entirely online. She no longer went anywhere without a mask and spent most days at home in the woods of Chatham County. She gripped her handmade "Black Lives Matter" sign as we assembled for the half-mile march to the Alamance County Courthouse, where a thirty-foot-tall Confederate monument stood behind barricades. Citizens and community leaders of this county had been demanding the removal of the statue with increasing urgency, but this march was not about the statue.

It was, as Drumwright said on the day he announced the march, about the systems that "shadow the monument"—bigotry, white supremacy, and police brutality. The nonpartisan march was also about getting out the vote, which was one reason I wanted to bring my daughter. I knew that we'd chant, "This is what democracy looks like," and I wanted Beatrice to hear that and feel the swell of pride I feel whenever I say those words. Of course, I also knew that there would be people jeering from the sidelines and honking horns from Confederate flag–flying pickup trucks. I was prepared for that.

But I wasn't prepared for what happened.

The police blocked off Main Street for the march, and although Drumwright insisted we take our time—we had elders and babies with us, he reminded us—it took only about twenty minutes to get to the courthouse.

FACING

TOP Marchers followed a police escort down Main Street.

CENTER LEFT Protesters knelt in memory of George Floyd and others killed by police violence. After approximately nine minutes of silence and prayer, they were given a thirty-second warning and then pepper-fogged by police.

CENTER TOP RIGHT The second round of pepper-fogging and violence happened inside police-constructed barricades that surrounded the courthouse. Protesters intended to listen to speeches and then march to the polls.

CENTER BOTTOM RIGHT Protesters struggled to hold on to one another before being wrestled to the ground by police.

BOTTOM More than twenty people were arrested that day, including an *Alamance News* photographer and citizens who planned to vote after the march. It was the last day of same-day voter registration.

(All photos by Anthony Crider.)

YIELD TO
PEDESTRIAN
IN CROSSWALK

POLICE
POLICE

JOURNALISM TODAY AND YESTERDAY

Reports of the I Am Change Legacy March to the Polls showed up immediately in local, state, and national news outlets, including the local conservative paper the *Alamance News*, the *New York Times*, the *Washington Post*, and *Rolling Stone*. In early 2021, Sylvester worked with journalists Carli Brosseau and Julia Wall as narrator on an Emmy award–winning short documentary about Alamance County's bitter divisions and police violence, *The Sound of Judgment*, produced by the *Raleigh News and Observer* and ProPublica. Brosseau and Wall were among eleven journalists caught in the pepper spray on October 31.

Before the October 31 march, most local reporting about police violence, antiracist activism, and Black Lives Matter protests against the Confederate memorial came to Alamance County residents through the *Alamance News*, under direction of (or even written by) president and publisher Tom Boney. In an op-ed titled "What of Rev. Drumwright?" published November 5, 2020, Boney is plainly on the side of the police: "So when Drumwright stopped for four to five minutes, blocking the intersection of North Main and Harden streets, they must have been irritated. Certainly the drivers who couldn't proceed to cross Main Street were—and understandably so."*

Politically biased reporting is hardly new—during Reconstruction, newspapers like the *Raleigh Sentinel* and the *Charleston Mercury* were often heavily influenced by the political and white supremacist leanings of their editors-in-chief and by white Southern Democrats in general. But accurate and in-depth reporting about race and racial violence is also not new. When Brosseau and Wall began their eight-month investigation of the intense Black Lives Matter protests in Graham, they talked to people on both sides of the issue, from police to protesters to neo-Confederates. Their work "tells a lot about the context of racism in America," said Nikela Patel, chair of the Online News Association, which awarded Brosseau and Wall an Online Journalism Award for Excellence in Social Justice Reporting in 2021. "The journalists put you into the person's stories and you can empathize with them. A particularly newsworthy, noteworthy element is essentially telling the story of a place over many decades, how generation after generation can drive these mentalities and these conflicts."†

The time, skill, and bravery required for this kind of detailed, long-form reporting has a historical precedent in the Black-owned newspapers that date back to Northern papers like *Freedom's Journal*, Frederick Douglass's *North Star*, and newly emerged Reconstruction-era papers published in the South, like Raleigh's short-lived *Journal of Freedom* or Charlotte's long-lived *Star of Zion*. These papers spoke directly to a Black audience about issues like voting rights, military service, and Freedmen's Bureau affairs. Though they shared an activist bent—the *New York Times* described the publication of the *Journal of Freedom* as "a bold push on behalf of Negro suffrage in the South"—the papers considered an essential, and previously overlooked, audience of readers and citizens.‡

Investigative journalism about white supremacy and racial violence was further advanced by groundbreaking reporters like Ida B. Wells, an activist journalist and editor who traveled throughout the South in the 1880s and 1890s. Wells's painstaking, risk-taking investigative work exposed the lies printed by white-owned newspapers about Black people, particularly lynching victims, accused of what she deemed the "thread-bare lie that Negro men assault white women."** Her activism was inspired by the 1892 lynching of three close friends; after writing and speaking out about the injustice, her newspaper offices were destroyed, and she and her family were threatened.

Wells connects to our story in a few ways; first and foremost was her bravery. Second, her pamphlet *The Red Record: Tabulated Statistics and Alleged Causes of Lynching in the United States* inspired the digital site A Red Record, housed at the University of North Carolina at Chapel Hill, which aims to document "lynchings in the American South, starting with North Carolina." She also knew, corresponded with, and was likely introduced to her husband, attorney and journalist Ferdinand Lee Barnett, by her ally Albion Tourgée.††

---

* Tom Boney, "What of Rev. Drumwright?," *Alamance News*, November 5, 2020, https://alamancenews.com/what-of-rev-drumwright/.

† Catherine Clabby, "N&O, ProPublica Win Online Journalism Award for Reporting on Racial Justice in NC County," *Raleigh News and Observer*, October 18, 2021. www.newsobserver.com/news/politics-government/article255075512.html.

‡ "Journal of Freedom (Raleigh, N.C.) 1865-186?," Library of Congress, accessed May 30, 2025, www.loc.gov/item/sn88074095/.

(*continued*)

** Ida B. Wells-Barnett, "The Offense," in *Southern Horrors: Lynch Law in All Its Phases* (New York: New York Age Print, 1892), www.gutenberg.org/files/14975/14975-h/14975-h.htm#THE_OFFENSE.

†† Carolyn L. Karcher, *A Refugee from His Race: Albion W. Tourgée and His Fight against White Supremacy* (Chapel Hill: University of North Carolina Press, 2016), 41, 210–11.

Along the way we repeated the names of Black people murdered by police and police violence: George Floyd, Breonna Taylor, Sandra Bland. We stopped in front of Wyatt Outlaw's address, now occupied by a Baptist church.

We sang about being ready for change. "Whose streets?" Drumwright called out. "Our streets!" we yelled back. Gray police drones buzzed over our heads. Unmasked spectators filmed and photographed us from the sidewalks.

With my hand nestled in Bea's hoodie, I could feel tension coiled in her neck and shoulders. I wondered if the march, with its heavy police presence, was too much for her, especially in a year when she'd already experienced so much sadness—a sick grandfather, first grade reduced to Zoom sessions, no playgrounds or beach trips or playdates. But she kept her sign raised, and we marched along.

We arrived at the courthouse a little before noon and knelt for eight minutes, forty-six seconds—the time we then believed it took for the police to kill George Floyd. His family was in attendance, and we were going to listen to them speak.

"I want to go home," Bea whispered, head down. "I want to be in the woods."

I put my arm around her, still kneeling, and told her she was safe. I pointed out the trees near the street—she thinks of trees as her friends—and the other children who were there. A little girl in a fairy costume. A baby in a stroller. I pointed out an older woman in a beautiful black-and-white dress, kneeling next to her cane on the pavement.

At the end of our vigil, we stood and looked around. Drumwright, who'd thanked the police for their escort, told us to wait while the speakers assembled. He had a permit for the march, but something about it was complicated—they had not been allowed to set up the PA system and speaking platform in advance.

There were so many police—some of them in regular sheriff's deputy uniforms but others in tactical gear, like soldiers; some of them standing on the roof of the courthouse with guns, like snipers; some of them chatting amiably with unmasked white bystanders. An officer told the crowd near me that we needed to clear the streets, which were still blocked off. I didn't hear cars honking or backed-up traffic or any warning about what would happen if we *didn't* clear the streets, but I wasn't here to get arrested. I grabbed Bea's hand and looked for an empty place where we could stand and still hear the speeches.

Maybe thirty seconds after the officer told us to move, the screaming started. And the choking and coughing and crying. My eyes stung and watered. I could see a cloud of vapor coming toward us, and I knew that we'd been tear-gassed or pepper-sprayed. I won't forget my daughter's horrified face when she realized that the air she was breathing was literally choking her. "Mommy!" she cried. "Why is this happening?"

I hoisted Bea onto my hip and moved into an alley where another woman was standing with her child. Other people, including children, elderly, and disabled people, were also choking and coughing behind their masks. Someone brought us water, and we drank it and rinsed our eyes. I did not see a single police officer offer aid to any of the 200 protesters now struggling to breathe, see, and comfort loved ones.

"I want to go home," Bea said again. Some of the pepper-fogged marchers were reconvening around the courthouse; at this point, just before noon, it looked like they would continue the march. But Bea and I were done. Though I did not want to be intimidated by what I saw as a deliberate and cruel show of police violence, my greater responsibility was to my daughter. Only six years old! We began our walk back to the car, the landscape suddenly more ominous.

"Why is this happening?" she'd demanded to know.

The answer is so dark I was almost afraid to tell her. It was happening because some people with power, like police, would rather pepper-spray children, elderly people, and disabled people than wait for them to move. Some people would rather cut the sound to a PA system than hear a faith leader issue a demand for change. And some people would rather arrest peaceful protesters than see them vote.

All of this is, of course, part of the history of racism and brutality against Black people that shadows our country. There was no avoiding that truth as we walked down the street where Wyatt Outlaw was lynched 150 years ago. His blood was "under our feet," Drumwright said during the march. How do you tell a six-year-old what lynching is? And that it still happens today?

• • • •

It was hard to pick up the pieces.

In the coming days I met with Dreama, Sylvester, and many other folks who were there—some friends and former students of mine who'd gone to the march because I invited them. My friend Jennifer Shaw, who went with her daughter and stayed through the whole march, went home and wrote a minute-by-minute account of everything she remembered. Here is her contemporaneous documentation of the part of the march that I missed when I left with my daughter:

- The speakers spoke for about 45 minutes. Part of the crowd was across the street, and you would occasionally hear shouting and the police dragging away someone while people/bystanders yelled. The Reverend tried to keep the crowd focused on the speakers.
- There were so many law enforcement people! There were rows of officers behind the speakers and above them on the courthouse steps. They had on gas masks. And one was in khaki camo with a machine gun. He didn't appear in police clothes, and I don't know who he was. When things got crazy, he pointed a long gun at all of us in the crowd. Then suddenly the line of officers moved down the steps and moved over to the audio speakers and all hell broke loose. The people speaking on the podium shouted to stop touching it and the officers behind them started pepper-spraying. There was no warning. There was an older woman in a scooter/wheelchair who happened to be near the audio speakers (we were only about 20 ft. from the podium as well). Her scooter seemed to be jammed and since she didn't move quickly enough the police pepper-sprayed her. There was so much commotion, and people were trying to help her get up and move away but the pepper spray was blinding and the only way out of the barricades was past the woman's scooter. That's when a man next to us started to move the barricade so we could get out.
- There were two young boys next to us outside the barricade and the police were dragging one of them away and the second boy was holding onto him around the waist. The police grabbed the first boy and pulled him to the ground by his hair.
- It was complete chaos—people were screaming—we tried to leave and go back across the street and back to our car. Apparently, the

> police had sprayed pepper spray on the sidewalk across the street too. People were moving away quickly and our eyes and throats were burning again and we hurried to get past the area and walk back to the church where our car was parked.

Three days after the march, on Election Day, my husband, Richard, and I marched with Bea and her two-year-old sister, Harriet, at a follow-up voting rights march in Graham. I wanted to show that we weren't scared, that we wouldn't be intimidated, but it was too soon. Seeing the crowd, a larger gathering than we'd experienced on Halloween, Bea immediately got nervous. A protester burned a bundle of sage near a police car and Bea started crying—she thought it was more pepper fog, and we chose to leave the march. Even now, she doesn't trust police or believe they're there to keep her safe.

I struggled—and still do—with guilt over my decision to take a six-year-old to the October 31 march. Because as much as I want to believe that I was right to do so, I know that I should have seen the warning signs and protected her. The hostile neo-Confederates. The aggressive police. The drones. The roof-posted snipers.

When I was pregnant with Bea, Richard and I marched with Moral Mondays, part of the Poor People's Campaign against North Carolina's Republican-led legislature's attacks on our social safety net, including legislators' refusal to expand Medicaid and hefty cuts to unemployment benefits and public education. We marched right into the general assembly, led by Reverend William Barber II, for a planned act of civil disobedience. Police gave a warning that anyone who did not want to be arrested should leave now, and we did—Richard because he was serving as volunteer legal counsel, I because I didn't want to risk our baby's safety. The orderly and safe experience of that protest, and others I took Bea to in Raleigh when she was younger, was nothing like what we saw in Graham, and Bea said she never wanted to go back.

But in early 2021, not long after the production of *The Spirit of Wyatt Outlaw*, members of the Alamance County Community Remembrance Coalition invited me and Sylvester on a church-led bus trip through Atlanta to see Martin Luther King Jr.'s birthplace and then on to Montgomery, Selma, and Birmingham to see major sites of resistance and triumph during the civil rights era. Sylvester and I signed up right away, but the trip was postponed because of high COVID rates. The trip was rescheduled for April 2022, but this time Sylvester had a conflict: a performance of Bertolt Brecht's *The Life of Galileo*. Bea would be eight years old, and I had the idea that it could be a useful, healing experience—a chance to reset some of the ideas she had about peaceful protest, its purpose and outcomes and place in history. I asked whether she wanted to go.

"Sure!" she said. Early 2022 was still a time of minimal travel for our family, other than trips to Virginia to see relatives. Bea loved travel, hotels, movement, so her answer didn't surprise me.

I warned her about the long bus ride and about how the trip would have sad and serious parts, as well as a slower pace than she was sometimes used to (many of the participants were older). Did she want to take time away from school and play for a weeklong history lesson?

She did, she promised. She was sure. And it turned out to be one of the most profound trips I've ever taken.

Early one April morning, we boarded a charter bus in Burlington with a couple dozen other folks. We traveled first to Atlanta, where we visited the King Center and homeplace. We saw the last flowers Martin Luther King Jr. sent to Coretta Scott King—silk roses, because he feared the end of his life was near. We traveled to Birmingham and stood inside Sixteenth Street Baptist Church, gazing up at the stained-glass Wales Window for Alabama, an image of a Black Christ donated by the people of Wales after the 1963 Klan bombing. We ate fried fish, greens, and chocolate-frosted cake at a community college in Selma and then began a walking tour, led by Dianne Harris, who'd been a teen foot soldier in the movement. We visited the Voting Rights Museum, the Rosa Parks Museum, and the Montgomery waterfront. At the National Memorial for Peace and Justice, we saw the weathered steel plinth that represented the lynchings in Alamance County—the space for Wyatt Outlaw not yet engraved. We read the names for Chatham, our home county, and Bea gasped and teared up when she read her sister's first name in the entry for Harriet Finch.

All the while, Bea was in the gentle care of men and women from Alamance County. She got to count them on bus trips to make sure we didn't leave anyone behind and talk to them at the hotel breakfast bar. She got to push our new friend Dale Walker, a retired minister, in her wheelchair through the Legacy Museum in Montgomery and up the aisle of the church in Montgomery where the Reverend Martin Luther King Jr. once preached.

Maybe most importantly, she saw adults, Black and white, young and old, supporting one another as they grappled with the lessons and untold stories of the past. She saw us dumbfounded as we learned that, in the century before Klan members attacked it, Sixteenth Street Baptist Church was condemned and demolished by white city officials who deemed it too tall. She saw us shaking our heads as Dianne Harris told us about the impossible "literacy tests" faced by Black voters in Alabama: How many jellybeans in this jar? How many bubbles in a bar of soap? How many drops of water in the Alabama River?

One of the most powerful things about hearing history directly from a person who lived it, instead of reading it from a plaque on a wall, is that they can respond to the people in the room. Ms. Harris noticed Bea in our group and connected with us through her own complex relationship to defiance as a young person—how she didn't want to disobey the teachers who told her not to march (some of them also participated in the teachers' marches), how she tried to tell her mother the truth about what they did and planned to do. In the end, she could not help but follow the singing marchers on March 7, 1965, later known as "Bloody Sunday." Harris assured her brother, when he reminded her that they'd promised not to march, that they'd stay in the back.

"We *attempted* to march," she told us. The truth, she said, was important, and she did not step foot on the Edmund Pettus Bridge before being turned back by screaming people attacked by state troopers, violent posse men on horseback, and tear gas. They fled back to the church that had been their sanctuary, where they were given first aid. Once home, she got what she called "the whipping of my life."[7]

But throughout this time her mother helped house visiting activists, and later she allowed Harris and her brother to ride a bus to Montgomery on March 24 for the last leg of the march. They camped with other young activists and stayed up all night listening to musicians like Harry Belafonte, Nina Simone, Sammy Davis Jr., and Joan Baez who'd come to support the cause. The next day, they marched with 25,000 people and heard King give his "How Long, Not Long" speech.

Her mother voted that fall and in every election for the rest of her life. Harris has also never missed an election, state or local, since she turned twenty-one. And the work she began in 1965 continues today. "I transport people to the polls," she said. "I man the telephone to see if people need rides. I'm in a sorority, and we canvass voters all around Selma. I have my very own bullhorn."

Back on the bus, I told Bea that Dianne Harris was special because she had lived through an important moment in history and was living through it now, in her focus on voting rights and voter access to the polls. I walked behind Bea, who wore the same green hoodie she'd worn at the march in Graham, as she walked across the Edmund Pettus Bridge and stared out at the water, her blonde hair whipping in the wind.

On October 31, Bea and I didn't mean to walk into history, but like a

This embroidery journal by Belle and her daughter Beatrice was made during their trip to civil rights sites in Georgia and Alabama in 2022. (Photo by Belle Boggs.)

couple hundred other people, including kids, we had. That day made an indentation in our lives, the same way it did for Dreama and Sylvester and Ebony and Jenny.

But so had this trip. On the sometimes-lengthy bus rides, we started an embroidery journal, stitching in the names of places we'd been. Burlington, where we began, then Atlanta, Montgomery, and Selma. I did my best to outline the front of Sixteenth Street Baptist Church and MLK's childhood home. Bea stitched a slice of chocolate cake, the Edmund Pettus Bridge, and a tree she admired in Atlanta. We blocked in three rust-colored plinths to represent the Legacy Museum. We stitched the bus at the start of the trip and the bus on our last day in Montgomery, when it broke down next to Dr. King's church.

When we finished, the little embroidered circle looked like our journey—imperfect, winding, surprising, deliberate.

PART FOUR

RECKONING AND RESPONSIBILITY

CHAPTER SEVENTEEN

JOSEPH R. HOLMES AND WHAT'S POSSIBLE

On a late spring morning in 2023, we traveled north from Graham on our way to an even smaller town in Virginia. We made our way through Alamance's rural community of Pleasant Grove and into Caswell County, which shared the period of Klan murders and attacks on Black people that Governor Holden deemed an insurrection in 1870 and tried, unsuccessfully, to stop. In these densely wooded counties, it was still possible to picture that time period—the terrified flight of Black families, the roving bands of disguised, horse-riding Klansmen. From Caswell, still home to a chapter of North Carolina's KKK, we crossed the border into Virginia's Halifax County.

We were looking for a story we hoped would help us better understand Wyatt Outlaw's life and what was possible about his remembrance in Alamance. By then we'd learned so much about the lynchings and assassinations of the Reconstruction era—murders of patriotic, peace-loving people who were exercising their newly won rights to vote, to assemble, to work for a fair wage, and to help others do the same.

These stories of heinous violence weighed heavily on us, but we wanted to know how the inspiring work of these Black men and women could be communicated to future generations. What was possible to honor men like Wyatt?

We'd learned that in York County, South Carolina, a plantation house in Historic Brattonsville had been restored to its Reconstruction-era appearance—bricks cleaned, shutters repaired and painted—not to celebrate the white people who profited from enslavement but to tell the story of James Williams, a man enslaved in the county. Williams escaped from slavery during the Civil War and joined the Union army. He returned to York County, where he served as captain of an all-Black militia. He was well-respected and politically powerful—this was why he was targeted. After his 1871 abduction and murder by the Klan, the county coroner brought his body to the plantation house known as Brick House, which functioned by then as a general store.

This is where his community mourned him in 1871 and where some 150 years later visitors from all over can learn about his impressive and historically important life, which motivated not only the 1871 Civil Rights Act but also an immigration of a large group of local Black families to Liberia. Notes taken by federal investigators after Williams's assassination became crucial evidence during South Carolina's Ku Klux Klan trials.[1]

And we'd also heard about Virginia's Charlotte County, where we were headed on this June day—a place neither of us had traveled before. As we followed the rural roads of Halifax County, we expected to see Trump signs and Confederate flags, but all we encountered were green pastures and woods and little houses with yellow "Thank You, Jesus" yard signs. Eventually we crossed into Charlotte County, which offered long stretches of emptiness—no houses, no plowed fields, not even a power line. Charlotte County has only 11,500 residents, which is less than the total population of Graham. Cell service dropped, and Sylvester, who had driven five miles below the speed limit the whole trip, said something about ghosts. We kept the windows down and talked about the questions we'd ask. *How much backlash has there been? What's the payoff?*

A little before noon, our appointed meeting time, we arrived in the town of Charlotte Court House, the county seat, and parked on a side street adjacent to the historic courthouse. Designed by Thomas Jefferson, it sits on a corner lot surrounded by oak, cherry, maple, and magnolia trees. A square, red-brick Roman revival building, the courthouse—no longer used for trials and court sessions—has four massive white columns supporting a white pediment. The red brick is rumpled and aged, like parchment or old linen, and the dark green shutters are thick with many coats of glossy paint. A large metal bell hangs above the door.

On the lawn, a historical marker notes that the last debate by Patrick Henry and the first by John Randolph took place here. Henry spoke against states' rights; Randolph, for them. They both won their elections. Both owned slaves, though the marker, installed in 2017, doesn't mention this. On the other side of the lawn sat a replica of a Confederate cannon, donated by the Sons of the Confederate Veterans in 2006. Behind it is a Confederate statue—the familiar armed soldier atop a tall plinth, which is engraved with words of tribute: "Noble deeds are a people's inspiration." We read that it was installed in 1901, thirteen years before the statue in Graham was erected.

But more prominent, for us, was a state historical marker honoring Joseph R. Holmes. The silver and black marker was dense with text, as if its creator was squeezing in as much as possible. We stood there reading it to ourselves, then aloud.

Holmes was not a "former slave" but "formerly enslaved"—enslavement was a thing that was *done to him* rather than his identity. He "campaigned for civil rights and education." He "served as a delegate to the Virginia Republican Party conventions in 1867" and "was elected to represent Charlotte and Halifax Counties." These four verbs—campaigned, served, elected, represent—all point to what he did and make you think of the people who must have trusted and depended on him.

He was "shot dead here on the courthouse steps" on May 3, 1869. Four men, "all white," were charged with his murder and are named on the sign: "Brothers John and Griffin S. Marshall, along with William T. Boyd and Macon C. Morris."

They "fled and were never tried."

But, the sign concludes, "The murder drew international attention to the plight of freedpeople during Reconstruction."

International attention: People cared. Here is the possibility of, if not justice or accountability, then at least recognition. In smaller letters, at the bottom of the sign: "Department of Historic Resources, 2020."

On the plaque are "702 characters, including spaces," Kathy Lee Erlandson Liston informed us. We'd contacted her after coming across Joseph Holmes's remarkable—and remarkably similar to Wyatt's—story in the *Washington Post* and then in a *Charlotte Gazette* article by Liston. She wrote the marker's text herself and got it approved by the Virginia Department of Historic Resources (the easy part) and Charlotte County's conservative, all-white board of supervisors (more difficult).[2]

A retired archaeologist, Liston is a petite white woman with short dark hair and a vivacious but frank manner. She wore slim dark jeans, white

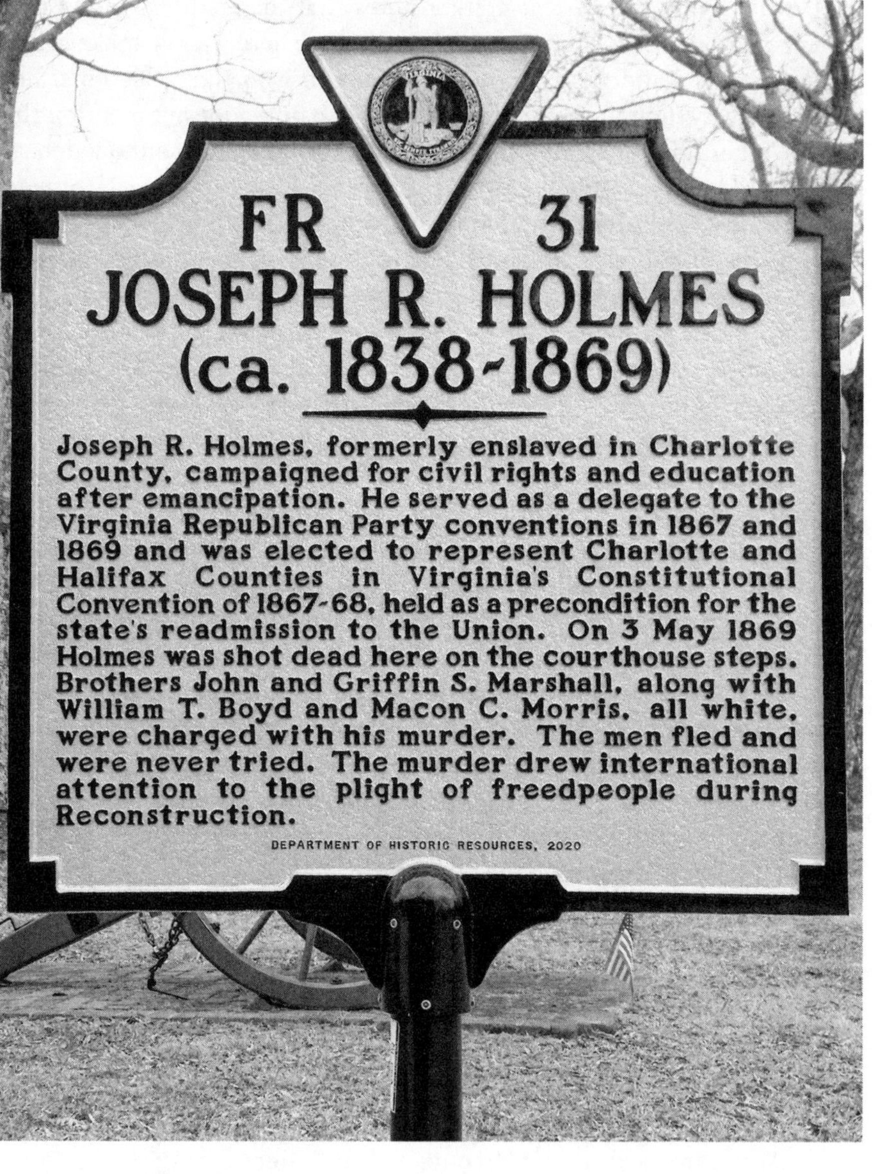

Joseph R. Holmes historical marker, Charlotte Court House, Virginia. (Photo by Kathy Lee Erlandson Liston.)

sneakers, and an olive-green button-down and frequently reached for sparkly purple readers, the result of a lifetime of squinting at old documents. Gesturing at the sign, she told us that people have asked her, "Why put it *there*?" She turned and made a frame with her hands. "We wanted people to see the courthouse steps, where Joe died, *and* the Confederate monument and that silly cannon as they learn about him."

Joseph R. Holmes is "Joe," to her, as he was known in his thirty-one-year life. She first came across his story after finding a trove of documents in the plantation she and her husband bought and restored twenty-five years ago. She began searching for descendants of the enslaved people who had worked and been buried on their property or who had lived in town. She posted what she found on Black genealogy sites online, and in 2012 she heard from Lisa Henderson, a direct descendant of Jasper Holmes, Joseph's brother. Henderson told Liston that she'd always heard she was distantly related to a Black man who'd been killed on the courthouse steps in Charlotte County for his political views. Liston dug some more.

Finally, in the county clerk's office, after reading through thousands of documents that had been rolled up and bound with red cotton tape, she unearthed witness statements detailing the murder. Holmes was lynched on a Monday, a court day, near five in the afternoon, so plenty of people, white and Black, saw what happened. They gave their statements the day after the murder, during the coroner's inquest.

Holmes had been on his way to the courthouse to obtain warrants for the arrest of four white men who'd been overheard bragging about killing a Black man and threatening to kill Holmes. They pistol-whipped him and shot him twice, once on the lawn and once as he reached the courthouse steps. He died on the property: the courthouse, the symbol of the laws of equality and freedom he was working to uphold.

"There's debate about whether Joe had a gun, but everyone agrees that he never fired at anyone," Liston said. The murderers escaped, aided by others in the community, but lived public lives. One even became a police officer, another a sheriff, foreshadowing the controversial but commonplace hiring (including in Alamance County) of officers with blood on their hands.

Holmes's inspiring life and tragic lynching parallel Wyatt Outlaw's in a number of ways. He believed in education and worked to found schools for freedpeople. He owned land—eleven and a half acres, bought with his earnings as a shoemaker. He was active in Republican politics, representing his community at the state constitutional convention, and believed in peace, voting rights, and the rule of law. He was respected by both white and Black citizens but was targeted specifically by Democrats who opposed the free exercise of rights by Black people and who were especially galled by the idea that a Black man might enforce the peace.

Like Wyatt's murderers, the men who killed Joseph Holmes were not held accountable. Instead, they were able to live and travel freely, without fear of prosecution.

And as with Wyatt, there were rumors: Someone else did it; maybe Holmes deserved it or did something to draw the violence to him. All these stories, passed along and repeated by white people, were shared without anyone looking at any of the materials Liston has seen—she knew this because she unbundled the papers herself. She showed us the photocopied witness statements, pointing to the similarities between accounts and the fact that the witnesses were both white and Black.

And yet, we could see differences in how their communities have held and passed on their stories.

To Liston, Wyatt's story is remarkable because he was remembered. His name is in academic books and novels and in the memories of older folks in town. But to us, Charlotte County's readiness to erect Joseph Holmes's sign was unimaginable. The all-Republican, all-white board of supervisors had only one member, chairman Gary Walker, who spoke and voted against the marker.

"I'm just wondering how many other requests we open the door to, that Uncle So-and-So or Granddaddy So-and-So did a lot for Charlotte County 160 years ago, too?" he asked in a meeting. "Not that he's not a worthy recipient, don't anybody get me wrong, I'm not saying that."[3]

The day before the unveiling in October 2021, the *Washington Post* ran a story about Liston and Henderson's work to unearth and recognize Holmes's accomplishments. The story notes Walker's resistance and his suggestion that the contributions of another Black resident, House of Delegates member Dabney Smith, might make a better tribute: "Other than the fact that Mr. Holmes was killed on the square makes it exciting to talk about, that doesn't mean he meant more to Charlotte County than Mr. Smith."

Pointedly, the article also mentions that Walker approved the placement of the replica cannon, as well as his co-ownership of Roxabel Plantation, where two of Holmes's killers lived. The plantation is now a wedding and events venue, and nowhere on the website advertising it—even under the "History" tab—do its owners acknowledge the presence and work of slaves to build and maintain the property or the fact that two of its residents "got away with murder," as Liston puts it.

This was all familiar: placing white-owned business interests above accurate and complete representations of history. Walker's equivocation and refusal to acknowledge that Joseph Holmes, like Wyatt Outlaw, had historical significance meriting a marker and permanent remembrance. The idea that Black leaders are interchangeable and that there is room only for one, at most, on a courthouse lawn. The minimizing reference to "Uncle So-and-So," "Granddaddy So-and-So," as if only a family member could feel a desire to see Holmes memorialized. And also: as if descendants' desires, memories, and need to know where they came from don't truly matter.

Less familiar to us was the ease with which Liston called across the courthouse lawn to a sheriff's deputy to ask whether the unused courthouse was open. Could he get us a key?

"Can he get us a key?" Sylvester chuckled, shaking his head. It was hard to imagine Graham law enforcement offering to let anyone from the Alamance County Community Remembrance Coalition into a closed courthouse.

The deputy jiggled the doorknob, which stuck, and then gained entry through a back door. He opened the large front door for us, and we stepped inside a brick-floored courtroom with low wooden benches, large white columns, and a balcony overlooking the bench. The officer, who was white, stepped respectfully to the side as Liston explained that this courtroom had hosted the speeches before the sign's unveiling and that the room was so full they had to turn people away.

That Saturday, a sheriff's deputy had been on hand in case protesters showed up, looking for trouble. But the event was peaceful, attended not only by Holmes's descendants and the many Black and white Charlotte County residents who'd contributed or shown interest in the new sign but also by the county sheriff, who is Black, and several white deputies who sat, off-duty but uniformed, inside the courtroom to listen.

"You told me you'd be up in a deer stand that day," Liston joked with Jeremy Jones, the officer who had let us into the courthouse. Jones was a captain in the sheriff's department and the son of a longtime sheriff.

Jones smiled, almost bashfully. "I remember. But I was here."

That, too, was new.

• • • •

Charlotte Court House is a small town—756 residents, as of the 2020 census. There isn't much to see: the historic courthouse, a new brick county courthouse, a Dollar General. There's a library, a law office, a pharmacy. After our tour, Liston suggested we get something cold to drink, and we crossed David Bruce Avenue to Mimmo's, an Italian-style lunch spot with wraparound windows shaded by red awnings. Tall stacks of pizza boxes sat on the counter inside the door, and about half of the tables were occupied by families, couples, and friends.

Right away, Liston was greeted warmly by a tall white man with white hair. They chatted amiably, and on our way to our table, she leaned close to Belle and said, "That's him—Gary Walker."

She explained that after the *Post* article came out, Walker didn't like the negative attention to his dismissive comments. He'd been trying to make things up to her ever since, but she remained unimpressed. He had to live in this town, just like she did, and there were consequences to the things you say, the stands you take.

Liston, unlike Walker, isn't from here. She grew up in Baltimore County, where her dad was a reporter for the *Baltimore Sun*, and moved to Brazil as a young teenager when he became the paper's Latin American bureau chief. In Rio de Janeiro, she had friends of every shade of skin and economic level and was a "baby flower child," as she puts it, living a life of adventure and precocious experiences, eventually finding a career in archaeology and cultural resource management. "Where are all the flower children now?" she asked, looking around at the old folks, families, and lunching ladies seated at small wooden tables inside her town's one café.

Charlotte County seemed an odd relocation choice for someone with Liston's worldly pedigree. It's a "deep red" county, as she put it, about 70 percent white and 27 percent Black, with the remaining 3 or 4 percent divided between Asian, Hispanic, and Indigenous residents.

Hardly any of the young people in Charlotte County stay put, Liston told us—there's little to keep them here if they're not interested in working as home health aides, drinking sweet tea at Mimmo's, or attending historical reenactments. In 2023, fewer than 70 percent of households in Charlotte County had broadband Internet access. This included Liston, who had to connect via a hotspot or drive into town to send email.

For a while, even after the 2016 election, Liston focused on keeping politics out of her relationships, even as she investigated the town's long-buried history of enslavement and white supremacist violence, partially through records she found on her property. She and her husband worked on restoring their home and land and helped neighbors trace their ancestors to people buried in the slave cemetery on their property. They hosted an annual Christmas open house, where Republican friends mixed with Democrats. But as the 2020 election heated up, things began to change. Liston parted ways with her "oldest, best girlfriend" over an argument about Michelle Obama that escalated—Liston had commented that she looked beautiful in a yellow gown, and her friend became incensed. How could Liston say that, knowing how her friend felt about the former First Lady? "We'll never speak again," Liston said, shaking her head.

Things reached a breaking point on January 6, 2021, when hard-right rioters breached the US Capitol carrying Confederate flags, assaulting police officers, breaking furniture, and causing nine deaths, including the deaths of five officers. "Something inside of me changed," Liston said. "I'm not a big patriot. But I was so pissed off that those people *dared* to do it."

She sipped her iced tea, then added, "We have not associated with any of our Republican friends since the insurrection."

We sat with that complicated and lonely truth, so close to Sylvester's and yet so different. She chose this place; Sylvester was raised in his. Both had dedicated years of their lives to researching and spreading the word about men who were murdered more than 150 years ago. The social consequences were real for both of them, though Liston had not been followed by police nor feared for her safety. She conversed easily with the man who opposed her efforts most vocally, and the historic marker was now a clearly visible, prominent, permanent fixture on the courthouse lawn. There is no such marker for Wyatt, and no clear path to one, either.

Sylvester leaned back, folded his hands, and asked her the question that had been most on his mind: "What's your motivation for all of this? Why is Joe's story so important to you?"

"Joe is very personal to me. I get emotional when I talk about Joe," Liston said. But, she clarified, it wasn't about race to her. "I hate injustice. I hate things that are unfair. And it was just so unjust and unfair, what happened to him."

She paused and then added, "It would be just as unjust and unfair if he were white. I'd feel the same."

• • • •

But Holmes wasn't white, and what happened to him, and what is still happening to Black men and women who challenge white supremacy, cannot be separated from race. Joseph Holmes had a target on his back because he was a Black man who helped rewrite Virginia's constitution with a progressive Reconstruction agenda; because he advocated for voting rights for Black men; because he opened a school for Black children and bought land for his Black family. All of these acts upended the strict, brutal order constructed by white supremacists.

Even more offensive to white supremacists than the elevation of Black men to power was Holmes's insistence that white men were subject to the same laws as everyone else. As a member of Virginia's Committee on

Taxation and Finance, he investigated and tried to stop corruption by those long used to having the power of government all to themselves. On the day he died, witnesses stated that Holmes was headed to the courthouse to obtain a warrant for the arrest of four white men who'd claimed that they shot a Black man and who threatened to kill Holmes. Holmes's very existence, like Wyatt's, was a threat to white supremacy because he knew the law and was determined to uphold it. White men were no longer free to maim, kill, and steal from Black men and women as they had been before emancipation and the passage of the Fourteenth Amendment. As of 1868, one year before Holmes was killed, Black men and women not only had the right to protect their lives and property but could tell their truth in a court of law.

Like the men and women who stormed the Capitol on January 6, the four men responsible for Holmes's death committed their crime in broad daylight, in front of many witnesses. According to witness testimony, these men confronted Holmes on the courthouse lawn. William Boyd hit Holmes with his cane, and John Marshall pistol-whipped him before shooting him at point-blank range. Holmes made it to the steps before being shot again, and he collapsed and died on the building's threshold.

Liston told us that her editor at the *Charlotte Gazette*, which finally published an article she wrote about Holmes in February 2020, initially resisted her use of the word "lynching." But Liston persisted, explaining in the second sentence, "Although the killers used guns instead of a rope, Holmes was for all intents and purposes lynched for daring to demand equality for all." The inclusion of this single word was her biggest victory, she told us.[4]

But before we left the café, she told us that not every objection to the marker came from white Republicans. A Black man, around her age, urged her to reconsider: "If I bring young people by here, all they'll see is that white men killed a Black man." This aligned with the fears and resistance that Sylvester had heard from older Black folks in Graham.

The same man came up to her later, though, and told her, "I'm glad you did this. I was wrong. It's a good thing for the Black people of this community."

After lunch, we hustled back across the street to stand again before Holmes's sign. A slight breeze ruffled the cherry tree leaves, and the Confederate monument seemed to recede into the distance as we admired the sign again. Though they weren't able to move or remove the monument, Liston worked with two other community members, one white and one Black, to create another contextualizing sign that would explain when, how, and why the monument was erected, as well as what it means to many Black residents. That sign was placed later, in 2023, and is now being studied as a possible model for the hundreds of other towns unsure of what to do about their Confederate monuments. Liston believes it is the first such sign in Virginia. It is also likely to increase visibility to Holmes's story, which is already a stop on Virginia's Black History Trail.

Liston urged us to work toward a marker for Wyatt. She told us she would help us, and for a brief moment, in this tiny town where sheriffs open locked doors and supervisors try to make nice with activists, we could picture it: a handsome, permanent sign, every space filled to tell Wyatt's story. We promised to stay in touch and climbed into Sylvester's SUV to head home.

The sky was milky with a thick haze as we traveled south. It reminded Belle of late-summer humidity over the Haw River, while Sylvester once again thought of ghosts. We didn't know it yet, but it was smoke from the Canadian wildfires, drifted so far south it traveled with us into Graham, where it settled, a dense and ugly vapor.

We passed the hardware store where white men filmed themselves unpacking semiautomatic weapons after the peaceful George Floyd protests. Passed the soda shop where our friends were arrested for singing. Passed the Confederate monument and its tall, $32,000 black fence and the courthouse steps where Sylvester and dozens of other activists were pepper-fogged on Halloween 2020.

Sylvester slowed his under-the-speed-limit driving to a crawl as we rounded the courthouse. Where could we place our signs, our envisioned monuments and historical markers? The dirt collected from the site of Wyatt's death went down to Alabama, where it will be rotated in and out of an exhibit at the Legacy Museum and where a weathered steel plinth, representing Alamance County, is engraved with his name. The glass jar of dirt from the same site, kept in Alamance, sits at the African American Cultural Arts and History Center in Burlington, waiting for a traveling display.

There's no room, no space in Graham set aside for Wyatt's story.

No room, at least, until we make room.

CHAPTER EIGHTEEN

SPREADING THE WORD

Alamance County is not without spaces and people dedicated to the mission of sharing an honest picture of local history. But their considerable efforts tend to be made on top of many other responsibilities.

Shineece Sellars, who balances her work as executive director of the African American Cultural Arts and History Center in Burlington with a career as a real estate agent and financial advisor, said "running a museum was never part of the plan," but she sees the work's importance every day through the enthusiastic response of visitors, who sometimes make planned tours and at other times happen upon the small storefront museum.[1]

Her mother, the late Jane Sellars, filed paperwork to begin the AACAHC in 2017, but Shineece said "the work started long before then." Jane Sellars was a lifelong Alamance County citizen and educator with a strong interest in genealogy and history; she founded the center to "collect and preserve Alamance County's African American history in many varied forms; cultural, architectural, artistic, familial, industrial, commercial, and generational." Jane Sellars did not live to see the AACAHC housed in a brick-and-mortar building but spent years sharing her collection—which included oral histories, photographs, and family heirlooms collected from residents across the county—as a way of sparking conversation at community events and school visits.

Sylvester viewing the Wyatt Outlaw exhibit at the African American Cultural Arts and History Center in Burlington, North Carolina. The painting leaning against the wall, which imagines what Wyatt might have looked like, is by Rodney Blackwell. (Photo by Carey Kirk.)

Today, the AACAHC is open five days a week to the public. Admission is free. It is the only museum dedicated to the African American experience in Alamance County.

"Most visitors are drawn to Wyatt Outlaw," James Shields, manager of the AACAHC, told us. "People come in, and they have never heard of him." Shields, an avid historian who previously led tours at Guilford College about

A display of pre-integration yearbooks from Jordan Sellars High and Central High in Burlington is popular with visitors. (Photo by Carey Kirk.)

the Underground Railroad, said it is his job not only to teach visitors about Wyatt Outlaw but also to give context about the Reconstruction era in Alamance County.[2]

In addition to viewing the Outlaw and Reconstruction exhibit, visitors can pull up a chair to peruse yearbooks from the county's African American schools as well as newspaper reports from the 1969 police killing of Leon Mebane, an unarmed Black fifteen-year-old, during the Burlington race riots.

Other exhibits highlight the community's African American business and economic history as well as the military service of African Americans from Alamance. As an army veteran, Sylvester was surprised to see a photograph of "Lil'" Paul Hunter, whom he remembered singing gospel songs in his powerful and passionate tenor voice at Children's Chapel UCC. Sylvester credits Hunter as one of his inspirations for becoming a singer but did not know until seeing AACAHC's exhibit that he was also an army veteran.

In addition to Shineece Sellars's work on the AACAHC, she serves as a board member for other community organizations. "In a lot of these meetings I'm the only person of color, and I'm usually the youngest. This is why we're here."

Sylvester was surprised to see a photo of a church soloist he did not realize was also a veteran. (Photo by Carey Kirk.)

James Shields, museum manager, and Shineece Sellars, executive director of the African American Cultural Arts and History Center. (Photo by Carey Kirk.)

Who Was Wyatt Outlaw, a comics pamphlet by Nic L. Cassette and Forward Motion Alamance. (Courtesy of Nic Cassette.)

James Shields agreed that the work is critical and is enthusiastic about speaking with white visitors, who will sometimes want to defend the Confederate statue. He invites them to sit down and "talk about why it's there."

"How we reckon with our history says a lot about us," said Shields. "Let's have a conversation."

In 2020, artist Nic L. Cassette, a member of the activist group Forward Motion Alamance, created *Who Was Wyatt Outlaw*, a black-and-white comics pamphlet that depicts Outlaw's life and death in Graham, along with a zine called *They Tried to Kill the Black Vote*, which illustrates an X-Men-style fight over Black voter suppression in American history, and a special *Villains* zine depicting longtime Sheriff Terry Johnson's civil rights abuses. Forward Motion Alamance members handed out the zines at protests, and Cassette encourages people to copy and share them.

CHAPTER NINETEEN
COUNTENANCE

BELLE

I've been thinking about the word "countenance"—the noun, meaning the expression on a person's face, and the verb, to consent or give permission.

It's kind of an old-fashioned word, maybe something you'd hear in a spelling bee or be assigned to learn in high school. I remember giving my Alamance County high school students a lot of vocabulary words about the face and its expression—"mien," for example, and "visage"—especially when we were reading nineteenth-century fiction. I taught them "countenance," the noun and the verb.

I came across the word again while doing research at UNC's Wilson Library, in the Southern Historical Collection, when Sylvester and I pulled a selection of materials in our research about Wyatt Outlaw. Among the papers and documents was a small book, printed in 1870: *Ritual, Constitution, and By-Laws of the National Council, U. L. of A.*

The Union League was a patriotic society that began in the North during the Civil War and moved into Southern states during Reconstruction as a way of supporting Republican ideals and encouraging newly enfranchised Black men to vote. The league was a place where Black men could discuss the issues of the day; make political, educational, and business contacts; and understand the importance of political participation. Education, political power, and economic security were all highly prized by these new citizens.

As a league leader, Wyatt likely had a copy of the bylaws, exacting in their directions for where to stand, what to say, how to outfit the room where meetings were held. Outlaw most certainly would have been familiar with the oral obligation, which was used to initiate new members. They swore to "support, protect, and defend the Constitution and Government of the United States of America" and to vote only for "those who advocate and support the great principles set forth by this League, to fill any office of honor." They promised to "aid and defend the working men of the nation, and in all lawful methods endeavor to secure them the right to labor and enjoy the full fruit of their labor." And they would not, they pledged, "countenance or employ anyone who is in any manner hostile to the working men of the nation."[1]

This oath stands in stark contrast to the hateful things written and said about the Union League by white supremacists at the time and for many years after—that the league was responsible for violence done by the Ku Klux Klan, that it was corrupt and secretly enslaved its members. The group's emphasis on the rights of workers was not mentioned, nor the fact that Union Leaguers were the carpenters, mechanics, masons, metalsmiths, railroad workers, and teachers of their communities.

But the oath, made by those who had so recently had their labor and liberty stolen, is very clear. I will support and protect the Constitution and government. I will vote for people who believe, as I do, in the principles of the Constitution. I will help the working people and will do so lawfully. And I will not put up with anyone hostile to my fellow working people.

The first day that Sylvester and I took out the Union League handbook, August 1, 2023, Donald Trump was indicted on three federal charges of conspiracy to commit election interference: defrauding the United States, obstructing an official government proceeding, and depriving people of the right to have their votes counted.[2]

The second day we examined the book, August 14, Trump and eighteen of his allies were indicted on forty-one counts of election interference by Fulton County district attorney Fani Willis.[3] These included perjury, giving false statements and writings, forgery in the first degree, and solicitation of violation of oath by a public officer. Both indictments—against a man who has since been convicted of failing to pay his taxes and defrauding banks—were revealed after we carefully turned the pages of this book that was over 150 years old.

When I mentioned the coincidence to Sylvester, he said, "Maybe we should go to Wilson Library more often."

• • • •

I don't say the Pledge of Allegiance and haven't since I was a child; Bea stopped saying it at six, after she was pepper-sprayed by police in a get-out-the-vote march.

But I like this idea of countenance, expressed within the Union League oath—my face turns toward those who help and side with workers and away from those hostile to them. I saw it in the actions of local activists like Kris Loy, Maurice Wells, Avery Harvey, and Carey Kirk, who stood side by side, night after night, in Wyatt Outlaw Park, holding signs and engaging with passersby after the January 6 insurrection. I saw it in the patience and fortitude of the folks who provided court support, waiting outside the Alamance County Courthouse on chilly mornings while their fellow activists faced trial. I saw it in the attorneys, journalists, photojournalists, chefs, and artists who donated time and food and talent to every march, court date, and community action in Graham and Burlington.

But Graham and Burlington are not my home. I live one county south, in rural Chatham County, which like Alamance has increasingly become a bedroom community for larger metropolitan areas. Unlike in Alamance, my county commissioners and other elected officials are overwhelmingly Democratic. Because of racial gerrymandering that intentionally dilutes the votes of Democrats, my state and national representatives are also safely Democratic. The Jim Crow–era Confederate statue that stood before our historic courthouse was removed in 2019, after the county commissioners voted to have it removed.

Until I learned about Wyatt Outlaw and his Union League, I never considered Chatham, at least the part of Chatham I live in, as a good place to organize. In election seasons, I volunteered for the Democratic Party in Burlington and Siler City, driving twenty miles or more to canvass voters in neighborhoods I needed a map to navigate. But after working side by side with Sylvester for two years, observing and admiring his long-held relationships across Alamance County, I understood that my own impact could be greater at home, within communities I knew well. In 2022, I got involved with a small group of women who were working to reelect our county's only Black school board member, a twenty-year board veteran I'd known and looked up to for more than a decade. She was being challenged by a white newcomer endorsed by the right-wing extremist group Moms for Liberty. We sprang into action, holding rallies, talking with our neighbors, and engaging with voters outside the polls. Our candidate was reelected by a mere 462 votes.

With the help of Down Home, our local teachers' union, and other grassroots organizations, this group has continued to build power. In 2024, we focused our energy on helping some of the most essential workers in our community: teachers, instructional assistants, cafeteria staff, office staff, and bus drivers, who were grossly underpaid and leaving the profession in large numbers. We knew that the children in our county were suffering too, learning in overcrowded classrooms or without permanent, certified teachers. We worked within existing power structures to demand increased teacher pay in 2024–25, attending and speaking at school board and county commissioner meetings alongside parents, teachers, grandparents, and students from across the county. We faced opposition from commissioners wary of increasing taxes, and we did not get everything we asked for, but our small and scrappy community group ultimately prevailed, and commissioners budgeted $2,000 raises for every teacher in the county.

During the 2024 presidential election season, Chatham County also received help from Down Home, which brought in a team of organizers to knock on doors and talk to Chatham voters about health care access, abortion rights, and full funding for public schools. Bea and Richard and I wore our "Elect Working People for Everything" T-shirts to canvass in neighborhoods across the county. I'm proud that, like five other rural counties where Down Home organized, Chatham reversed national electoral trends, moving leftward instead of rightward to cast ballots for candidates who care about working people and our families.

In Chatham County, that meant overperforming our expected outcomes by 6 percent and reelecting another long-standing Democratic leader on our school board, a former educator and principal who helped us achieve teacher raises in the spring.[4]

I learned to turn my face toward the people closest to me—kids, teachers, neighbors—from Wyatt Outlaw, the other Union League leaders of his time, and the members of Down Home North Carolina, who, with or without knowing it, follow his example too. This locally focused work, divided across more than 150 years of history, makes it possible for me to believe in and work for a better South and a better community.

• • • •

Sylvester once told me about a time, about a year after he left active duty, when he decided to try writing a new version of "The Star-Spangled Banner."

He sat down at his home in Graham with a pencil and staff paper. He

Wales Window for Alabama, designed by John Petts.
Photograph by Carol M. Highsmith, 2010.
(Courtesy of the Library of Congress Prints and Photographs Division.)

wrote a three-part soprano, alto, and tenor arrangement for the song. He finished it, plugged it into music notation software, and replayed it.

At first he was pleased. But something made him hold off on sharing it, even though he was often asked, given his background as an Army Band musician, to perform patriotic music. One afternoon, in the mill-turned-coffee-shop where we often met to talk and write, I asked him why he'd arranged the song and why he hadn't performed it.

Sylvester took his time thinking about the question, gazing out the paned windows at the Haw River. He drew a breath. "I always knew I wanted to write this; I wanted to put my imprint on the song while maintaining its original integrity," he said and then paused. "But I felt like it would be wrong, in Graham, to share it while Black and Brown lives, Black and Brown history, matters less to police and even to society itself than white lives, white history. It would be wrong to share it while North Carolina's Republican legislature works to suppress the Black vote, to suppress Black history, to take rights away from people."

I asked, "When will you share it?"

This was easier to answer. "You know, when more churches have a darker-skinned Jesus in their window, that's when I'll know the tide has turned," he said.

I was surprised at first, as Sylvester had been talking about things I saw as outside of church: voter suppression, police brutality, history. But then I remembered the ruthless attacks on churches, the endless rebuilding that Black pastors and parishioners have had to do, all across the South and all across the country.

I thought of the Wales Window for Alabama, with its sorrowful Black Jesus. Donated by the people of Wales, including hundreds of schoolchildren, and designed by artist John Petts, the window was installed two years after the attack on Birmingham's Sixteenth Street Baptist Church that killed four little girls. The large stained-glass window is mostly composed of cool tones—blue, purple—and takes its inspiration from Matthew 25:40: "Truly, I say to you, as you did it to one of the least of these my brothers, you did it to me" (ESV). YOU DO IT TO ME, reads the bottom of the window, in notable present tense. A rainbow blooms between Christ's outstretched arms. His large hands are unmistakably those of a workingman, a carpenter. The right hand pushes against the frame, while the left is open, palms-up, signaling forgiveness. Bea and I brought a small print back from our visit to Sixteenth Street Baptist Church, and I gave it to Sylvester. It sits on Sylvester's desk, next to papers, books, computer and recording equipment, and a glass-encased baseball card of Andruw Jones.

I'm still waiting to hear Sylvester's arrangement of "The Star-Spangled Banner," but that's okay. There's a lot of work to do in the meantime.

CHAPTER TWENTY

IT TAKE A LONG PULL TO GET THERE

SYLVESTER

The familiar pounding in my chest got louder and louder as I realized we were getting closer to curtain. Backstage was chaos as the production crew prepared, presetting props, testing microphones, and running light cords. My hands were sweaty; my head was spinning.

It was May 4, 2024, and I and five other local artists were commissioned by the Culture Mill and Carolina Performing Arts to curate an event called the Commons Festival. Six Black artists would create six separate pieces and premiere them in front of a live audience at this intimate black box theater. Meetings, residencies, rehearsals, and other curatorial activities had ensued over that previous year.

The string of assassinations of Black political leaders during Wyatt's time became more evident as Belle and I continued our research. We come across other heroes in various counties throughout the South with similar fates—the "other Wyatts." Armed with this information, I'd set out to utilize what had become a new voice for me, the form of art my great friend Walter Boyd had encouraged me to take on just three years earlier: playwriting.

Johnny Lee Chapman III, Sylvester Allen Jr., and Cortland Gilliam performing in *The First and Final Meeting of Jim, Joe, and Wyatt*. (Photo by Rode Diaz.)

Walter was gone now, having passed away in August 2023. I couldn't call him up in the middle of the night and ask him questions about Wyatt. I didn't have him to text at any time when I had questions about Jemima Phillips or the Long family or any speck of dust on Alamance County land I came across. This time it was on me.

This time I would call it *The First and Final Meeting of Jim, Joe, and Wyatt*.

Cortland Gilliam, poet laureate for Chapel Hill, and Johnny Lee Chapman III, astute wordsmith and movement artist, both already members of what we called the festival cohort, were recruited to play Joe and Jim, respectively. Maybe it was the franticness of writing and producing a play, but only then, standing backstage with the others, did I finally realize that, unlike in *The Spirit of Wyatt Outlaw*, I would be playing Wyatt Outlaw myself tonight. That was an eerie thought, akin to the way I felt holding Jacob A. Long's recollections in the Wilson Library across this very campus. I would live in his "house," walk in his "shoes," and eat his "food." After chasing Wyatt's story for so long, I would *be* Wyatt Outlaw.

• • • •

We'd scavenged the PlayMakers Repertory Company's costume shop, trying to find clothing of the Reconstruction era. We'd found tables and painted them. We'd searched antique stores for period-appropriate woodworking tools. I'd stayed up till 5:00 a.m. multiple nights composing music to underscore the stage movements. But tonight was the night. I could feel the moment getting closer. It was almost showtime.

Cortland put on his Panama hat and dark-brown corduroy blazer—a perfect fit for his long arms and tall stature. Lee pressed his tan poor-boy cap over his dreads and draped a brown leather travel bag over one shoulder. I buttoned the sleeves of my Victorian shirt and laid my collar down in front of the backstage mirror.

The three of us circled up backstage to give thanks to each other and honor the men we would portray after the long process of rehearsals, table reads, stumble-throughs, discussions, and gathering of props and set pieces, all with the intention of telling a story of three people whom history threatened to leave behind. No more writing, no more thinking, no more repainting props or rehanging lights. It was time.

Thirty minutes away from Graham on the campus of UNC–Chapel Hill, the same campus where Belle and I had sat in Wilson Library, holding Wyatt's 1867 Union League commission in our hands, I walked out in costume at 5:05 p.m. to a half-full crowd in the 139-seat CURRENT ArtSpace + Studio and uttered the first words of my impromptu preshow curtain speech.

"This feels like a dream," I said in almost a whisper, just loud enough to reach the ears of the farthest member of the audience. I paused in reflection. It felt surreal. I knew we were telling an important story, and I could feel that the people in the room could sense that, too. We sat in deep silence as the rain came down on the roof over our heads.

Blinded by the spotlights, seeing only silhouettes of the small crowd, I was reminded of the first words of my first play back in Saxapahaw: *You may have heard by now the legend of Wyatt Outlaw.* Once again, time stopped. Though dimly lit, I peered into the faces of those who'd registered for the festival, bought tickets, and took time on this stormy weekend to drive in and see the performance.

I could see just well enough to know that Belle was there in the fourth or fifth row, as she had been for *The Spirit of Wyatt Outlaw* a few years back. My partner, Karla, slipped in just in time for the house lights to dim. There were others I knew to be comrades in the fight for justice. Their presence reminded me of the activists who sat in the Haw River Ballroom amphitheater for the first play and of the activists we'd interviewed over the last few years.

And it was in that silence after the first few words of the curtain speech that I realized the work Belle and I had done had come full circle. We'd interviewed so many people and read so many books, articles, papers. Followed closely as activists went through court proceedings after having been arrested for peaceful protests. Heard stories of courage and sacrifice from seemingly ordinary people. The question I had in the beginning all of a sudden had a clearer answer. Why did it mean so much to them?

What I've learned is this: Wyatt's life and death represented a bigger idea and introduced in Alamance the practical application of that idea. And the idea was this: that every person, no matter how rich or poor, no matter how big or small, no matter how young or old, can have a voice and can inspire others if they can find courage to put the self aside and live for the collective. That you, no matter how ordinary you may see yourself, can leave an extraordinary legacy. Wyatt embodied these ideas.

There is no known picture of Wyatt, but if I were to draw him, he might wear a cape, carry a sword and shield, and ride on horseback through the streets of Graham during the 1860s, watching over the town like some kind of Avenger. Though that seems like an exaggerated "tall tale" depiction, it would have been nice to walk through a museum as a child in Graham and see that kind of display and then hear the tall tale behind it. And then to know it was based on a real person. And that person was here. That person was someone who looked like me and was from my own hometown. That is the image the white folks in power attempted to steal from me—steal from us.

Wyatt did extraordinary things. Led efforts to build a church and school. Inspired people to vote and participate in public life. And he did all that in the face of imminent danger. He did it under intense pressure. He did it with audacity. Because he knew it had to be done. He inspired change against all odds. Perhaps most important to remember: He was not a superhero; he was just a man.

Back to the theater.

After I finished my curtain speech, the lights went out and we began the play, *The First and Final Meeting of Jim, Joe, and Wyatt*. Using blood-red lighting, we depicted the three of them onstage moving as if they were reliving their assassinations over and over. Upstage, a projection screen displayed blurred images of little-known Black Reconstruction-era leaders and families, as if to say, *We know you all were here, but we can't really see you*. The narrator of the story then starts to tell about a dream he had in which Joe, Jim, and Wyatt meet to discuss their fears and excitement. In the dream they are human, they are real, not just words on a page. Wyatt discusses his suspicion that the KKK is up to something, that they should all be careful but not stop in their pursuit of the advancement of newly freed people. Joe and Jim discuss their strategies for dealing with the threats. They all share gumbo, hoecake,

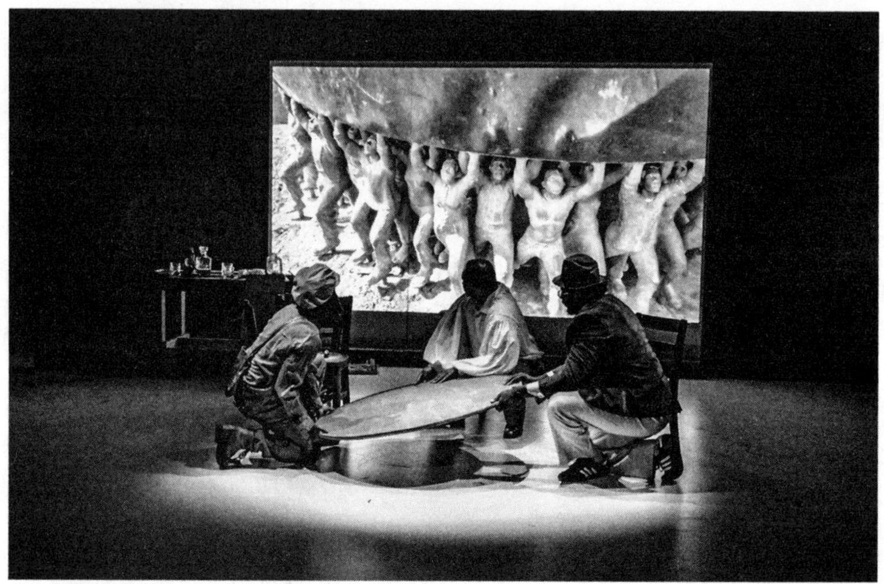

Jim, Wyatt, and Joe as "Unsung Founders." (Photo by Rode Diaz.)

and gifts with each other. The play closes with a tableau of the *Unsung Founders* memorial table at McCorkle Place, a central park on the UNC–Chapel Hill campus. The sculpture, donated by the class of 2002 and installed in 2005, is a two-foot-tall polished granite table supported by some 300 bronze figures representing free and enslaved men and women who "helped build the Carolina that we cherish today."

The idea of the tableau came from visiting the memorial and realizing how miniature the figures were that depicted the enslaved. When I saw it for the first time I thought, *They should be bigger.* I wanted them to be giants.

The play takes a few people, once footnotes in history, and makes them something bigger . . . and multiplies them. Multiplied not just by activists in Wyatt's era but by today's activists. Today's Outlaws. And that's what I find to be most interesting. What the whitewashers of history are afraid of. Multiplication. Because that's what you get when you try to kill one Outlaw. You only make more of them.

• • • •

Avoiding humiliation in the face of reprehensible circumstances, even when self-inflicted, seems a particular way of storytelling in the small-town American South. I knew that one day I wanted to be a part of the *reshaping* of that storytelling. Writing *The Spirit of Wyatt Outlaw* and *The First and Final Meeting of Jim, Joe, and Wyatt* allowed me to be a part of that reshaping. Writing *The Legend of Wyatt Outlaw* has too. In the end, the courage to write, to confront the system, was less about what I believed I was capable of and more about what I knew I had to do.

Because it wasn't just Graham, North Carolina, history that needed a rewrite. I'm more convinced now that this is an American problem. An American story. It doesn't just start with Wyatt and end with today's Alamance outlaws. These outlaws were everywhere.

Joseph Holmes was assassinated in Charlotte County, Virginia. Jim Williams was assassinated in York County, South Carolina. This is an American problem that requires an un-American solution. It's coming to terms with what the Civil War really was about and what really happened in the Reconstruction era. And how these lynchings, or assassinations, were often led by municipal and county leaders, even sheriffs. And how that history affects how we interact with each other today. Yes, the un-American thing. To tell the truth about our past and not let pride get in the way of learning something new.

In the age of social media, we all have a choice: Promote truth or promote misinformation. *Stick to an idea of America that makes me, my family, and my friends comfortable, or humble myself to something that feels less good: relearning what we got wrong the first time around.*

"We are *all* descended from slaves," South African–born Tesla CEO and billionaire Elon Musk said in an interview with Black television journalist Don Lemon in 2024, as if to imply that we've all had a fair and equal shot.[1] To ignore the particularly brutal reality of American chattel slavery is one thing, but to act as if the end of slavery was the end of injustice for Black people in America reaches another level of dishonesty. From the deconstruction of the Reconstruction era to the Black Codes, to redlining and gentrification, to lynchings and voting rights suppression, the denigration and degradation of Blackness in this country, racism, and injustice didn't stop after the Civil War. Any collective frustration on the part of the Black community is the result of the whole truth, not part of it. That's the point.

This country, over the course of its history, has tried to paint us as perpetrators, doers of crime, lower than or less than. It's the effort to strip us of our dignity rather than acknowledge it. To deprive us of our history and identity, leaving us twisting in the wind, and then tell us that whatever we don't have is entirely our own doing.

But the stories of Wyatt Outlaw, Joseph Holmes, and Jim Williams defy that narrative. The stories of today's outlaws defy that narrative. Their stories, woven together, compose a symphony of distinguishment, sacrifice, and perspicacity. Their stories are important, not just because of how they died or the pain they experienced but because of what they represent.

Even as someone who served in the military, and maybe especially so as a Black man stationed at Fort Lee, I can say with honesty that some of our American pride is built on shifting sand. It's built on omission or a false reconstruction of history.

One of Wyatt's murderers stated that he was killed for his "mouthy" behavior. But Wyatt's voice was one they couldn't drown out for good. His work showed up in the efforts and activism of the people on the ground, local people whose deeds would often go unsung. These activists had become outlaws because they had to. Because we live in a society where telling the truth about history makes you an outlaw. Fighting for justice makes you an outlaw. Fighting for true equality makes you an outlaw. And these outlaws have paid the price in many ways and for many years.

Dreama rose to the challenge as a candidate for county commissioner in Alamance in 2020. The smear campaign was relentless, and she lost the race, but she went on to make an impact across the state as codirector of Down Home NC, a progressive rural organizing nonprofit.

Kris joined the fight for justice and accountability in Alamance through various activist groups as well as with Down Home. But his presence at peaceful protests and subsequent arrests have made it almost impossible to find substantial employment.

Michael Harris has never stopped, driving tirelessly to different towns in the United States to "apply pressure" to unjust systems. In July 2022, Michael was punched repeatedly in the face by police during an arrest as he and several others protested the killing of Jayland Walker at the hands of an Akron police officer. He continues to protest where he sees police violence and injustice.

Some outlaws have talked about the ongoing hardships from the traumatic experiences they have endured throughout their encounters with law enforcement and neo-Confederates and how working as a leader in the movement has taken a toll on their mental health.

"The charges is the least of my worries. . . . It's the mental health," Avery Harvey said in an interview for a documentary with ProPublica in 2021. "People come to me and say . . . 'This happened to my son.' I know you got people. I go in these communities every day and they look at me like I'm a superhero. But I can't help. And I don't know what to do."[2] Avery was instrumental in bringing attention to the constant injustices of local police and pointing out the needs of the underserved in the lower-income Black communities of Alamance County. Avery is not a superhero. But he is a hero to many.

I think in our lives we search for heroes. When I was a kid, watching baseball players do extraordinary things on TV made me want to emulate what they did. What became more important, though, was knowing about the heroes from my own hometown. Wyatt isn't the only hero, but he's important to our story. Our Alamance story. Therefore, our American story.

Wyatt Outlaw is now a hero of mine, like Andruw Jones, whom I watched soar across center field to catch line drives for the Atlanta Braves in the 1990s. Joseph Holmes is now a hero of mine, like my stepfather, Willie, who made the best out of what he had and set the best example he could for me to follow. And I'm glad I know now of Jim Williams, who was little-known to the rest of the world but who inspires me to summon courage when it is needed, just like he did.

Because it's hard to be a true hero without those who look up to you knowing of your sacrifice. The outlaws in Alamance County were inspired by Wyatt's story—not just his death, but his brilliant life. And though we don't know every detail of it, we know enough to understand that he and the activists of his time fought together. They endured together. And they should be remembered together.

Zora Neale Hurston wrote, "There is no greater agony than bearing an untold story inside of you."[3] I don't believe that goes only for an individual. That can go for a town as well. And in a small town like Graham, North Carolina—like Alamance County—the community can't truly come together without bearing the full truth of it. The full untold story inside of us, from enslavement to the Reconstruction era to Black Lives Matter. Let us ask, Who are we? How did we come to this internalized division? And how do we heal from that division? And how do we finally squash the persistent practice of pride over truth? Maybe it's too much to ask for a nation built on a long list of falsehoods. Maybe it would be "too long a pull." Maybe.

But maybe it starts with something simpler. Maybe it starts with a stage play, a book, or a conversation at the local pub. Maybe it starts at the ballot box. Maybe it starts in backyards where kids catch lightning bugs. Maybe it starts in break rooms at weaving plants and barbecues put on by grassroots organizations. Maybe it starts with school board meetings and history classes.

I *do* know this history matters. It's important because it informs who we are and who we know we don't want to be. It's important to the unsung heroes and to those who would be inspired by them. To the church women who wore "crowns" in the pews and the men who shined their shoes every Saturday afternoon for Sunday's service. To everyone who's given testimony, from Jemima to the churchgoers of today who have spoken of injustice, inequity, and struggle. To all those who don't know their ancestry past a couple of generations but who wish to know more in order to extend *their* understanding of who they are, how their communities came to be, and who tried to stop their progress.

It matters to Samuel Merritt, Wyatt's great-great-grandson, who has come to know Wyatt as a town hero, an example, and something to be proud of, even as his own trajectory, from a small, segregated North Carolina town to the directorship of the state's public health lab, inspires others.

It matters to the outlaws of this town. The ones whose eyes were pepper-sprayed with hate at the Alamance County Courthouse, right in front of the Confederate statue.

It matters to Audra Faucette, who was misinformed as a child about Wyatt and told a narrative that could have been easily spread throughout the town, replacing the story of a courageous town commissioner and constable with a legacy of shame and indignity.

It matters to my mother, who still remembers having to go to the back of the restaurants as a child and whose stepfather was made to feel less than human when his sharecropping money was kept by the white man who saw him as less than smart, less than responsible, all because of his skin color.

It matters to Omega and Brenda Wilson, who fought for over a decade to save St. Luke Christian Church from erasure and who have fought since to bring clean water and modern utilities to the West End of Mebane.

It matters to the families of George Floyd, Trayvon Martin, Ahmad Aubrey, and countless other families who've lost loved ones on account of prejudice, ignorance, and hatred. Because the prejudice that America still holds toward the Black community only fuels violent actions from racists who feel justified in those killings.

And it matters to me. It matters because it explains, in part, the racial tension that I feel in my own hometown at times. It explains why I get the feeling that some store owners would prefer that I find somewhere else to shop. It explains why so many friends had racist parents, parents whose houses I couldn't go into as a child. It matters to people like me who have spent their lives as writers and composers and performers, putting on works that attempt to fill in the holes left by history.

In the opera *Porgy and Bess*, Jake, a fisherman, sings,

It take a long pull to get there
But I'll anchor in the Promised land
In the Promised Land.[4]

I've been using those lyrics to describe my frustrations ever since I got a chance to perform the opera, starring Rhiannon Giddens, at the Tanger Center while writing this book. Now, when I drive past the new $32,000 fence surrounding the Confederate statue in Graham, put up as a way of mitigating the need for constant police patrol with taxpayer dollars, I just smile and say, "It take a long pull to get there." Or when I learn of businesses like Liberation Station, a Black-owned children's bookstore, having to move out of Raleigh because of death threats and intimidation, I say, "It take a long pull to get there."[5] When I see clips like the Don Lemon and Elon Musk interview, where Musk tried to water down the Black struggle in America by saying we're all descendants of slaves, I shake my head and say, "It take a long pull to get there."

Conrad, the marble Confederate soldier that stands in front of the Alamance County Courthouse, is a reminder of the white supremacy that Jacob A. Long hoped to leave behind after his death. It is a reminder of allegiance, even in the face of truth, to remain at the top of the pecking order. Where does Wyatt Outlaw fit in such people's story? How do you tell the whole truth, nothing but the truth, and remain the hero in the end? They couldn't. They could only conclude that Wyatt—his image, his truth, his impact—must be blurred.

CHAPTER TWENTY-ONE

THE SPIRIT OF WYATT OUTLAW

What We Owe the Living

SYLVESTER

I sometimes wonder what Alamance County would have looked like without its racist past. America, for that matter. What would it be like for every person in the Black community to be able to sift through the depths of their family history, to be able to find the sense of familial grounding that I believe every human soul craves, longs for, stands on? To know more definitively from what countries our families originated? What if the Reconstruction era had truly been used for reconstruction and there had been no backlash to minority progress? What heights would we have achieved by now without the burning of Black Wall Street, the massacre in Wilmington, the desecration of Black families systematically, the implementation of Jim Crow, the Black Codes?

At the time of the writing of these final pages, Conrad, the Confederate statue in Alamance County's Court Square, is still standing; Terry Johnson is still the sheriff; and Donald J. Trump, a convicted felon who was also impeached for inciting an insurrection against the federal government, has been reelected president. As he did in 2020, he won the closely contested swing state of North Carolina—but this time, he won the other swing states too. On January 20, 2025, he was inaugurated for a second term, just a few days after a final report by Special Counsel Jack Smith concluded that had Trump's election interference charges made it to trial, there was sufficient evidence to convict him.

On this cold, cloudy Inauguration Day—which fell bitterly on Martin Luther King Day—Belle went with her daughters to a day of service at a local high school, packaging hygiene supplies for hurricane victims in western North Carolina. I taught music lessons to ten different students, ranging in age from five to seventy-one years old, in Burlington.

The small town of Graham, which I drove through to get to work, was still unwilling to take responsibility for telling the story of Wyatt Outlaw to its townspeople. There is no statue or bust or plaque or marker in the place where Wyatt died. No sign in the town square commemorating a detailed account of the murder of 1870 nor a visible written commitment to racial reconciliation.

Graham is a normal-looking, even quaint-looking town. The soda shops, pubs, and cinemas that show classic and second-run movies host steady foot traffic from open to close on any regular day. Police details still block off the west side street on Thursdays at 7:00 p.m. for band performances and good, clean family fun in the summertime. Hundreds of people shop, talk, laugh, or eat ice cream while standing on or near the road where the KKK marched Wyatt to his demise in February 1870. It's as if Wyatt never existed.

And as I drove the roundabout, past the courthouse and past Conrad, I couldn't help but notice that not one Black business remained in the square. Not one barbershop, restaurant, or record store. Deadbolted on the lonely northeast corner of Court Square sat a dark, empty space where Dionne's consignment clothing shop, The Muse, once stood. Even Dionne was gone now.

Despite the cold—maybe because of the cold—I thought about warmer times in my county and in this square.

In June 2024, a few weeks before Belle and I finished the first draft of this book, I was invited to attend a reception for gubernatorial candidate Josh Stein, held at the house of former Burlington mayor Ian Baltutis. Under a tent on the grassy back lawn in front of rows of standing tables draped with white cloth, I spoke with activists and delegates and political figures about how we could positively influence the future of the city, the state, and the country overall. After a hopeful exchange with Mr. Stein about his campaign and a quick plug about the book Belle and I were writing, I then entered a spirited gabfest with the Reverend Walter Allison, member of the NAACP Alamance chapter, and another older Black gentleman, who also grew up in Graham.

After some laughs and talk about the weather and music, the reverend started a monologue about his love of playing trumpet when he was in high school and how that dream came to a halt with the distraction of racial tension among the students in the schools, to include the riots of 1969 that led to the death of Leon Mebane in front of a grocery store on Rauhut Street in Burlington.

Further into the conversation, the three of us having now formed a huddle, the two men reminisced about the Black Bottom, a long-extinct downtown district that housed businesses owned and patronized by Black townspeople. Surrounded by a mostly white guest list, they told me about how the urban renewal project of the 1960s and '70s eventually either destroyed or moved all of the businesses in the district. Billiard halls, grocery stores, barbershops, smoke shops, theaters, dentists were gone; some were moved farther northeast to Rauhut Street, while most simply disappeared.

I'd never heard of it. They said these places thrived when they were kids, but they all went away. The only business from Black Bottom now is Lawrence Slade's barbershop, L&M. I thought, what a concept! Black business districts. Black economy. Black growth. And in Alamance County. I settled quickly into that huddle, hanging on every word of their stories.

After that conversation, I contemplated the stark difference between what those gentlemen described and what I saw in the county today. Those are not stories I would have learned in school. And I took that moment with me as an example of how powerful storytelling can be from one generation to the next. Just as powerful, though, is the intentional manipulation of history, even in the school systems.

Undeniably, the infiltration of the United Daughters of the Confederacy and its members' Lost Cause narrative into our school systems had a massive influence on the beliefs of many, in the South especially, about what the Civil War was fought over, how it ended, and who's owed what as a result. All of the happenings of the past—chattel slavery, the destruction or incompleteness of official record, the whitewashing of the nation's history, and the often-brutal means taken to confuse and scramble Black identity—have left us with questions, holes in the answers, and a deep frustration. The George Floyd protests, or even the 1969 Burlington riots, came as no surprise given the ever-present tension that's gone unresolved in the aftermath of the Civil War.

• • • •

About a week after that campaign event, Belle and I met with Dr. Samuel Merritt, Wyatt Outlaw's great-great-grandson, at the park we've come to know as Wyatt Outlaw Park, the spot where Wyatt was hanged in 1870. During a previous interview, Belle and I had asked about a family Bible my friend Walter Boyd told us about before he died. We wanted to see it in person, so Dr. Merritt agreed to meet on a scorching summer day in Graham on his way from Raleigh to Atlanta.

Wearing shades and melting in the sun, we waited at the park's granite benches as Dr. Merritt wrestled through Chapel Hill traffic to get to us. Belle noticed the smell of mint from plants growing around the park, while I studied the behavior of the townspeople as they trod the crosswalks to and from the historic county courthouse. A mother and daughter, both white, wandered into the park, searching for their family name among the park's inscribed bricks, and I wasn't surprised when Belle engaged them in conversation, telling them why we were there and what was significant about the park.

"Wyatt Outlaw," the teenage girl said. "That's a pretty sick name."

Her mother agreed, approvingly. Belle turned to me, and I finished the story she started.

"In fact, historians believe he was hanged from an elm tree right where you are standing."

They looked at the names beneath their feet like they might find his own there, and I told them there wasn't anything to show what happened on this spot, not yet. They thanked us and told us they'd read our book when it came out.

Dr. Merritt arrived sharply dressed, as he is every time I see him. Even in his eighties, he walks with a lift that would remind you of someone sixty years younger.

Almost immediately he began to show us pictures of his grandmother Nancy Outlaw, Wyatt's grandchild. She was light-skinned with a head full of black hair, standing in front of a slick black Pontiac.

Dr. Merritt set a large box down on the granite bench, opened it, and pulled out the oldest Bible I'd ever laid my eyes on. It was Wyatt's family Bible, the one that had his handwritten birth date in it. The binding on the book was worn, so it took two of us to hold the heavy book steady. Under the intensity of the hot sun, and as locals peered curiously into our meeting as they traveled the nearby sidewalks, we flipped through the pages, noticing the handwriting generations old, mixed in with the printed biblical text.

I realized at that moment the significance of what we were doing: holding Wyatt's family Bible in the very place, the very spot, where he was hung in 1870. I remembered holding the letters of Jacob A. Long, one of the Klansmen who killed him, at UNC's Wilson Library. This was a full circle moment that started when I first heard Wyatt's story when I was a teenager. It was a strange and unearthly experience to hold in my hands the real-life family artifacts of someone who'd become a ghost story in his own town.

After showing us more pictures and telling us fascinating stories about his childhood, Dr. Merritt closed the family Bible. He had to get going to see his daughter, a doctor who lived in Atlanta.

He placed the Bible in its box and set it gently on the granite bench. I asked him a final question.

"What does it do to a person to learn more and more about your family history?"

"It fills in all the gaps," he said.

He closed his eyes, searching for a fitting analogy. When he found it, he stretched his arms, one to the front and one to the back, and described images of ancestors, family members from different generations, all holding hands in a long line.

"You're on a march," he began. "All holding hands. There are older folks behind you, and the younger folks up front. Time passes."

He paused and lowered his arms, fingertips touching the Bible's protective box.

"Because the people behind you will soon drop off, and pretty soon you're at the end of the line of marchers. When you drop off you better have told the person in front what you needed to or else the story gets lost."

He opened his eyes. I thanked him for the explanation and was stunned by the power of the metaphor, which brought to mind the Sankofa symbol of the mythical bird, reaching backward for a precious egg. This is what we were doing: going back to fetch what we forgot so we could pass it to the next generation.

• • • •

After Dr. Merritt left, Belle looked up and noticed the big clock at the corner of the park closest to the statue, how both the hour and minute hands had been removed. A fancy clock in a park officially named for the time Graham had been in existence, "Sesquicentennial," yet the face of the clock marked no time at all. The broken clock faced the spot where Wyatt was hung.

I wondered what we could have been without the obstacles. And then I thought, *Look where we are anyway. Look how far we've come despite the obstacles, the hate, the voter suppression.*

How strong must we be? How brilliant must we be in order to orchestrate, individually and collectively, a push forward to Black progress over hurdles so high you have to bust through them instead of jumping over?

Dr. Samuel Merritt (*standing*) shares the Outlaw family Bible and photos with Sylvester in downtown Graham. (Photo by Belle Boggs.)

What Michael Harris (the author of "Pressure" in chapter 11) said about momentum, about how he keeps going, still sits with me today. We stand on the backs of our ancestors. We're still chucking wood in the fire that they started. For one small town, one of those ancestors is Wyatt Outlaw: a carpenter, a bondsman, a constable, a commissioner, a Union League leader, a son, a father, a husband. And now his spirit is shaping the future of Alamance County.

I think Wyatt would be proud to see some of the progress we've made, especially since 2020. That year, Alamance County elected Ricky Hurtado to the North Carolina House of Representatives, making him the first Latinx Democrat elected to the state's general assembly. Seneca Rogers, a Black man and public school advocate, was appointed to the Alamance–Burlington Board of Education in 2023. In that same year, Dejuana Bigelow and Bryant Crisp were elected to their city councils. In 2024, Seneca Rogers and Tameka Harvey, two candidates endorsed by Down Home, were both elected to the Alamance–Burlington Board of Education.

In fact, in 2024 Alamance County bucked the national and statewide "red wave" trend of rightward electoral results, moving in the *opposite* direction instead. This was clearly the impact of grassroots organizing groups like Down Home, along with other groups and individuals who remember the voter suppression of 2020 and are determined to be heard.

So, what do we owe the living? I know we owe them the truth. We owe them a fair shot at prosperity. We owe the living a proper education and sturdy housing. We owe the living a real shot at the American dream. We owe the underserved and underheard the same protections as the privileged. We owed Tamir Rice. We owed Michael Brown. We owed Fred Cox. We owed Breonna Taylor. We owed George Floyd. We owed Sonya Massey. Some debts can't be paid.

We owe the living representation in the public sphere and a fair shot to build their own homes, their communities, their neighborhoods for sustainment, something that can be passed down to future generations. Even if there was no district like Black Bottom again in Burlington, that doesn't mean we couldn't see Black businesses all over Main Street and Church Street and Webb Avenue. Black musicians on the street corners and Black-owned concert halls, filling the air with harmonies and rhythms and melodic lines impossible to ignore. More Black representation in city hall. That's a small Southern town that would feel more inclusive, more like home.

As Belle and I walked through Wyatt's story together, we had to become outlaws ourselves, joining a band of other outlaws in their pursuit of justice, fairness, and progress. *Outlaw* is an image far from that of a kid in a three-piece suit carrying a new Bible up the stairs of a church, where he'd get lost in the music and listen to sermons of right and wrong, good and evil, and angels and demons. It was a transformation for the earnest teacher who drove across the bridge into Saxapahaw looking for a job.

Along the way, we noticed just how many people there were eager to get Wyatt's story out. Eager to unblur his face. So in that sense, Wyatt is no longer just a ghost, no longer just an idea. He is real, and he walks among us

Children celebrating 2020 electoral wins in downtown Graham.
(Photo by Anthony Crider.)

in Alamance County, where countless people are being driven by his spirit, shocked by his audacity, and strengthened by his courage. Belle and I are only two of those people. And we're all writing, listening and researching, telling and retelling the story of this town together.

In fact, I'd go so far as to say *they* are the story. Every person who has been moved to action. Every lawyer who's shown up to defend a peaceful protester in court. Every medic who's applied an ice pack to the wounded. Every pastor who has prayed for this town. Every author, every playwright who's put pen to paper for truth. Every museum curator. Every journalist and photojournalist. Every giver of food and mutual aid. Every dissenter waiting their turn at a commissioner meeting. Everyone who's sung for justice. We are the story of this town. We are the story of this country. We are the spirit of Wyatt Outlaw.

NOTES

INTRODUCTION

1. Dreama Caldwell, Zoom interview by Belle Boggs, November 13, 2020.

2. "GPD News Release—Officer Involved Shooting," Graham Police Department, July 14, 2020, www.cityofgraham.com/wp-content/uploads/2020/07/Public-address-Officer-involved-shooting-1.pdf.

3. Allen Kim, "North Carolina Racetrack Ordered Shut Down after Holding Races to Near-Capacity Crowds despite Virus Restrictions," CNN, June 9, 2020, www.cnn.com/2020/06/09/us/ace-speedway-race-rally-trnd/index.html.

4. Alamance County commissioner, interview by Belle Boggs on Zoom, January 13, 2021.

CHAPTER ONE

1. Jacob A. Long, "Introduction," *Alamance Gleaner*, May 28, 1914.

2. United States of America v. Johnson, No. 1:12-CV-01349, Complaint ¶ 3 (M.D.N.C. December 20, 2012), www.justice.gov/iso/opa/resources/55620121220953110360.pdf.

3. National Association for the Advancement of Colored People, Alamance County Branch v. Peterman et al., No. 1:20-CV-613, Consent Temporary Restraining Order (M.D.N.C. July 6, 2020), www.acluofnorthcarolina.org/sites/default/files/tro_granted-_7-6-20.pdf.

4. W. E. B. Du Bois, "The Beginnings of Slavery," *Voice of the Negro* 2 (1905): 102.

5. Bess Beatty, *Alamance: The Holt Family and Industrialization in a North Carolina County, 1837–1900* (Baton Rouge: Louisiana State University Press, 1999).

6. Harry McKown, "April 1854—The Fayetteville and Western Plank Road," *This Month in North Carolina History*, April 2008.

7. Carole Watterson Troxler, "'To Look More Closely at the Man': Wyatt Outlaw, a Nexus of National, Local, and Personal History," *North Carolina Historical Review* 77, no. 4 (2000): 403–33, www.jstor.org/stable/23522167.

8. *Trial of William W. Holden, Governor of North Carolina, before the Senate of North*

Carolina, on Impeachment by the House of Representatives for High Crimes and Misdemeanors (Raleigh: "Sentinel" Printing Office, 1871), 1363.

9. "An Act concerning Slaves and Free Persons of Color," 1816, Documenting the American South, https://docsouth.unc.edu/nc/slavesfree/slavesfree.html.

10. Quoted in Troxler, "'To Look More Closely at the Man,'" 409–10.

11. Ana Rosado, Gideon Cohn-Postar, and Mimi Eisen, with the Zinn Education Project team, *Erasing the Black Freedom Struggle*, 2022, www.teachreconstructionreport.org/.

12. Fallen Officers Memorial Service 2020, posted May 18, 2020, by AlamanceCountyNC, YouTube, www.youtube.com/watch?v=GluwVR7egTA.

CHAPTER TWO

1. Omega Wilson and Brenda Wilson, interview by the authors, Mebane, NC, July 2022. All quotes from the Wilsons in this chapter are from this interview.

2. Geneva Smitherman, *Talkin and Testifyin: The Language of Black America* (Detroit: Wayne State Press, 1986), 150.

3. "Mother Emanuel AME Church," United States Civil Rights Trail, accessed May 21, 2025, https://civilrightstrail.com/attraction/emanuel-ame-church/.

4. Biff Hollingsworth, "Founded in 1865: African American Churches at the End of the Civil War," June 26, 2015, *Southern Sources: Exploring the Southern Historical Collection* (blog), University Libraries, University of North Carolina at Chapel Hill, https://blogs.lib.unc.edu/shc/tag/first-baptist-church-chapel-hill/.

5. "An Act concerning Slaves and Free Persons of Color, General Assembly of the State of North Carolina, 1831–32," Nat Turner Project, accessed May 21, 2025, www.natturnerproject.org/north-carolina-gen-assemb-1831-32.

6. "Our History," Sixteenth Street Baptist Church, accessed May 21, 2025, www.16thstreetbaptist.org/our-history/.

7. "The 16th Street Baptist Church (Birmingham, Alabama) Holds Its First Service," African American Registry, accessed May 21, 2025, https://aaregistry.org/story/birminghams-16th-street-baptist-church-holds-its-first-service/.

8. Al Sharpton on Henry Louis Gates Jr., *The Black Church: This Is Our Story, This Is Our Song*, episode 1, aired February 12, 2021, on PBS.

9. Elie Mystal, "Let's Talk about the Taking of Black Land," *The Nation*, March 7/14, 2022.

10. Margaret Garb, "No Place Like Home: St. Louis' Eminent Domain History," Washington University in St. Louis, Center for the Humanities, September 22, 2017, https://humanities.wustl.edu/features/Margaret-Garb-St-Louis-Eminent-Domain.

11. William A. James Sr., "Vinegar Hill Remembered: Eminent Domain, Urban Removal, and the Demolition of a People's Soul," *Vinegar Hill Magazine*, March 6, 2024, https://vinegarhillmagazine.com/vinegar-hill-remembered-eminent-domainurban-removal-and-the-demolition-of-a-peoples-soul/.

12. Mindy Thompson Fullilove, *Eminent Domain and African Americans: What Is the Price of the Commons?*, Perspectives on Eminent Domain Abuse vol. 1, Institute for Justice, February 14, 2007, https://ij.org/report/eminent-domain-african-americans/.

13. Joseph Naughton, "Bethel African Methodist Episcopal Church," Hill District Digital History, accessed May 21, 2025, https://hillhistory.org/items/show/9.

14. Peter Smith, "Black Church, NHL's Penguins Reach Historic Land Use Accord," Associated Press, April 14, 2023, https://apnews.com/article/pittsburgh-penguins-historic-black-church-bethel-reparations-08dfa73ed59ee66d31cfec3a3c5381be.

15. Bill Nichols, "First Public Radio Station in Jackson Due in Early 1983," *Clarion-Ledger* (Jackson, MS), September 8, 1982, 29.

16. Omega Wilson and Brenda Wilson, "Our Right to Basic Health Amenities," *Perspectives in Primary Care*, Harvard Medical Center for Primary Care, December 16, 2022, https://info.primarycare.hms.harvard.edu/perspectives/articles/our-right-to-basic-public-health-amenities.

17. "Timeline," West End Revitalization Association, accessed May 21, 2025, www.wera-nc.org/timeline.htm.

18. Danielle Purifoy, "Community Organizing Mattered around Mebane—but the Struggle Isn't Over," *Scalawag*, August 27, 2016, https://scalawagmagazine.org/2016/08/community-organizing-mattered-around-mebane-n-c-but-the-struggle-isnt-over/.

19. "Our Photo Gallery," West End Revitalization Association, accessed May 21, 2025, https://weranc.org/our-gallery/.

CHAPTER FOUR

1. "Jury Ordered to Fully Investigate Graham Lynching," *Durham Morning Herald*, August 26, 1920.

2. "John Jeffress," A Red Record: Revealing Lynching Sites in North Carolina, accessed May 21, 2025, https://lynching.web.unc.edu/the-people/john-jeffress/.

3. Spencie Love, *One Blood: The Death and Resurrection of Charles R. Drew* (Chapel Hill: University of North Carolina Press, 1996), 1.

CHAPTER SIX

1. John B. Gordon, *Reminiscences of the Civil War* (New York: Charles Scribner's Sons, 1903), 114, https://docsouth.unc.edu/fpn/gordon/gordon.html#gord105.

2. Samuel Merritt, interview by the authors on Zoom, December 11, 2023. All quotes from Merritt in this chapter are from this interview.

CHAPTER EIGHT

1. Matthew Turi, interview by the authors, Chapel Hill, NC, June 1, 2023.

2. Turi, interview.

3. Union League of America, *Ritual, Constitution, and By-Laws of the National Council, U. L. of A.: Together with All Necessary Information for the Complete Working of Subordinate Councils* (New York: M. B. Brown, 1870), 6.

4. James Boyd, *Raleigh Daily Standard*, July 30, 1870.

5. "William W. Holden to the Senators and Representatives in the Congress of the United States from North Carolina," March 14, 1870, NC Pamphlets, VI Governors' Messages, p. 49, North Carolina Collection, Wilson Library, University of North Carolina at Chapel Hill.

6. "William W. Holden to His Excellency, the President of the United States," March 10, 1870, NC Pamphlets, VI Governors' Messages, p. 47, North Carolina Collection, Wilson Library, University of North Carolina at Chapel Hill.

7. Jacob A. Long, "To the People of North Carolina," 1908, North Carolina Collection, Wilson Library, University of North Carolina at Chapel Hill, 1. Long's quotations in the following paragraphs are from the same source, pp. 2, 3, 4, 5, and 7.

8. Alexander H. Stephens, "Cornerstone Speech," March 21, 1861, Savannah, Georgia, www.battlefields.org/learn/primary-sources/cornerstone-speech.

9. Jacob A. Long, "Introduction," *Alamance Gleaner*, May 28, 1914.

10. Wyatt Outlaw Union League of America Commission, 1867, #569-z, Southern Historical Collection, Wilson Library, University of North Carolina at Chapel Hill.

CHAPTER NINE

1. Gordon P. Kelly, *A History of Exile in the Roman Republic* (New York: Cambridge University Press, 2006), https://assets.cambridge.org/052184/8601/excerpt/0521848601_excerpt.htm.

2. R. Hargus Taylor, "Outlaw, George," NCpedia, accessed January 16, 2025, www.ncpedia.org/biography/outlaw-george; Rebecca B. Littleton, "Outlaw, David," NCpedia, accessed January 16, 2025, www.ncpedia.org/biography/outlaw-david.

3. Scott Reynolds Nelson, "Red Strings and Half Brothers," in *Enemies of the Country: New Perspectives on Unionists in the Civil War South*, ed. John C. Inscoe and Robert C. Kenzer (Athens: University of Georgia Press, 2001), 39.

4. Carole Watterson Troxler, "'To Look More Closely at the Man': Wyatt Outlaw, a Nexus of National, Local, and Personal History," *North Carolina Historical Review* 77, no. 4 (2000): 411, www.jstor.org/stable/23522167.

5. Fergus Bordewich, *Klan War: Ulysses S. Grant and the Battle to Save Reconstruction* (New York: Knopf, 2023), xiv.

6. Scott Reynolds Nelson, Zoom interview by Belle Boggs, January 11, 2021.

7. Wade Harrison, phone interview by Belle Boggs, January 21, 2025.

8. Nelson, "Red Strings and Half Brothers," 44.

9. Elsie Freeman, Wynell Burroughs Schamel, and Jean West, "The Fight for Equal Rights: A Recruiting Poster for Black Soldiers in the Civil War," *Social Education* 56, no. 2 (1992): 118–20 (revised and updated in 1999 by Budge Weidman), www.archives.gov/education/lessons/blacks-civil-war.

10. *Trial of William W. Holden, Governor of North Carolina, before the Senate of North Carolina, on Impeachment by the House of Representatives for High Crimes and Misdemeanors*, (Raleigh: "Sentinel" Printing Office, 1871), 1198.

11. Eric Foner, *Reconstruction: America's Unfinished Revolution* (New York: Harper Perennial, 2014), 283.

12. *Minutes of the Freedmen's Convention, Held in the City of Raleigh, on the 2nd, 3rd, 4th, and 5th of October, 1866* (Raleigh: Standard Book and Job Office, 1866), 24. https://docsouth.unc.edu/nc/freedmen/freedmen.html.

13. The definitions of "union" and "loyal" are from *The New Oxford American Dictionary*, 2nd ed. (New York: Oxford University Press, 2005), 1837.

14. Wyatt Outlaw Union League of America Commission, 1867, #569-z, Southern Historical Collection, Wilson Library, University of North Carolina at Chapel Hill.

15. Union League of America, *Ritual, Constitution, and By-Laws of the National Council, U. L. of A.: Together with All Necessary Information for the Complete Working of Subordinate Councils* (New York: M. B. Brown, 1870), 4.

16. Union League of America, *Ritual, Constitution, and By-Laws*, 7.

17. Union League of America, *Ritual, Constitution, and By-Laws*, 7.

18. Union League of America, *Ritual, Constitution, and By-Laws*, 7.

19. Scott Reynolds Nelson, *Iron Confederacies: Southern Railways, Klan Violence, and Reconstruction* (Chapel Hill: University of North Carolina Press, 1999), 108.

20. Foner, *Reconstruction*, 287.

21. Nelson, *Iron Confederacies*, 107.

22. Nelson, *Iron Confederacies*, 107.

23. Nelson, *Iron Confederacies*, 113.

24. *Trial of William W. Holden*, 1250.

25. *Trial of William W. Holden*, 1262.

26. Nelson, *Iron Confederacies*, 110.

27. *Trial of William W. Holden*, 1312.

28. *Trial of William W. Holden*, 1313. The next two paragraphs also draw on this page.

29. *Trial of William W. Holden*, 1314.

30. *Trial of William W. Holden*, 1321.

31. *Trial of William W. Holden*, 1325.

32. Equal Justice Initiative, *Reconstruction in America: Racial Violence after the Civil War, 1965–1876*, chap. 3, "Documenting Reconstruction Violence," 2020, https://

eji.org/report/reconstruction-in-america/documenting-reconstruction-violence /#racial-terror-and-reconstruction-a-state-snapshot.

33. Kathy Liston, "Lynching a Legislator: The Joseph R. Holmes Story," Racial Terror: Lynching in Virginia (website), January 31, 2024, https://sites.lib.jmu.edu /valynchings/lynching-a-legislator/.

34. Equal Justice Initiative, *Reconstruction in America*, chap. 3, "Documenting Reconstruction Violence," https://eji.org/report/reconstruction-in-america /documenting-reconstruction-violence/#racial-terror-and-reconstruction-a-state -snapshot.

35. Equal Justice Initiative, *Reconstruction in America*, chap. 2, "Freedom to Fear," https://eji.org/report/reconstruction-in-america/freedom-to-fear/#chapter -2-intro.

36. "The Map," A Red Record: Revealing Lynching Sites in North Carolina (website), accessed May 21, 2025, https://lynching.web.unc.edu/the-map/.

37. Equal Justice Initiative, *Reconstruction in America*, chap. 2, "Freedom to Fear," https://eji.org/report/reconstruction-in-america/freedom-to-fear/.

38. William W. Holden, "A Proclamation, by His Excellency, the Governor of North Carolina," *Daily Standard* (Raleigh), July 27, 1870.

39. *Public Laws of the State of North Carolina, Passed by the General Assembly* [1869–1870], ch. 267, sec. 2 (Raleigh: Jo. W. Holden, 1870), https://dn720407.ca.archive .org/0/items/proclamationsbygoonort/proclamationsbygoonort_djvu.txt.

40. *Trial of William W. Holden*, 1401.

41. *Trial of William W. Holden*, 1372.

42. *Trial of William W. Holden*, 1349.

43. *Trial of William W. Holden*, 1350–52.

44. *Trial of William W. Holden*, 1221–22.

45. *Trial of William W. Holden*, 1316; also applies to the following two paragraphs.

46. *Trial of William W. Holden*, 1316.

47. *Trial of William W. Holden*, 1316–17; also applies to the following four paragraphs.

48. *Trial of William W. Holden*, 1882.

49. Kidada Williams, *I Saw Death Coming: A History of Terror and Survival in the War against Reconstruction* (New York: Bloomsbury, 2023), 75.

50. *Trial of William W. Holden*, 1376–77.

51. *Trial of William W. Holden*, 1385.

CHAPTER TEN

1. Christina Sharpe, *Ordinary Notes* (New York: Farrar, Straus and Giroux, 2023), 343.

2. Sharpe, *Ordinary Notes*, 351.

3. Sharpe, *Ordinary Notes*, 17.

4. Sharpe, *Ordinary Notes*, 240.

5. Sharpe, *Ordinary Notes*, 40–41.

6. Sharpe, *Ordinary Notes*, 41.

7. Sarah Schwartz, "Map: Where Critical Race Theory Is under Attack," *Education Week*, updated March 21, 2025, www.edweek.org/policy-politics/map-where-critical-race-theory-is-under-attack/2021/06.

8. Sharpe, *Ordinary Notes*, 31.

9. Equal Justice Initiative, *Lynching in America: Confronting the Legacy of Racial Terror*, 3rd ed., 2017, https://eji.org/wp-content/uploads/2005/11/lynching-in-america-3d-ed-110121.pdf.

10. Clarence Page, "Postcards from an Ugly Period," *Chicago Tribune*, August 21, 2021.

11. Somini Sengupta, "Racist History in America's Past Stirs Emotions at Exhibition," *New York Times*, January 4, 2000, www.nytimes.com/2000/01/24/nyregion/racist-hatred-in-america-s-past-stirs-emotions-at-exhibition.html.

12. Parul Sehgal, "The First Photos of Enslaved People Raise Many Questions about the Ethics of Viewing," *New York Times*, September 29, 2020, www.nytimes.com/2020/09/29/books/to-make-their-own-way-in-world-zealy-daguerreotypes.html.

13. Sharpe, *Ordinary Notes*, 31 (italics in the original).

14. Sehgal, "First Photos of Enslaved People."

15. Equal Justice Initiative, "34 Documented Mass Lynchings during the Reconstruction Era," in *Reconstruction in America*, chap. 3, "Documenting Reconstruction Violence," https://eji.org/report/reconstruction-in-america/documenting-reconstruction-violence/#34-documented-mass-lynchings-during-the-reconstruction-era.

16. Sharpe, *Ordinary Notes*, 31.

CHAPTER ELEVEN

1. International Civil Rights Center and Museum, Greensboro, North Carolina.

CHAPTER TWELVE

1. *Trial of William W. Holden, Governor of North Carolina, before the Senate of North Carolina, on Impeachment by the House of Representatives for High Crimes and Misdemeanors* (Raleigh: "Sentinel" Printing Office 1871), 1363.

2. Arch T. Allen III, "A Study in Separation of Powers: Executive Power in North Carolina," *North Carolina Law Review* 77, no. 6 (1999): 2049, 2058.

3. "North Carolina State Senate, 1870–1872" (table), Carolana.com, accessed May 21, 2025, www.carolana.com/NC/1800s/nc_1800s_senate_1870-1872.html.

4. *Trial of William W. Holden*, 1364–65.

5. *Trial of William W. Holden*, 1366.

6. *Trial of William W. Holden*, 1367.

7. *Trial of William W. Holden*, 1193.

8. *Trial of William W. Holden*, 1299.

9. *Trial of William W. Holden*, 1194.

10. *Trial of William W. Holden*, 1196.

11. *Trial of William W. Holden*, 1194.

12. *Trial of William W. Holden*, 1369.

13. Steven Hahn, *A Nation under Our Feet* (Cambridge, MA: Harvard University Press, 2003), 274–75.

14. Scott Reynolds Nelson, "Red Strings and Half Brothers," in *Enemies of the Country: New Perspectives on Unionists in the Civil War South*, ed. John C. Inscoe and Robert C. Kenzer (Athens: University of Georgia Press, 2001), 40–43.

15. Carole Watterson Troxler, "'To Look More Closely at the Man': Wyatt Outlaw, a Nexus of National, Local, and Personal History," *North Carolina Historical Review* 77, no. 4 (2000): 406, www.jstor.org/stable/23522167.

16. Troxler, "'To Look More Closely at the Man,'" 409–10.

17. Alfred Avins, "The Right to Be a Witness and the Fourteenth Amendment," *Missouri Law Review* 31 (1966): 473–79, https://scholarship.law.missouri.edu/cgi/viewcontent.cgi?article=1954&context=mlr.

18. *Trial of William W. Holden*, 1364.

19. Scott Reynolds Nelson, *Iron Confederacies: Southern Railways, Klan Violence, and Reconstruction* (Chapel Hill: University of North Carolina Press, 1999), 100.

20. General Assembly of North Carolina, "Slaves and Free Persons of Color: An Act concerning Slaves and Free Persons of Color," 1831, Documenting the American South, https://docsouth.unc.edu/nc/slavesfree/slavesfree.html.

21. Troxler, "'To Look More Closely at the Man,'" 414.

22. *Minutes of the Freedmen's Convention, Held in the City of Raleigh, on the 2nd, 3rd, 4th, and 5th of October, 1866* (Raleigh: Printed at the Standard Book and Job Office, 1866), https://docsouth.unc.edu/nc/freedmen/freedmen.html.

23. Nelson, *Iron Confederacies*, 102–3.

24. Nelson, *Iron Confederacies*, 102.

25. Nelson, *Iron Confederacies*, 102.

26. *Trial of William W. Holden*, 1353.

27. *Trial of William W. Holden*, 1311–28.

28. *Trial of William W. Holden*, 1918.

29. Nelson, *Iron Confederacies*, 112.

30. Nelson, *Iron Confederacies*, 113.

31. *Trial of William W. Holden*, 1366.

32. "The Outrage at Graham," *Greensboro Patriot*, March 18, 1870. Accessed through A Red Record: Revealing Lynching Sites in North Carolina, https://lynching.web.unc.edu/wp-content/uploads/sites/9169/2015/04/The_People_s_Press_Fri__Mar_18__1870_.jpg.

33. *Trial of William W. Holden*, 1310.

34. Allen W. Trelease, "Stephens, John 'Chicken' Walter," NCpedia, January 1, 1994, https://dev.ncpedia.org/biography/stephens-john-walter.

35. *Trial of William W. Holden*, 1363.

36. "Wyatt Outlaw," A Red Record: Revealing Lynching Sites in North Carolina (website), accessed May 22, 2025, https://lynching.web.unc.edu/the-people/wyatt-outlaw/.

37. Jason Tomberlin, "June 1870: The 'Kirk-Holden' War," This Month in North Carolina History, *North Carolina Miscellany* (blog), University Libraries, University of North Carolina at Chapel Hill, June 1, 2006. https://blogs.lib.unc.edu/ncm/2006/06/01/this_month_june_1870/.

38. Nelson, *Iron Confederacies*, 114.

39. "Address to the Colored People of North Carolina," NCpedia, accessed May 22, 2025, www.ncpedia.org/anchor/primary-source-address.

40. "Address to the Colored People of North Carolina," December 19, 1870, Documenting the American South, Academic Affairs Library, University of North Carolina at Chapel Hill, https://docsouth.unc.edu/nc/address/address.html.

41. Troy L. Kickler, "Holden Impeachment," North Carolina History Project, accessed May 22, 2025, https://northcarolinahistory.org/encyclopedia/holden-impeachment/.

42. William J. Barber II with Jonathan Wilson-Hartgrove, *The Third Reconstruction: Moral Mondays, Fusion Politics, and the Rise of a New Justice Movement* (Boston: Beacon Press, 2016), 115.

43. Ronnie W. Faulkner, "Convention of 1868," NCpedia, accessed January 20, 2025, www.ncpedia.org/government/convention-1868.

44. Barber with Wilson-Hartgrove, *Third Reconstruction*, 117.

45. "Alamance County Confederate Monument, Graham," Commemorative Landscapes, Documenting the American South, accessed May 22, 2025, https://docsouth.unc.edu/commland/monument/10/.

46. Isaac Groves, "Alamance Confederate Monument's History a Common Southern Story," *Burlington Times-News*, October 13, 2017, www.thetimesnews.com/news/20171014/alamance-confederate-monuments-history-common-southern-story.

47. *Whose Heritage? Public Symbols of the Confederacy*, Southern Poverty Law Center, February 1, 2019, www.splcenter.org/20190201/whose-heritage-public-symbols-confederacy.

48. Richard Reid, *Freedom for Themselves: North Carolina's Black Soldiers in the Civil War Era* (Chapel Hill: University of North Carolina Press, 2008).

49. Heather Leah, "Abandoned Colonial Settlement, Stop on Underground Railroad, Falling Apart in Snow Camp," WRAL.com, October 29, 2020, updated October 31, 2020, www.wral.com/abandoned-colonial-settlement-stop-on-underground-railroad-falling-apart-in-snow-camp/19361075/.

50. *Guide to North Carolina Highway Historical Markers*, North Carolina Office of Archives and History, October 30, 2019, 7–10, https://files.nc.gov/ncdcr/NC-Historical-Markers-Guide-Final-Oct-30-2019-PDF.pdf.

51. *Trial of William W. Holden*, 1929.

52. *Trial of William W. Holden*, 1366, 1309.

53. *Examining the Demographic Compositions of U.S. Circuit and District Courts*, Center for American Progress, February 13, 2020, www.americanprogress.org/article/examining-demographic-compositions-u-s-circuit-district-courts/.

54. John Eligon, "Speaking Black Dialect in Courtrooms Can Have Striking Consequences," *New York Times*, January 25, 2019, www.nytimes.com/2019/01/25/us/black-dialect-courtrooms.html.

55. *Trial of William W. Holden*, 1309.

56. Joe Fisher, "Dueling Protests Come to Alamance County over Confederate Monument," WRAL.com, May 20, 2021, www.wral.com/dueling-protests-come-to-alamance-county-over-confederate-monument/19688734/.

57. Grace Holland, Miles Moraitis, "Digging Deeper: NC NAACP Sues Alamance County to Bring Down Graham Confederate Monument," WFMYNews2.com, April 1, 2021, www.wfmynews2.com/article/news/local/digging-deeper-nc-naacp-sues-alamance-county-to-bring-down-graham-confederate-monument/83-e5796f96-4538-4e38-baa5-881b4c0a056a.

58. Adam Powell, "Commissioners Discuss Confederate Statue in Heated Meeting," *Mebane (NC) Enterprise*, August 18, 2020, www.mebaneenterprise.com/news/article_9799bfaa-e18c-11ea-9a8c-531fd8c6b1ea.html (site discontinued).

59. "Justice Department Releases Investigative Findings on the Alamance County, N.C., Sheriff's Office," United States Department of Justice, Office of Public Affairs, September 18, 2012, www.justice.gov/opa/pr/justice-department-releases-investigative-findings-alamance-county-nc-sheriff-s-office.

60. Dreama Caldwell, Zoom interview by Belle Boggs, November 27, 2020.

CHAPTER THIRTEEN

1. Constitution of North Carolina, December 18, 1776, https://avalon.law.yale.edu/18th_century/nc07.asp.

2. Ronnie W. Faulkner, "Constitution of 1835," North Carolina History Project, accessed May 22, 2025, https://northcarolinahistory.org/encyclopedia/constitution-of-1835/.

3. *Public Laws of the State of North Carolina Passed by the General Assembly at the Sessions of 1866–'67* (Raleigh: Wm. E. Pell, State Printer, 1867), https://archive.org/details/publiclawsofstat186667nor/page/n5.

4. "War's End and Reconstruction," North Carolina Historic Sites, accessed May 25, 2025, https://historicsites.nc.gov/resources/north-carolina-civil-war/wars-end-and-reconstruction.

5. *Trial of William W. Holden, Governor of North Carolina, before the Senate of North Carolina, on Impeachment by the House of Representatives for High Crimes and Misdemeanors* (Raleigh: "Sentinel" Printing Office, 1871), 1993.

6. *Trial of William W. Holden*, 1994.

7. *Trial of William W. Holden*, 2002, 2019.

8. *Trial of William W. Holden*, 2019.

9. *Trial of William W. Holden*, 1781–82.

10. *Merriam-Webster.com Dictionary*, "citizenship," accessed May 19, 2025, www.merriam-webster.com/dictionary/citizenship.

11. Center for the Study of Citizenship, Wayne State University, "What Is Citizenship?," accessed May 19, 2025, https://csc.wayne.edu/what-is-citizenship.

12. Trevon D. Logan, "Do Black Politicians Matter? Evidence from Reconstruction," *Journal of Economic History* 80, no. 1 (2020): 1–37, https://doi.org/10.1017/S0022050719000755.

13. Scott Reynolds Nelson, *Iron Confederacies: Southern Railways, Klan Violence, and Reconstruction* (Chapel Hill: University of North Carolina Press, 1999), 107.

14. Nelson, *Iron Confederacie*, 107.

15. *Merriam-Webster.com Dictionary*, "assassination," accessed May 19, 2025, www.merriam-webster.com/dictionary/assassination; *Cambridge Dictionary*, "assassination," accessed May 19, 2025, https://dictionary.cambridge.org/us/dictionary/english/assassination; *Britannica*, "assassination," accessed May 19, 2025, www.britannica.com/topic/assassination; *Oxford English Dictionary*, "assassination," accessed May 19, 2025, www.oed.com/dictionary/assassination_n?tl=true.

CHAPTER FOURTEEN

1. Eric Foner, *Freedom's Lawmakers: A Directory of Black Officeholders during Reconstruction*, rev. ed. (Baton Rouge: Louisiana State University Press, 1996), xi–xxxii.

2. "National Assessment of Adult Literacy," National Center for Education Statistics, accessed June 16, 2025, https://nces.ed.gov/naal/lit_history.asp.

3. *Trial of William W. Holden, Governor of North Carolina, before the Senate of North Carolina, on Impeachment by the House of Representatives for High Crimes and Misdeameanors* (Raleigh: "Sentinel" Printing Office, 1871), 135–37.

4. Fergus Bordewich, *Klan War: Ulysses S. Grant and the Battle to Save Reconstruction* (New York: Knopf, 2023), 152.

5. Andrew Stanton, "Donald Trump's Lawyer Admits Jan. 6 Was a 'Criminal, Shameful' Riot," *Newsweek*, February 8, 2024, www.newsweek.com/donald-trump-lawyer-january-6-criminal-shameful-riot-jonathan-mitchell-1868262.

6. Ross Douthat, "Why Jan. 6 Wasn't an Insurrection," *New York Times*, January 12, 2024, www.nytimes.com/2024/01/12/opinion/jan-6-not-insurrection.html.

7. Chris Cameron, "These Are the People Who Died in Connection With the Capitol Riot," *New York Times*, January 5, 2022, www.nytimes.com/2022/01/05/us

/politics/jan-6-capitol-deaths.html; Zachary Snowdon Smith, "Capitol Riot Costs Go Up: Government Estimates $2.73 Million in Property Damage," *Forbes*, April 11, 2022, www.forbes.com/sites/zacharysmith/2022/04/08/capitol-riot-costs-go-up-government-estimates-273-million-in-property-damage/.

8. Tom Dresibach, "A Capitol Police Officer Assaulted during the Jan. 6 Riot Says He Feels 'Betrayed,'" *Morning Edition*, NPR, January 6, 2025, www.npr.org/2025/01/06/nx-s1-5197697/a-capitol-police-officer-assaulted-during-the-jan-6-riot-says-he-feels-betrayed.

9. Bordewich, *Klan War*, 132, 157–58.

10. Bordewich, *Klan War*, 132, 149.

11. Scott Reynolds Nelson, *Iron Confederacies: Southern Railways, Klan Violence, and Reconstruction* (Chapel Hill: University of North Carolina Press, 1999), 114.

12. Bordewich, *Klan War*, 151.

13. Senate Bill 256 (Public) filed Tuesday, March 8, 2011, "To Pardon William W. Holden from the Judgment Imposed upon Him by the Senate on March 22, 1871, on Conviction of Articles of Impeachment," UNC School of Government Legislative Reporting Service, https://lrs.sog.unc.edu/bill/pardon-governor-holden.

14. "Tillis Introduces the No More Political Prosecutions Act of 2024" (press release), Thom Tillis, U.S. Senator for North Carolina (website), June 21, 2024, www.tillis.senate.gov/2024/6/tillis-introduces-the-no-more-political-prosecutions-act.

CHAPTER FIFTEEN

1. All quotations from Dreama Caldwell in this chapter come from three interviews with Belle Boggs: Zoom interviews on November 13 and 17, 2020, and an in-person interview in Greensboro, NC, on July 1, 2024.

2. "Memorandum of Agreement" between DHS, ICE, and Alamance County, NC, ICE.gov, January 10, 2007, www.ice.gov/doclib/287gMOA/sheriffsofficeof alamancecounty.pdf.

3. Gregory Drumwright, press conference, Graham, NC, October 14, 2020.

4. Daniel Ayers, Zoom interview by Belle Boggs, November 19, 2020. All quotes from Ayers in this chapter are from this interview.

5. Jennifer Gonnerman, "Kalief Browder, 1993–2015," *New Yorker*, June 7, 2015, www.newyorker.com/news/news-desk/kalief-browder-1993-2015.

6. Dolan Reynolds, "Alamance-Burlington School System Delays Start of School until Sept. 5 Due to Mold Issues," CBS17, August 23, 2023, www.cbs17.com/news/north-carolina-news/alamance-burlington-school-system-delays-start-of-school-until-sept-5-due-to-mold-issues/.

7. Ebony Pinnix, interview by Belle Boggs, July 9, 2024. All quotes from Pinnix in this chapter are from this interview.

8. Fergus Bordewich, *Klan War: Ulysses S. Grant and the Battle to Save Reconstruction* (New York: Knopf, 2023), 37.

CHAPTER SIXTEEN

1. Taylor Lang, "Body Camera Footage Showing Arrest of Bobby Harvey Released," WXII-12.com, October 11, 2019, www.wxii12.com/article/body-camera-footage-showing-arrest-of-bobby-harvey-released/29439770.

2. Megan Allman, "No Charges to Be Filed against Graham Police Officer in Shooting Death of Jaquyn Light," WFMY News Digital, July 17, 2020, www.wfmynews2.com/article/news/local/alamance-county-district-attorney-releases-report-graham-officer-involved-shooting-jaquyn-light/83-8090415e-22cb-403a-9c60-808f3d036675.

3. "May 18 2020 Regular Commissioners Meeting," posted May 19, 2020, by AlamanceCountyNC, YouTube, www.youtube.com/watch?v=updyPNHdDCU&t=4708s.

4. "Search Continues after Man Swimming in Lake Norman Went Missing," WCNC Charlotte, June 28, 2020, www.wcnc.com/article/news/local/crews-looking-for-missing-swimmer-in-catawba-county/275-5f5d0b52-cf67-443a-bc8b-6d5c2222da4f.

5. Faith Cook, "Alamance Mom Says Driver Tried to Run Over Her 12-Year-Old Daughter and a Friend," Facebook Live video on the *News & Observer* website, August 25, 2020, www.newsobserver.com/news/local/crime/article245236730.html.

6. Eric Leverson, "Former Officer Knelt on George Floyd for 9 Minutes and 29 Seconds—Not the Infamous 8:46," CNN.com, March 30, 2021. www.cnn.com/2021/03/29/us/george-floyd-timing-929-846/index.html.

7. Dianne Harris, presentation to tour group in Selma, Alabama, April 20, 2022.

CHAPTER SEVENTEEN

1. Thelisha Eaddy, "Embracing Life, Death of a Formerly-Enslaved Person Positions York Co. Site to Help Tell Obscure Era of U.S. History," South Carolina Public Radio, May 31, 2022, www.southcarolinapublicradio.org/sc-news/2022-05-31/embracing-life-death-of-a-formerly-enslaved-person-positions-york-co-site-to-helpcclarify-an-era-of-us-history.

2. Kathy Liston, interview by the authors, Charlotte County, VA, June 6, 2023. Additional quotes from Liston in this chapter are from this interview.

3. Gillian Brockell, "He Was Killed on the Courthouse Steps. Now, a Virginia County Honors Its First Black Elected Leader," *Washington Post*, October 22, 2021, www.washingtonpost.com/history/2021/10/22/joseph-holmes-charlotte-county-marker/. This is also the source of the information in the next two paragraphs.

4. Kathy Lee Erlandson Liston, "A Murder in Charlotte Court House," *Charlotte Gazette*, February 11, 2020.

CHAPTER EIGHTEEN

1. Shineece Sellars, interview by the authors, Burlington, NC, January 30, 2025. Additional quotes from Sellars are from this interview.

2. James Shields, interview by the authors, Burlington, NC, January 30, 2025. Additional quotes from Shields are from this interview.

CHAPTER NINETEEN

1. Union League of America, *Ritual, Constitution, and By-Laws of the National Council, U. L. of A.: Together with All Necessary Information for the Complete Working of Subordinate Councils* (New York: M. B. Brown, 1870), 6.

2. United States of America v. Trump, No. 1:23-cr-257, Indictment (D.D.C. August 1, 2023), www.justice.gov/storage/US_v_Trump_23_cr_257.pdf.

3. Fulton County Superior Court indictment, filed August 14, 2023, *New York Times*, https://int.nyt.com/data/documenttools/georgia-indictment-trump/daed97d37562a76f/full.pdf.

4. "What We Won This Tuesday—Down Home Outliers in a Red Wave," Down Home North Carolina, November 7, 2024, https://downhomenc.org/2024/11/07/down-home-outliers-in-a-red-wave-organizing-works/.

CHAPTER TWENTY

1. Taylor Telford, "5 Key Moments from Elon Musk's Interview with Don Lemon," *Washington Post*, March 18, 2024, www.washingtonpost.com/technology/2024/03/18/elon-musk-don-lemon-interview/.

2. Carli Brosseau and Julia Wall, "Sound of Judgment" (video), May 21, 2021, ProPublica, www.propublica.org/video/sound-of-judgement.

3. Zora Neale Hurston, *Dust Tracks on a Road* (New York: Harper Perennial Modern Classics, 2010), 176.

4. George Gershwin, "It Take a Long Pull to Get There," *Porgy and Bess*, lyrics by Ira Gershwin and DuBose Heyward, 1935.

5. Anna Johnson, "Downtown Raleigh Bookstore Dedicated to Black Children, Authors, to Close after Threats," *News & Observer* (Raleigh), April 4, 2024, www.newsobserver.com/news/business/article287339905.html.

INDEX